TRI-FAITH AMERICA

Tri-Faith America

HOW CATHOLICS AND JEWS HELD POSTWAR AMERICA TO ITS PROTESTANT PROMISE

Kevin M. Schultz

OXFORD
UNIVERSITY PRESS

OXFORD
UNIVERSITY PRESS

Oxford University Press is a department of the University of Oxford.
It furthers the University's objective of excellence in research, scholarship,
and education by publishing worldwide.

Oxford   New York
Auckland   Cape Town   Dar es Salaam   Hong Kong   Karachi
Kuala Lumpur   Madrid   Melbourne   Mexico City   Nairobi
New Delhi   Shanghai   Taipei   Toronto

With offices in
Argentina   Austria   Brazil   Chile   Czech Republic   France   Greece
Guatemala   Hungary   Italy   Japan   Poland   Portugal   Singapore
South Korea   Switzerland   Thailand   Turkey   Ukraine   Vietnam

Oxford is a registered trade mark of Oxford University Press
in the UK and certain other countries.

Published in the United States of America by
Oxford University Press
198 Madison Avenue, New York, NY 10016

Library of Congress Cataloging-in-Publication Data
Schultz, Kevin Michael.
Tri-Faith America: How Catholics and Jews Held Postwar America
to Its Protestant promise / Kevin M. Schultz.
     p.   cm.
Includes bibliographical references and index.
ISBN 978-0-19-533176-9 (hardcover); 978-0-19-998754-2 (paperback)
1. United States–Religion–History–20th century. 2. Multiculturalism–Religious aspects.
3. Multiculturalism–United States. 4. Christianity and other religions–Judaism.
5. Judaism Relations–Christianity. I. Title.
BL2525.S3357   2011
200.973'09045–dc22   2010029149

9 8 7 6 5 4 3 2 1

Printed in the United States of America
on acid-free paper

Contents

Acknowledgments

Ideas develop best through conversation, so even though writing a book requires significant devotion to one's chair, the good ideas often emerge through discussions with friends and colleagues. Whatever ideas are worth anything in this book are almost certainly not my own.

This book began as a dissertation at Berkeley, and it was David A. Hollinger who nurtured the kernel that became the book. David was a wonderful mentor, truly humane in his advice, both academic and personal, and he's someone all academics should struggle to emulate. Also at Berkeley, Robin Einhorn taught me how to think about history and how to teach it to undergraduate and graduate students. Robert Post argued quite smartly for the importance of law, and Waldo Martin and Yuri Slezkine taught me to think about the work ideas do even if they are or seem to be sociologically insignificant when first pronounced. My fellow students were helpful as well, and made life in graduate school something I actually look back upon fondly. These friends and colleagues include Jason Sokol, Susan Haskell Khan, Molly Oshatz, Dan Geary, Jennifer Burns, and especially Paddy Riley. The project next ventured to Charlottesville, Virginia, where James Davison Hunter has built a marvelous institute for pursuing the big questions, his Institute for Advanced Study in Culture. While a postdoc there, I benefited greatly from conversations with Christopher McKnight Nichols, Shannon Latkin Anderson, David Franz, Josh Yates, Charles Mathewes, Jenny Geddes, Matthew Crawford, and the inimitable Slava Jakĕlic. To all of them, thanks aren't enough.

My most recent intellectual home has been the University of Illinois at Chicago, a wonderful and exciting place to teach, write, and think. The History Department there is filled with brilliant and welcoming people, including Leon Fink, Robert Johnston, Eric Arnesen, Michael Perman, Corey Capers, Christopher Boyer, Richard John, Jim Sack, Rick Fried, Sue Levine, and John D'Emilio. UIC's Institute for the Humanities gave me a year's sabbatical and a wonderful forum to test ideas and learn in an interdisciplinary way. Mary Beth Rose was an excellent director.

There were a lot of financial angels to the project. Foremost among them were my parents, who not only helped fund my academic pursuits but listened patiently to some of my more foolish ideas and asked questions that, importantly, were not steeped in historiography. For that and for many other reasons, they deserve my eternal gratitude. Meanwhile, the Jacob K. Javits Fellowship Program helped me pay for graduate school and take research trips. The Institute for Advanced Studies in Culture subsidized archival work and two years of valuable thinking time. UIC allowed me to go to conferences and on research trips. And the Jack Miller Center gave timely subvention funds. All of them were incredibly important.

Librarians, archivists, and editors exposed me to ideas I didn't even know were out there. Important among these were Mike Hovland at the U.S. Census Bureau, Janis Wiggins at the National Archives, and Dave Klaassen at the University of Minnesota's Social Welfare History Archives. Marc Stern at the American Jewish Congress was wonderfully supportive; without him entire chapters would have gone unwritten. Outside reviewers also took the time to think about the central ideas in the book and offer substantive critiques and advice. Special thanks to Mark Silk, Paul Harvey, the reviewers from Oxford University Press, and the anonymous reviewers from journals where parts of this manuscript were previously aired. Thanks too to the *Journal of American History* for allowing me to reprint parts of what appears here as Chapter 7 and to the *American Quarterly* for allowing me to reprint parts of what appears here as Chapter 5. Editorially speaking, Susan Ferber has hovered over this project for longer than she probably cares to remember, but throughout she has been a wonderful guide and has prevented me from saying some really silly things. Thanks much for that.

Life experiences also enhance the way we understand and think about history, and no one has taught me more about life than my wife, Terra. She's reminded me that stories are part of what's most interesting about history. She's asked some of the hardest questions and forced me to think about many things differently. She deserves my deepest gratitude and, of course, my love. She's also given me three of the greatest joys of my life, Thaddeus, Eleanor, and Quincy. They've certainly made this project more fun, if slower to progress. Nevertheless, their energy, light, and promise have presented me with new ways to think about the past and to enjoy the present. Thanks too to Lilly the dog.

TRI-FAITH AMERICA

Introduction

WHEN A GERMAN U-boat torpedoed the USS *Dorchester* in February 1943, the four chaplains aboard the American vessel—a Catholic, a Jew, and two Protestants—performed their military duty admirably. After the captain gave the order to abandon ship, the four men distributed life jackets to the dozens of young soldiers who had run to the upper decks without grabbing their own vests and then encouraged the young soldiers to take the plunge into the icy Atlantic. Quickly, though, all the extra life jackets were gone, and several soldiers remained unprotected. The soldiers panicked. They hadn't even made it to the battlefields of Europe, but here they were, facing imminent death.

Without hesitation, the four chaplains did something heroic. In a move that came to symbolize wartime sacrifice and interfaith tolerance between Protestants, Catholics, and Jews, the four chaplains unbuckled their own life vests and handed them to four young soldiers without giving a second thought to the faith of the recipient. The chaplains knew their decision would likely be their last. Survivors of the wreck last saw the four chaplains praying arm in arm as the ship began its descent to the bottom of the sea. Alexander Goode, a young, bespectacled Brooklyn-born rabbi, was reciting the Sh'ma—the affirmation of the unity of God—just as the waters engulfed the ship forever.[1]

Family and friends mourned the four men immediately, but by the end of the war, the U.S. armed services began to realize the public relations potential of the selfless deaths. Harmony, bravery, sacrifice: the story could touch even the most stoic citizen. Here were Protestant, Catholic, and Jew praying and dying together, three faiths as one, vital symbols of American unity. Two years after their deaths the armed services awarded each of the four chaplains a posthumous Distinguished Service Cross before a press corps assembled specifically for the event. Later it gave the rights to the story, free of charge, to Warner Brothers, which began production of a film called *Four Men of God*. Before long, a depiction of the Four Chaplains, thereafter always honored with capitalization, became a United States postage stamp. According to one observer, the action of the Four Chaplains "proved the utter uselessness of all . . . sharp religious controversy."[2] The ethnic, religious, and racial divisions that had been predominant in pre–World War II America no longer had a place in the defining traits of good Americanism. With enemies such as Hitler, Mussolini, and Hirohito, the ideal of tolerance was sacrosanct, and during the war years the kind of tolerance that was lionized most was that between Protestants, Catholics, and Jews.

After the war, the story of the Four Chaplains was not easily forgotten. Partly this was because the federal government and various other organizations sought to keep the themes of tri-faith religious tolerance in the public eye, and the story of the Four Chaplains was a perfect vehicle. It also helped that the father of one of the fallen chaplains was Daniel A. Poling, a fiery conservative Protestant who edited the influential *Christian Herald* and wrote a religious column for the *New York Post*. When Poling's son died aboard the *Dorchester*, Poling was able to insert a letter entitled "Americans All" into the Congressional Record. The letter told of how a Catholic clergyman had come to comfort him the night he learned of his son's death. Poling wrote: "Where the boy was going and where he now is, there are no schisms and no divisions—all are one in the Father of us all."[3] This kind of interfaith generosity was especially meaningful coming from someone of Poling's conservative religious pedigree.

In this spirit, in 1947 Poling decided to build a Chapel of Four Chaplains in Philadelphia. To gain some interfaith publicity for his venture, he invited several political leaders, including a young Catholic congressman from Massachusetts, to attend a December 15, 1947, fund-raiser.

John F. Kennedy readily accepted. The Four Chaplains event would emphasize his war record and put him on a national stage with other big-name politicians. But just two days before the event, Kennedy changed his reply. The reasons for his last-minute change of heart remain unclear. Kennedy claimed he had accepted the invitation thinking he had been invited as a representative of veterans or of American political leaders. Only later did he discover that he was invited to serve as the fund-raiser's representative Catholic. He pointed out he was one of just three speakers, including Herbert Lehman, a Jewish politician from New York, and

Charles Taft, past president of the Protestant Federal Council of the Churches of Christ in America. Kennedy was not comfortable serving as the "official representative" of a religious organization. "Therefore," he said, "I felt I had no credentials to attend in the capacity in which I had been asked."[4]

Poling had a more critical interpretation of Kennedy's withdrawal. "The record is unmistakably clear," Poling wrote Kennedy several years later. "You accepted an invitation, and then at the request of His Eminence, Cardinal Dougherty, you abruptly canceled the engagement." In Poling's mind, Kennedy had reneged in order to placate Philadelphia's domineering Dennis Joseph Cardinal Dougherty, who evidently felt it unworthy of a Catholic to attend a fund-raiser for what would be, after all, a Protestant chapel.[5]

Frustrated though he was, Poling let the issue go. His priority was on constructing a chapel to honor his son and his son's fallen comrades, not on providing bad press to a very junior, if very famous, member of the House of Representatives. The Protestant chapel with an interfaith theme was completed in 1951. The story of the Four Chaplains and the chapel constructed in their honor was cited throughout the 1950s as a symbol of America's widespread religiosity, and also of its three-pronged religious pluralism. In 1954, President Eisenhower listed the *Dorchester* event as one of the four most significant episodes in American religious history.[6]

Just nine years later, what had been a minor inconvenience for Poling became a portentous sign of a changing America. The tri-faith platitudes of wartime—always made under the watchful eye of the Protestant majority—were now being used to demand that the nation live up to its pluralist creed. Congressman Kennedy was now a senator and on the verge of becoming president, and millions of Americans were truly concerned about having a Catholic in the White House. They read newspaper and magazine stories that questioned Kennedy's allegiances, most of which suggested that Kennedy would be unable to lead the country without the forceful intrusion of the Pope.[7] One story that seemed to confirm this fear was the fund-raising episode surrounding the Chapel of Four Chaplains. Indeed, Poling breathed life into the story in his 1959 autobiography, *Mine Eyes Have Seen*. "At least once," Poling wrote in his book, "John Kennedy of Massachusetts submitted, apparently against his own inclinations and better judgment, to [the Catholic Church's] dictates."[8] With Poling's prodding, the 1947 fund-raising debacle gained renewed life in the press.

As the election neared, Poling sent a telegram to his friend the Reverend K. O. White, pastor of the First Baptist Church in Houston, Texas. Houston was where Kennedy had decided to confront "the Catholic question" once and for all by speaking to a conference of Protestant ministers. Poling knew White would be invited to hear Kennedy's speech, so in his telegram Poling asked

White to question Kennedy about the Four Chaplains incident and see if Kennedy would admit to the cardinal's influence.

At the nationally televised event on the evening of September 12, 1960, White listened to Kennedy's keynote remarks, where Kennedy famously said: "I believe in an America where the separation of church and state is absolute, where no Catholic prelate would tell the President (should he be Catholic) how to act, and no Protestant minister would tell his parishioners for whom to vote. . . . I believe in an America that is officially neither Catholic, Protestant nor Jewish—where no public official either requests or accepts instructions on public policy from the Pope, the National Council of Churches or any other ecclesiastical source—where no religious body seeks to impose its will directly or indirectly upon the general populace or the public acts of its officials." Kennedy resoundingly concluded: "If this election is decided on the basis that forty million Americans lost their chance of being President on the day they were baptized, then it is the whole nation that will be the loser, in the eyes of Catholics and non-Catholics around the world, in the eyes of history, and in the eyes of our own people." Kennedy not only put Protestants on the defensive by warning them that they would look like bigots if they preached anti-Catholicism but also affirmed the tri-faith image of the nation by repeatedly mentioning Protestants, Catholics, and Jews together, as Americans all.[9]

When it came time for questions, White stood up and paraphrased Poling's description of the Four Chaplains fund-raising debacle. He asked Kennedy to rebut the accusation or to apologize. "I never discussed the matter with the Cardinal in my life," Kennedy told White and the rest of the audience. With tension in his voice, Kennedy said Poling had misled him about the purpose of the chapel: "The chapel . . . has never had a Catholic service," Kennedy angrily pointed out. "It is not an interfaith chapel. Therefore, for me to participate as a spokesman . . . for the Catholic faith . . . would have given an erroneous impression." Rightly feeling that some Protestants were alleging his blind allegiance to the Vatican, Kennedy asked: "Is this the best that can be done after 14 years? Is this the only incident that can be charged? . . . I have voted on hundreds of matters, probably thousands of matters, which involve all kinds of public questions, some of which border on the relationship between church and state. Quite obviously that record must be reasonably good or we wouldn't keep hearing about the Poling incident."[10]

His rebuff met with sustained applause. Pointing out that a minor incident from more than a decade earlier was the only time Kennedy's Catholicism might have affected his public life played no small part in defusing the whole issue. After the speech, overt anti-Catholicism moved to the margins of the campaign, and less than two months later the American people elected John F. Kennedy president of the United States. To underscore his election as an achievement of religious pluralism in America, during his inauguration Kennedy flanked himself with a Protestant pastor, a Roman Catholic cardinal, a Jewish rabbi, and a Greek Orthodox archbishop.

The story of the Four Chaplains and the chapel built in their honor sheds light on several significant issues in 1940s and 1950s America. First, it demonstrates the widespread acceptance of a new tri-faith image of America, a national image that was, for the first time, inclusive of both Catholics and Jews in what only recently had been widely referred to as a "Protestant country." By the time of World War II, even a fiery conservative Protestant labeled Catholics and Jews "Americans all." The federal government, the U.S. armed services, and many other Protestants, Catholics, and Jews celebrated the Four Chaplains as emblems of the new tri-faith nation.

But the story also demonstrates how that tri-faith image challenged the nation in unexpected ways, forcing it to alter the way power was meted out, who was deserving of social, political, and cultural recognition, and what that recognition would mean for the way the country conducted its business. Even if the image of America as a tri-faith nation was always something of a sociological myth, it produced very substantive results.

This book is intended to develop these two points. Part I, "Inventing Tri-Faith America, Ending 'Protestant America,'" charts the decline of the nineteenth-century notion that the United States was a "Christian nation" as the country increasingly adopted the tri-faith vision during the first half of the twentieth century. The tri-faith idea had its origins in the 1910s and 1920s, emerging in direct response to the revitalized Ku Klux Klan and the nativism that surfaced immediately following World War I. Several pluralist visions arose in the 1910s and 1920s, but the tri-faith vision took center stage in the shadow of European totalitarianism in the 1930s. By World War II, it had become America's standard operating procedure, and during the first decades after the war, the public religiosity demanded by the Cold War and the numerous social transformations of the postwar era led to widespread recognition of the perceived tri-faith character of the United States. The 1940s and 1950s were the tri-faith image's triumphant years, when many if not most Americans conceived of their nation as being predominately made up of Protestants, Catholics, and Jews, much in the same way social commentators had reflected on the divides between capital and labor in the 1930s and between black and white in the 1960s. Indeed, one of the central arguments of this book is that between these two periods—the capital-labor divide of the 1930s and the racial divide of the 1960s—sits another ideological division that has been mostly forgotten, that of Tri-Faith America. Part I charts its birth and maturation.

The second part of the book, "Living in Tri-Faith America," examines the variety of ways in which the tri-faith image allowed certain ideals to gain widespread airing from the mid-1940s to the early 1960s. For instance, the idea that persistent communalism was a good thing first won widespread acceptance in Tri-Faith America. It was negotiated, among other places, in the streets and on the school boards of suburbia, as Protestants, Catholics, and Jews used the inclusive tri-faith ideal to challenge any lingering Protestantism that might still surround the national image. Similarly, the high wall of separation between church and state that conservative Protestants have struggled against ever since was erected in Tri-Faith America too. This was, after all, the time of the second disestablishment of religion in the United States, the result of the labors of Catholics and especially Jews fighting to ensure that their recently proclaimed first-class status in American life remained unthreatened by any residual Protestant superiority. The idea that minority groups should have special rights in a democracy also arose during these years, especially when it came from Catholics and Jews arguing that minority groups should be allowed to discriminate in the name of self-perpetuation. Discrimination, argued postwar Catholics and Jews, had different implications when it came from a minority fighting for preservation rather than from a majority trying to maintain supremacy. The notion that religion was purely a private matter got sanction during these years too, as Americans probed the question of how deeply the federal government could and should learn about one's religious affiliation. Unlike with almost any other social category, Americans of many religious groups fought together to establish a new right of religious privacy. Finally, the pluralism subtly acknowledged in the tri-faith concept helped soften the ground for the civil rights movement of the 1960s. Often this was a happy accident for the leading proponents of the tri-faith idea, such as the leaders of the National Conference of Christians and Jews, who frequently supported black civil rights throughout the twentieth century but whose support was often tepid and hesitant, fearful that pushing too strongly for racial equality might jeopardize their primary objective of religious goodwill. Nevertheless, the tri-faith ideal provided both a language to tap into and an audience ready to hear pluralist arguments, two factors that helped prepare the way for civil rights.

Taken together, the arrival of the tri-faith image and the subsequent development of these pluralist ideals demonstrates that, rather than surfacing in the 1960s or 1970s, anti-conformist and anti-consensus ideas circulated freely during the years following World War II. And it was not race, class, or gender that served as the central provocateur, but religion.

Winning widespread acceptance for the tri-faith ideal and then fighting to give that victory some meaning were no easy tasks. Protestants, as the majority, had to be convinced that the United States was not a Protestant country, and certain social and cultural differences made some aspects of Catholicism and Judaism truly threatening to an America in the throes of the Cold War. For one, many Protestants saw Catholics and Jews as clannish and divisive. After all, a Catholic in midcentury America was expected to marry a Catholic, participate in Catholic social events, send his or her children to Catholic schools, join Catholic social fraternities, play on or coach Catholic Little League teams, and go to Catholic religious services. Meanwhile, Jews joined Jewish organizations such as Hadassah and B'nai B'rith in record numbers during these years. Their faith often defined whom they socialized with, married, and worked alongside, as well as the lens through which they viewed American society. Furthermore, American Jews were easily identifiable as the group most actively pushing for the creation of a secular state, something potentially threatening when the country was waging war against an atheistic enemy.

There were ecclesiastical divisions as well. During a time when political, economic, and intellectual democracy was hailed as the foundation of the "American way of life," Catholicism operated under a hierarchy that mediated between the laity and "the truth," therefore seeming to limit free thinking. Worse still, the leader of the hierarchy, the Pope, was deemed infallible in matters of faith and morals. To non-Catholics, the act of separating faith and morals from politics and society was simply splitting hairs. In the land of the free, how free were Catholics? Could they think on their own? It did not help that Catholics conducted their worship in a foreign language and that Catholics could be absolved for even their worst actions through the seemingly simple act of confession. Although it was clear that Catholics were not prone to communism (which, after all, wanted to destroy the Church), wasn't it also true that Catholicism frequently thrived under authoritarianism? Wasn't authoritarianism the intellectual and institutional predilection of the Catholic Church and its followers? Was there a place for such tendencies in a democratic society? As easy as it might be to dismiss postwar anti-Catholics as simpleminded bigots, they raised serious questions. With many rational people questioning Catholics' role in a democratic society, American Catholics stood out as being a people apart.[11]

Jews too had to confront intellectual and rhetorical challenges that questioned their place in American society. Although the worst vestiges of antisemitism were declining in the late 1940s and 1950s, many Jews were still worried that their status as the "chosen people," their stereotype for clannishness, and their Talmudic deference to tradition (rather than reason) set them apart from a mainstream that lionized meritocracy, the open society, and rational thought. More important in setting postwar Jews apart from their fellow Americans, however, was the decision by several American Jewish organizations to challenge the remnants of embedded Protestantism in American society. If Catholics' demands for acceptance challenged the mainstream's proclivities toward democracy, Jews' demands for equality challenged its proclivities toward Christianity. If Catholics were notable for their lack of embrace of the Enlightenment, Jews were notable for reifying that secular tradition. Jews themselves were torn over whether or not equality had to mean secularism. But throughout the middle of the century, Jews were clearly the most prominent advocates of removing Christianity from the American public sphere. This was something plausibly treacherous during a religious revival that had as its context a war against godless communism.

This all suggests that post–World War II Catholics and Jews were using the tri-faith rhetoric to challenge something larger than simple lack of access to neighborhoods, schools, or social clubs. They were challenging the established moral authority in America. Whose ideals should govern the nation? they asked. Whose beliefs about truth, community, and the good society would prevail? Although the Cold War's demand for national unity mitigated the most divisive aspects of debate, all sides were aware of the stakes. This is why some Protestants fought so hard to prevent parochial schools from receiving public funds and public schools from losing their religion. To them, acknowledging this kind of pluralism was the first step on a slippery slope toward the loss of Protestant moral authority in America. This was why, in 1951, *Christian Century* (the de facto voice of established Protestantism) decried pluralism as a "national menace" promoting "instability" and the subversion of "the traditional American way of life."[12] Privately, President Franklin D. Roosevelt put it more bluntly in 1942. The United States was "a Protestant country," he said, "and the Catholics and Jews are here under sufferance." Speaking to two high-ranking members of his administration, one Catholic, one Jewish, Roosevelt added that it was "up to you" to "go along with what I want."[13]

This was the sentiment challenged and overcome in Tri-Faith America. Despite the stakes, or perhaps because of them, not all Protestants resisted this transformation, and these sympathetic folks were particularly important in the success of the tri-faith image, especially as it first developed in the 1910s and 1920s. Despite resistance from many other Protestants, this sympathetic lot fought hard to broaden Americans' concept of their country, expanding it from "a Protestant country" to a "Judeo-Christian" one. It also mattered that the United States was founded, politically and culturally, by Protestants whose central ideas regarding political theory emerged from a dissenting tradition. It is hard to imagine the eventual success of religious pluralism in America if those in the dominant position did not have a history of dissent and toleration. "There is, to be sure, a Protestant accent to the American concept of religious freedom," reported *Life* magazine in 1955. "Not only did Protestant sectarianism make [religious freedom] prudent, but Protestant enshrinement of the individual conscience made it popular."[14] How the nation left behind the idea that it was a "Protestant nation," how suburbs and courthouses became battlegrounds, and how the recognition of a pluralist ideal forced the nation to change are at the heart of *Tri-Faith America*.

There were, of course, many unforeseen consequences to the arrival of Tri-Faith America. For instance, the promotion of this new national image began a debate about the role of the state in adjudicating religious matters, and the argument that ended up winning was that ethnic, racial, and religious identities should not matter too much when it comes to governance. Ironically, the idea propounded by Jews and some Catholics that religious minorities might best be served by a secular state simply helped institutionalize a larger trend toward secularization in American life. This was especially true in the courts, which, beginning in the late 1940s, debated, steadily limited, and, by the early 1960s, removed both Bible study and school prayer from public schools. The cost of religious diversity was thus an increasingly secular state. This was never the goal of the strongest advocates of the tri-faith image. It was, rather, one of their worst fears. And in fact the long-term consequence of the creation of this more secular state was a slow reconfiguring of America's religious sociology in the 1970s and 1980s, when political conservatives of all faiths put historical antipathies behind them in order to fight what they saw as an emerging secularism. By the 1970s, the primary religious divisions were no longer between Protestants, Catholics, and Jews but between liberals of all three faiths and conservatives of all three faiths.[15] Indeed, it was those very Supreme Court cases of the early 1960s that helped propel the religious right into being, fueled by a mission to "take back their nation," meaning, of course, to take it back to Protestantism.

A second irony was that as the tri-faith idea became largely accepted, many Catholics and Jews were losing some of what made them sociologically distinct. Even though throughout the 1950s religious ceremonies were heavily attended and religious self-identifying was common, the decline of social barriers eventually led to the decline of distinctiveness. Old ethnic neighborhoods melted away as Americans moved into new suburbs. The orthodox requirements of faith seemed onerous to many of those enjoying the fruits of postwar prosperity. For both Catholics and Jews, these changes sparked heated debates about what it meant to be Catholic or Jewish in a society that no longer punished one for claiming such an identity. Thus as religion became central to the nation's very conception of itself, more and more of the congregation was becoming less and less interested in faith. Not only was the nation officially becoming more secular, but so were many of its citizens.

Both of these ironies are explored in the book's conclusion. But neither diminishes the importance of Tri-Faith America, when many Americans put aside the notion that theirs was a Protestant country. The cultural monism of previous decades no longer fit the image the country was striving to project. Although pluralism had been a sociological fact ever since the nation's founding, accepting, embracing, and celebrating that pluralism was something most Americans were not often willing to do. In Tri-Faith America, the country's citizens reexamined themselves, embraced pluralism, tried to figure out what that would mean for the nation, and sent the country on a course it has yet to complete. Tri-Faith America's arrival was never a foregone conclusion, its creation a work of both circumstance and labor, but its existence changed the way people thought of, discussed, and lived in the United States.

PART ONE

Inventing Tri-Faith America,
Ending "Protestant America"

1

Creating Tri-Faith America

IN 1934, EVERETT R. CLINCHY, a thirty-seven-year-old Presbyterian minister, published a short book with a red cover called *All in the Name of God*. America was not a Protestant nation, Clinchy declared in the book. Instead, it was a nation composed of three equal "culture groups"—Protestant, Catholic, Jewish. Each group had its own unique "way of living," had its own "folkways," and thought its way of living was superior to the others. But Clinchy contended that in order to survive in the face of the totalitarian demagogues emerging worldwide in the 1920s and 1930s, to beat back the prejudices on which they were capitalizing, to allow the United States to live up to its most cherished ideals, no group could be allowed to proclaim its superiority in American civic life. At a civic and social level, the three groups were equal. There could be no Protestant hegemony in America.[1]

Clinchy, a tall, wiry man with slicked-down hair and serious eyes, wrote the book immediately upon returning from Germany, where he witnessed firsthand the political rise of Adolf Hitler. What had happened there could happen in the United States, he worried. In the United States, many Protestants possessed suspicions about the supposed political ambitions of Catholics and the believed economic leverage of Jews. The Ku Klux Klan had reemerged during the 1910s and 1920s too, specifically targeting Catholics and Jews, not just African Americans. Meanwhile, some Catholics and Jews feared that Protestants were willing to do anything to preserve their social, cultural, political, and economic control, even if it meant resorting to violence. If the Klan "had found an American Hitler,"

Clinchy wrote, "it might have become to America what Hitler's Storm Troopers became to Germany."[2] What was needed to prevent an American embrace of totalitarianism was greater understanding between the nation's "three culture groups." Religious hatred had fueled Hitlerism, and religious goodwill was the antidote.

All in the Name of God thus sought to explain the origins of distrust between Clinchy's three faiths of America, and the book detailed the country's long history of religious intolerance. The title, in fact, was a gift from Clinchy's friend Francis Gilbert, who, while reading a draft of the book, grew so flummoxed at the amount of American blood spilled over religion that he threw up his arms and exclaimed, "And all in the name of God!"[3]

In 1928, at just thirty-one years of age, Everett R. Clinchy became head of the National Conference of Christians and Jews (NCCJ), the leading organization in a then growing movement to advocate tolerance, something that came to be called the Goodwill Movement. From his perch atop the NCCJ, Clinchy put forward a vision that the United States was not a Protestant nation but a tri-faith one, premised on a newly formulated idea called the "Judeo-Christian tradition." Used by permission of the Social Welfare History Archives, University of Minnesota Libraries.

Parallel to all the bloodshed, though, Clinchy saw an American past that had thrived because of the country's religious diversity. The United States was the first nation in the world to proclaim religious freedom, Clinchy argued. The Founders had paved the way for religious equality. George Washington had reached out to Catholics and Jews. Thomas Jefferson had written the Virginia Statute on Religious Freedom. James Madison had penned "Memorial and Remonstrance Against Religious Assessments," which made a case for religious freedom instead of mere tolerance. "The American ideal summons its citizens to regard all forms of inner religious belief and cultural tradition as personal characteristics which enrich and give desired variety" to the nation, Clinchy wrote.[4]

More than just calling for a hollow celebration of diversity, however, Clinchy argued that American democracy had thrived because the nation had accepted its diversity, however unevenly. Without accepting difference, the nation would have fallen into authoritarianism, into "cultural monism," as he called it, "a stream whose source is the idea of the totalitarian state." Clinchy added: "If what has been called the American experiment is to succeed, if we are to achieve at ever higher levels in this country a true and free democracy, with equal rights and opportunities for all, we must learn cordially to accept the fact of cultural pluralism and to adapt our patterns of behavior to it."[5]

As he surveyed the American social and cultural landscape of the 1930s, Clinchy thought the most important battles to be worked out were between Protestants, Catholics, and Jews. Denominational differences among Protestants had declined in importance since the Second Great Awakening. Catholics and Jews had immigrated in such numbers during the nineteenth and early twentieth centuries that they could not be ignored. If America was to continue to be a beacon of liberty, it would have to accept its fate as a tri-faith nation.

Advancing this argument became Clinchy's life mission. Indeed, several years before his book's publication, when he was just thirty-one, he had become president of the National Conference of Christians and Jews, the leading organization in a growing movement to advocate interfaith tolerance, something coming to be called the Goodwill Movement.

At its inception, though, this tolerant vision had a considerable opponent. The 1910s and 1920s had witnessed the return of the Ku Klux Klan, calls for "one hundred percent Americanism," and general widespread nativism. It was Woodrow Wilson who famously said in 1919, "Any man who carries a hyphen about him carries a dagger that he is ready to plunge into the vitals of this Republic." Clinchy's mission was to promote a vision of tri-faith cultural pluralism, all while combating an ascendant drive to keep America "native, white, and Protestant."

THE DRIVE TO KEEP AMERICA "NATIVE, WHITE, AND PROTESTANT"

One of the most far-reaching and influential visions of early twentieth-century America emerged from Hiram Wesley Evans, the Imperial Wizard of the newly revived Ku Klux Klan. In 1926, in an effort to understand "the Ku Klux Klan and its place among American institutions," the editors of the *North American Review*, a mainstream quarterly, asked Evans to write an essay describing the Klan's vision, aspirations, and methods. In subsequent issues, they published essays on the meaning of the Klan by a priest, a rabbi, W. E. B. Du Bois, and William Starr Myers, a prominent historian. But it was Evans's vision that most interested the editors.[6]

In "The Klan's Fight for Americanism," Evans painted a picture of hearty, free-dom-loving frontiersmen sowing the seeds of democracy from which every genera-tion of Americans had benefited. From "Roanoke and Plymouth Rock," he wrote, those who founded America had made an epochal break from Old World hatreds. They had created a society that embraced a panoply of freedom-loving values, in-cluding democracy, "fairdealing, impartial justice, equal opportunity . . . acceptance of individual responsibility as well as individual rewards for effort, willingness to sacrifice for the good of his family, his nation and his race before anything else but God, dependence on enlightened conscience for guidance, [and] the right to unham-pered development." It was a society that celebrated freedom and personal respon-sibility, and, Evans argued, when people were free and responsible, they blossomed. A particular interpretation of nineteenth-century America—without the labor struggles, the rise of corporate big business, or increased income disparities—was the prime example of what might be called the Klan's neo-republican vision.

But there was a problem. The millions of immigrants that had come to the United States in the last quarter of the nineteenth century were beginning to adulterate the nation that Evans loved so much. They were threatening its continued existence as a beacon of freedom. By 1920, nearly a quarter of the people living in the United States were either first- or second-generation immigrants. These newcomers—speaking different languages, following different faiths, perpetuating "Old World" customs, conglomerating densely in urban neighborhoods, seeming to vote in polit-ical blocs, smelling of different foods, favoring different social outlets, vying for low-paying jobs—appeared odd, foreign, and threatening to those with longer-standing American credentials. Combined with the internal migration of millions of African Americans from the rural South to the cities of the North and South, many blue-blooded Americans were fearful of what the United States was becoming.

It was this fearful group for whom the Klan claimed to speak. According to Evans, the initial stewards of the American idea were "Nordics" of "white racial background," imbued with "American racial instincts." Evans believed "that there can be no question of the right of the children of the men who made America to own and control America. We believe that when we allowed others to share our heritage, it was by our own generosity and by no rights of theirs. We believe that therefore we have every right to protect ourselves when we find that they are betraying our trust and endangering us. We believe, in short, that we have the right to make America *American* and for Americans."[7] Republican democracy could be revoked when its true owners felt it had been used illegitimately, and Evans's Klan intended to protect the country's proper heritage from the immigrant scourge.

Yes, Evans admitted, the Klan had its history of perverse anti-black violence during Reconstruction. But the new Klan, the second Klan, had a different vision. Black people were still "a special duty and problem of the white American," he wrote. But they had not come here willingly, and they never threatened to "adulterate" America with a separate vision of the country. Still, the African American's "limitations are evident," wrote Evans, and therefore "we will not permit him to gain sufficient power to control our civilization. Neither will we delude him with promises of social equality which we know can never be realized." But Evans did not offer a program to limit African American influence besides demanding stronger anti-miscegenation laws. In his view, African Americans had clear limitations but were too few in number to be truly threatening.[8]

The new immigrants were more problematic, though, especially the Catholics. Evans attacked the Catholic Church for being separatist, anti-democratic, and run by foreigners. Their hierarchy and their authoritarianism befouled the American idea. Drawing a fine distinction, Evans welcomed individual "American Catholics" who were trying to balance national and religious allegiances and who did not bind themselves to the dictates of the Catholic hierarchy. But he distrusted "Roman Catholics," who defended the authority of Rome and were thus incapable of American patriotism and American democracy. "We believe," he wrote, "that its official position and its dogma, its theocratic autocracy and its claim to full authority in temporal as well as spiritual matters, all make it impossible for it as a church, or for its members if they obey it, to cooperate in a free democracy in which Church and State have been separated." Clearly Evans did not have a full understanding of Catholic doctrine, but neither did many other Americans who found their fears articulated in his work.[9]

More problematic than doctrinal issues, Evans said, was that the Catholic Church had taken great pains to "prevent the assimilation" of its people. "Its parochial schools, its foreign born priests, the obstacles it places in the way of marriage with Protestants unless the children are bound in advance to Romanism, its persistent use of the foreign languages in church and school, its habit of grouping aliens together and thus creating insoluble alien masses—all these things strongly impede Americanization." In addition to this persistent communalism, Catholics had also created a political stranglehold on several American cities and were now threatening to push their way into national office. "They vote, in short, not as American citizens, but as aliens and Catholics!" he wrote. "They form the biggest, strongest, most cohesive of all the alien *blocs*."[10] They did not share his vision of America, and they showed no interest or desire to do so soon. Their goal, Evans said, was to use the democracy granted them by "old stock" Protestants to establish Catholic control over American politics. This would allow them to eliminate separation of church and state, prioritize Catholicism at the expense of Protestantism, destroy democracy in favor of authoritarianism, and eventually bring the United States back into the wars of religion that had divided Europe in the fifteenth and sixteenth centuries. "Rome shall not rule America," said Evans, "because Protestantism is an essential part of Americanism; without it America could never have been created and without it she cannot go forward."[11]

If the fusing of Protestantism and Americanism excised Catholics from the American experiment, it likewise left out Jews. And in fact, this second Klan received inspiration from a group of men furious about the death of Mary Phagan, a white Protestant girl in Atlanta whose 1913 murder was pinned on a Jewish factory owner, Leo Frank, who was eventually lynched for the crime. At the new Klan's inception, the core of the organization's members called themselves not the Ku Klux Klan but the Knights of Mary Phagan.[12] Antisemitism was from the beginning a key facet of the revised Klan.

As he did with Catholics, Evans differentiated Jews into those who had been in the United States for decades and those of more recent arrival. Those who had been in the United States for generations were acceptable because "when freed from persecution these Jews have shown a tendency to disintegrate and amalgamate." But the new immigrants, dismissed as "Judaized Mongols," showed a divergence from the American type so great "that there seems little hope of their assimilation."[13] Evans did not think Jews were nearly as powerful as Catholics, and so he did not demonstrate as much concern. But he still saw their persistent communalism and their potential economic power as a threat to his version of Americanism. The melting pot was not what he wanted. Neither was cultural pluralism. Buying into these ideas would threaten the American experiment.

The Klan would, therefore, fight to preserve what was righteous and good in the name of those who had made it righteous and good. To do so, Evans mobilized around the three "American racial instincts" he deemed most important to the preservation of democracy. They were encapsulated in the Klan's new slogan: "Native, white, Protestant supremacy." Each of the three components had played its part in creating the spirit of America, Evans said, and those lacking any of the three would be unable to understand the national spirit. "We are accused of injecting old preju- dices, hatred, race and religion into politics, of creating an un-American class divi- sion, of trying to profit by race and religious enmities, of violating the principle of equality, and of ruining the Democratic party," he wrote. This was simply not true, he said. The Klan was merely insisting "on our inherited right to insure our own safety, individually and as a race, to secure the future of our children, to maintain and develop our racial heritage in our own, white, Protestant, American way."[14] It would not be a violent fight, Evans hoped. His Klan "has never broken up a meeting, nor tried to drive a speaker to cover, nor started a riot, nor attacked a procession or parade, nor murdered men for belonging to the Knights of Columbus or the B'nai B'rith." But, he added, "we are prejudiced against any attempt to use the privileges and opportunities which aliens hold only through our generosity as levers to force us to change our civilization, to wrest from us control of our own country, to exploit us for the benefit of any foreign power—religious or secular—and especially to use America as a tool or cat's-paw for the advantage of any side in the hatreds and quar- rels of the Old World."[15]

Since World War I, Evans felt his organization had done a good job promoting its vision. It was on the ascendant. It attracted men in both the North and the South, with its stronghold in the Midwest. Its membership peaked in 1926 with more than three million members. Most were urban white lower- and middle-class men worried about their economic and social status, a huge swath of Americans. It was so popular that even the future racially liberal U.S. Supreme Court justice Hugo Black became a member because he thought joining would help his law career and help him combat the entrenched political power of the wealthy elite in his native Alabama.

Despite this widespread popularity, it would be too much to suggest that the second Ku Klux Klan represented the mind-set of most Americans. Its member- ship turned over significantly throughout the 1920s. It came under frequent attack for being too vociferous in its complaints. And it was all too easily dismissed as a collection of backward-looking cranks prone to violence. In the late 1920s, the Klan suffered a sharp decline, mostly because of ineffective and often immoral leadership, a broad campaign by journalists against the symbol of the Klan, and the increasing violence of its activities.[16]

But if the Klan's actions were suspect, many felt its vision was not. These were years of triumphant nativism, years filled with public proclamations of anti- Catholicism and antisemitism that often erupted into the national discourse and shaped social policy. The publicity in favor of Prohibition, for example, was overtly anti-immigrant and anti-Catholic, and, despite notable exceptions, the debate about Prohibition looked like a contest between Protestants and Catholics.[17] Meanwhile, the Klan was just one of many organizations that applauded Congress's decision to tighten immigration laws in 1924, with Evans himself referring to immigration restriction as one of the primary "achievements" of the second Ku Klux Klan. At the same time, some of the leading universities in the country began instituting quotas on the number of Jews they would admit. Henry Ford, one of America's best-known citizens, published in 1920 a notorious antisemitic forgery, *The Protocols of the Elders of Zion*, reviving fears of a Jewish plot to take over the world.

This nativist vision of the nation only picked up strength in the 1930s. For Jews, the Depression years were particularly difficult. Between 1933 and 1941, more than one hundred antisemitic groups were founded nationwide.[18] According to a 1938 poll, at least 50 percent of Americans had a low opinion of Jewish people and 35 percent felt that Jews were responsible for the atrocities committed against them in Europe. Four out of five Americans felt it was unimportant to open America's boundaries to Jewish refugees fleeing Hitler.[19] Demagogues gained in stature, the most famous of whom, the Reverend Charles Coughlin, spread his antisemitic screeds to at least fifteen million Americans on the radio. And American Jews were regularly suspected of shady business dealings, of being clannish, and of preserving their own communalism at the expense of the greater nation in which they were residing.[20]

Anti-Catholicism increased during the Great Depression as well. It became especially harsh in 1936, with the beginning of the Spanish Civil War. After the rightist general Francisco Franco attempted to overthrow the popularly elected left-wing government, civil war followed in Spain, and the Catholic Church openly sided with the right-wing rebels. Adolf Hitler and Benito Mussolini also supported Franco, a fact that seemed to confirm suspicions that the Catholic Church was simply the prototype for authoritarian governments. In 1938, a group of American Protestants who were angered by Franco's bombing of civilians complained not to Franco but to the American Catholic hierarchy.[21]

Catholics protested the accusations. The editors of the prominent Jesuit-run journal *America* felt that Catholics were being so slandered in the mainstream press that they initiated a "Bias Contest" to determine which media outlets displayed the most anti-Catholicism. The *Ladies' Home Journal, Esquire, Foreign Affairs,* and the *New York Times* were deemed four of the top ten offenders, demonstrating the deep penetration of anti-Catholicism in mainstream American life. According to *America*, these publications had obfuscated the Catholic Church's position on the Spanish Civil War, but some also had misled readers on Catholic notions about birth control, ecclesiastical control during the Middle Ages, and Catholic support for Italian Fascism.[22] Predictably, chastising the mainstream press did little to allay public suspicions.

On a day-to-day level, discrimination against Catholics and Jews was casually pervasive throughout the United States during the interwar years. Sociologists Claris Edwin Silcox and Galen M. Fisher toured the United States and Canada to investigate interfaith relations, and in 1934 they published their findings in a book called *Catholics, Jews and Protestants*.[23] They concluded that American Jews suffered widespread discrimination in employment, housing, and social fraternization, while American Catholics suffered broad discrimination in political and civic affairs. For instance, employment agencies said they found it necessary to secure information concerning an applicant's religion before they sent an applicant to an interview, fearing that a Catholic or Jewish applicant would not have a chance to secure employment at a Protestant-dominated firm. The firms, meanwhile, blamed the employment agencies for sending them only one kind of candidate.[24] Similarly, in small towns, Catholics and Jews had a hard time getting work as teachers, often the primary form of employment for women. This was largely because teachers were expected to teach not only disciplines such as history and literature but also religion, which was, almost always, centered on Protestantism. One Jewish woman camouflaged her religion and attended Protestant prayer meetings to allay suspicions, but she was eventually found out and had to leave her job. In big cities, foreign accents sometimes kept public schools from employing Jewish women.[25] "One came across so many Jewish men and Jewish women who had been trained to teach and were now engaged in social work that it seemed as if the very exclusion of unusually well-educated Jews from the teaching profession had contributed in part to the extraordinary efficiency of Jewish social service," concluded Silcox and Fisher.[26] In New York City, teachers formed separate federations for Protestant, Catholic, and Jewish teachers, because their needs were felt to be so different.[27]

In white-collar professions, Catholics and Jews also faced obstacles.[28] Banks, for instance, often hired Jews only in areas where knowledge of Yiddish was useful.[29] Jewish-owned firms often adopted non-Jewish names so they would not frighten away business. Many non-Jews began to suspect that businesses with vague-sounding names were simply masking Jewish ownership.[30] The amount and severity of discrimination increased in areas where Jews constituted more than a tiny percentage of the population. It was also more acute "in high society," where "the dislike of the Jew becomes exceedingly vocal and active."[31] Jewish successes, meanwhile, were understood not to be the result of any positive attribute such as "superior brains or superior ability" but had to have been the result of "a 'plot,' and thus the soil is prepared to harbor any seeds which the anti-Semitic propagandist may sow."[32] Silcox and Fisher noted that even though Jews saw discrimination as having a foundation in religion, non-Jews usually cited social reasons—clannishness, a sense of superiority, economic competitiveness—as the main reasons for distrust.

Real estate discrimination was also a problem. Real estate agents and landlords often encouraged the building of a Catholic church because it meant a stable and unwavering list of tenants and buyers in that neighborhood. But in some exclusive neighborhoods, Catholics were discouraged from moving in. Where they were allowed, they often were required or opted to live in a separate sphere, living on certain blocks, shopping at certain stores, and patronizing specific restaurants.[33] Jews faced harsher residential discrimination. Silcox and Fisher reported, "The invasion of any particular area by Jews is often accompanied by the withdrawal or flight of the Gentiles, unless—and often, even when—the Jewish newcomers are persons of recognized social worth." Non-Jews left Brooklyn for Queens once Jews had moved to Brooklyn in prominent numbers, for instance.[34] Furthermore, covenants appeared in numerous neighborhoods denying entrance to Jews and others who were deemed unworthy. Many non-Jews felt that "land values cannot be maintained without such restrictions." Equity was apparently more important than equality.[35]

During their field research, Silcox and Fisher saw "For Gentiles Only" signs in front of several resorts (one, more thorough sign said "For English-speaking Gentiles only").[36] Hotels barred Jews. Social clubs such as the Masons segregated Jews. The Western Golf Association allowed Jewish country clubs only associate membership.[37] Business clubs left out Jews as well, which meant Jews could entertain Gentile customers only at Jewish lunchrooms.

When they asked Gentiles why they had created these restrictions, Silcox and Fisher heard several rationalizations: the "feeling that Jews are 'dirty' and noisy"; that their foods produce "certain offensive odors"; that they were apt to use Sundays "for their day of entertainment or else for fixing whatever needs to be fixed, and that the resulting noise and hilarity disturb Sunday quiet"; and the Gentile fear that being overly friendly toward Jews would drive away certain peers, "and they do not wish to displease their friends."[38]

Catholics, meanwhile, were feared because of their suspect commitment to democracy. Thus only a handful of Catholic politicians ever made it into national politics. From 1909 to the early New Deal, Silcox and Fisher could not identify a single Catholic cabinet member. In 1933, there were only five Catholic senators (and no Jewish ones), forty-four Catholics in the House (out of 435 total Representatives), and only two Catholic governors in the entire forty-eight states. Reflecting the persistent fear of a Catholic political takeover, Silcox and Fisher said "so far as these major offices are concerned, there is no great evidence that the Protestant majority should worry unduly about Catholics and Jews running the country."[39]

Silcox and Fisher also found Catholic parochial schools to be a source of friction between Catholics and non-Catholics. In the early 1930s, the Catholic school system consisted of about 2,000 secondary schools and 8,000 elementary schools, with a total enrollment of about 2.5 million, which would eventually grow to 5 million students by the 1950s. The parochial schools first emerged in the middle of the nineteenth century, as a reaction both to overt Protestantism in public schools and to the desire to provide a unifying Catholic education to Catholic children. It was a costly venture, and Catholics often asked for financial assistance, arguing that by removing so many students from the public school system, they were saving taxpayers the cost of building new schools, hiring new teachers and administrators, and buying new equipment.[40] Non-Catholics, meanwhile, complained that the quality of Catholic education was poor and, more worryingly, that students were denied important lessons about living in a democratic society, which would lead to persistent national disunity and maybe even individual disloyalty. "To the extent to which the Roman Catholic parochial school system supplants the public-school system and teaches cultural elements foreign and antagonistic to those of the United States as a whole," said Donald Young, a usually fair-minded contemporary historian, "it delays the assimilation of Irish, Italian and other immigrants of that faith, and increases group conflict."[41] In 1922 supporters of the Klan successfully outlawed private schools in Oregon in an effort to oust Catholic parochial education. The United States Supreme Court overturned the decision, but public sentiment was clear. At a 1938 meeting of school superintendents in Atlantic City, debate became bitter when President Roosevelt's representative, the Reverend George Johnson, a Catholic, recommended that federal money be made available for parochial schools. Non-Catholics balked. "Let's not have any church— Catholic, Protestant or Jewish—using public money to make propaganda for any policy or belief peculiar to itself," said Dr. George Drayton Strayer of Columbia University. A dean from New York University warned that federal aid for Catholic schools might "cause the spirit of the Ku Klux Klan to ride again."[42]

In sum, Silcox and Fisher concluded: "There is no doubt whatever that there is a tendency in education, social work, etc., to postulate the prevailing Protestant point of view, even in its approximation to secularism, as the American point of view, and to regard other points of view as substantially 'minority reports.'"[43] The second Ku Klux Klan may have been an outlier, overly vociferous in its complaints and its actions, but it was set apart from the mainstream by its methods rather than by its vision. That Protestants, Catholics, and Jews would be able to fulfill Everett Clinchy's pluralist vision was never a foregone conclusion. The success of the tri-faith vision would be an act of will, dependent upon a general fear of total-itarian-type governments and creative and visionary leadership.

ORIGINS OF THE TRI-FAITH IDEA

During the 1910s and 1920s, amid the nativist revolt, many leftist intellectuals began arguing about the possibility of better recognizing America's "cultural plu-ralism," of embracing a "transnational America," of reinterpreting the meaning of "democracy" and the "melting pot." Some educators, meanwhile, were developing an educational theory premised on the notion that outsiders brought "cultural gifts" that could be shared with other students and thus enrich American society through the teaching of principles such as tolerance, respect, and an appreciation of others. A third impulse emerged during the Great Depression, as leftist activists began promoting what historian Michael Denning has called "the Cultural Front," which advocated the idea that all people are created equal regardless of race, reli-gion, class, or gender, and that the best way to combat racial, religious, and other prejudices was through economic equality.[44]

Each of these movements did its part to provide an alternative vision of the United States during the interwar years, and each encountered various levels of success. But the movement that was most transformative in challenging "native, white, Protestant supremacy" emerged in the realm of religion, and it was the tri-faith vision articulated by Everett Clinchy.

The first adventures in goodwill between Protestants, Catholics, and Jews oc-curred during the second industrial revolution of the late nineteenth century, which had encouraged the immigration of millions of Catholics and Jews in the first place. The visible plight of immigrants and the changing character of the nation's largest cities prompted a Social Gospel movement, a Protestant venture designed to use the words of Christ to inspire action against industrial poverty. Protestant ministers such as Walter Rauschenbusch and Washington Gladden were luminaries of the Social Gospel movement, and the Federal Council of Churches of Christ in America became the movement's institutional body. The Federal Council, an umbrella organization that counted most of the large Protes-tant denominations as members, established itself as an early lobbyist for liberal social causes, siding, for instance, with labor over capital in the famous Bethlehem Steel strike of 1910.

But it was also active on the streets of industrial America, and there Protestant Social Gospelers encountered a collection of Catholic and Jewish charitable agencies already at work. The American Catholic Church at first worked from a distance to meet the dire social needs of Catholic immigrants, through support of the labor movement and organizations such as the Knights of Labor. Further expenditures on social welfare were hampered by the fact that the American Catholic Church was growing so fast that most of the Church's energy and finances were directed at basic organizational and institutional development. Early Catholic welfare thus usually focused on each parish performing good works for the benefit of its own parishioners. This changed in 1910 with the creation of the National Conference of Catholic Charities, a loose organization of diocesan charitable organizations. Catholic charitable efforts were consolidated further during World War I when the National Catholic War Council took control of nearly all social and political activities of the American Catholic Church. After the war, the American hierarchy transformed the National Catholic War Council into the National Catholic Welfare Conference (NCWC), which quickly became the clearinghouse of social activities for the Catholic Church in America. Other organizations, such as the Knights of Columbus (founded in 1882), combined charitable efforts with social and religious components and were also pivotal parts of Catholic social outreach.

American Jews had been famous for their communal service for more than a century. To accommodate the millions of Jewish immigrants fleeing the European pogroms that began in 1881, American Jews built free Hebrew schools, established free Jewish libraries, and developed free legal services. Local *landsmanschaften*, or societies of immigrants who originated from the same town or region, offered free loans to Jews, deriving much of their capital from local donations. In 1899, the National Conference of Jewish Charities combined many of these efforts into one national body. Long-standing organizations such as B'nai B'rith (founded in 1843), which combined social, religious, and charitable activities, were joined by the National Council of Jewish Women (1893), the American Jewish Committee (1905), Hadassah (1912), the Anti-Defamation League of B'nai B'rith (1913), and the American Jewish Congress (1928).

Thus when Protestant Social Gospelers performed social outreach across the industrial cities of America, they encountered several Catholic and Jewish agencies with complementary missions. Calls to limit overlapping responsibilities emerged, and in the first years of the twentieth century the three groups began, occasionally and with much suspicion, to work together.[45] Civic crises usually prompted the first gatherings. A 1907 economic recession led several Protestant, Catholic, and Jewish agencies to consolidate their charitable activities in Pittsburgh, for example. A 1912 flood in Dayton, Ohio, led all the charitable organizations of Cincinnati and Dayton to federate, and together they created a community chest. By the early 1930s, community chests operated in more than four hundred cities in the United States and Canada. They were some of the first tri-faith organizations.[46]

Deeper social problems provoked other kinds of interfaith gatherings. In 1908, the growing specter of secularism led the Religious Education Association, founded by mainline Protestants five years earlier, to bring together Protestants, a few Jews, and a small scattering of Catholics to discuss methods in religious education that would combat the allures of an increasingly secular society. Despite hopes for increased interfaith gatherings, often only Protestants and Jews attended meetings, and sometimes attendance was limited to just Protestants, but before this there had never been sustained cooperation between the three faiths on a national level.[47]

These initial gatherings in the face of civic crises allowed religious leaders, however slowly, to begin to understand what the image of tri-faith unity meant. Speaking together, the three groups seemed to possess greater moral authority and, it seemed, the capacity to voice the moral concerns of the entire nation. Their public appearances together created a stirring image. To capitalize on this broader moral authority, in 1914 representatives of the three faiths came together in the Church Peace Union (now the Carnegie Council) to protest the United States' slide into World War I and "to co-operate in abolishing savage war and establishing the reign of peace through arbitration of international disputes."[48] Following their lead, other similar groups appeared. The tri-faith American Council of the World Alliance for International Friendship was organized in 1914 with a mission similar to that of the Church Peace Union.[49] During World War I itself, the federal government requested that representatives of the three faiths work together to aid the troops rather than do so separately, which was causing confusion.[50] Beginning in 1923, three of the largest civic organizations representing Protestants, Catholics, and Jews came together to speak out on social issues, proposing to hold meetings regularly and create something of a tri-faith moral bloc. The Social Service Department of the Federal Council, led by the Reverend James Myers, the Social Action Department of the NCWC, led by the Reverend John A. Ryan, and the Social Justice Commission of the Central Conference of American Rabbis, led by Rabbis Edward L. Israel and Sidney E. Goldstein, collaborated on a regular basis to draft statements on industrial relations, strikes, unemployment, and working conditions.[51]

Despite the appearance of amity in civic affairs, tri-faith cooperation ranged "all the way from the most friendly cooperation, on the one hand, to distrust and friction, on the other," according to several participants.[52] At a broad cultural and social level, "nonsectarian" still generally meant "blandly Protestant" within the United States, and until 1920, religious goodwill was simply a by-product of civic activities.

The rise of the second Ku Klux Klan and the more general spread of post–World War I nativism shifted the focus of interfaith efforts. In short, goodwill became a cause in itself. In 1920, as a direct response to Henry Ford's publication of *The Protocols of the Elders of Zion* and the continued growth of the second Ku Klux

Klan, several Protestants, a handful of Jews, and some Catholics created the American Committee of the Rights of Religious Minorities.[53] The committee's manifesto, signed by, among others, William Jennings Bryan, Charles Evans Hughes, Louis Marshall, and James Cardinal Gibbons, read, in part, "We appeal to all people of good will to condemn every effort to arouse divisive passions against any of our fellow countrymen; to aid in eradicating racial prejudice and religious fanaticism; and to create a just and humane public sentiment that shall recognize the Fatherhood of God and the brotherhood of man."[54] The mission was no longer simply to combat civic injustices but to fight intolerance. Other similarly directed groups quickly copied the American Committee's efforts at goodwill. The Central Conference of American Rabbis created a Committee on Goodwill in the early 1920s, inviting Catholics and Protestants to join. The American Good Will Union and the World Fellowship of Faiths emerged too.[55] Universities took part in the new spirit, and during the academic year 1924–25, the University of Iowa developed the first tri-faith School of Religion, relying on representatives from each of the three faiths to teach classes on their respective traditions as well as courses on interfaith goodwill. A Catholic priest associated with the school said, "The School of Religion has served to bring Catholics, Protestants and Jews together in various cooperative undertakings . . . [and] while each group continues to maintain its special student organization, their work has been unified in many ways." UCLA, Columbia, and Cornell soon developed similar schools.[56]

One of the most prominent if short-lived goodwill organizations emerged in 1922. The National Conference on the Christian Way of Life, established by the Rockefeller Foundation, originally fostered conversations on "industrial, racial, and international problems in the hope of discovering whether there is a modern Christian way of living." The group at first focused on interfaith harmony between Protestants and Catholics, but it eventually changed its name to the Inquiry due to the large number of Jewish scholars and philanthropists eager to participate.[57] As the Inquiry, the organization began to formulate a loose plan to alter the Klan-centered definition of Americanism. Jews' demands to be included, and Protestant and Catholic willingness to accommodate that demand, demonstrated that the triad of Protestant-Catholic-Jew was coming to be the norm in the interfaith Goodwill Movement.

THE NATIONAL CONFERENCE OF CHRISTIANS AND JEWS

The growing number of goodwill organizations and the divergent agendas of each group led many goodwill advocates to see a need to combine efforts and move beyond pronouncements into actions. This was the goal of the most important goodwill group founded during these years, the National Conference of Christians and Jews (NCCJ). The NCCJ traced its origins to 1924, when the Federal Council set up a committee to investigate the question "What makes a person join the Ku Klux Klan?" The committee's answer was that most Americans did not have accurate information about America's minority groups, especially Catholics and Jews, and this lack of information allowed prejudices to metastasize, fueled by bigots such as Henry Ford and Hiram Evans.[58] To fill this vacuum, the Federal Council created a Committee on Good Will, led by Federal Council leaders John W. Herring and S. Parkes Cadman, who hoped to "take such positive action as they could to bring about better understanding amongst the various cultural groups throughout the country" (and by "cultural groups" they meant Protestants, Catholics, and Jews).[59]

As with almost all the goodwill organizations of the era, Protestants initiated the Federal Council's Committee on Good Will, with Catholics and Jews as the sole invitees.[60] Protestant overtures were important because goodwill leaders were afraid that minority-led groups would look like fronts for religious outsiders clamoring for first-class status. According to Roger Straus, a Jewish activist associated with the Federal Council's Committee, "The leadership in this movement has come, as it should come, from the Protestant group."[61] Carlton J. H. Hayes, a Catholic participant, wrote in 1937, "I have always maintained that *in this country* Protestants have the major responsibility for assuring justice and true toleration to non-Protestants, not because they are Protestants but because they are [the] *majority* group."[62]

For their part, Protestant interest in interfaith groups had grown during the First World War, when Protestants became aware of the patriotism of Catholics and Jews and when the chaplaincy of the U.S. armed forces was structured along tri-faith lines.[63] For a variety of reasons, after the war this interest grew. Several Protestant clerics and laymen became openly embarrassed by the rise of the Klan and the nativism that spawned it. Newton D. Baker, an Episcopalian convert, prominent lawyer, and secretary of war under Woodrow Wilson, was shocked by the amount of nativism that emerged after World War I, and began to participate in a series of goodwill activities in and around his native Cleveland. After the anti-Catholic backlash during Al Smith's 1928 campaign for the presidency, Baker befriended Everett Clinchy and became the Protestant co-chairman of the NCCJ.[64] Meanwhile, S. Parkes Cadman, the son of British coal miners and one of the founders of the Federal Council, embraced goodwill in an effort to reduce suffering.[65]

A final, less amiable reason for Protestant interest was proselytization. Interfaith encounters, some Protestants argued, were perfect for creating converts. During the decades straddling the turn of the twentieth century, at least fifteen Protestant organizations emerged in order to convert recently immigrated Jews.[66]

There was no concerted effort to go after Catholics, although "in nearly every Protestant church there are some persons who have come out of Catholicism."[67]

This missionary zeal created discomfort for Catholics and Jews, and would hamper the advancement of the Goodwill Movement until World War II.[68] It also divided the Federal Council's Committee on Good Will.[69] In 1926, in the wake of the Scopes "monkey trial," one committee member said "that some of the fundamentalists in the Council were not going to permit us to do business in a gentlemanly way with the Jews."[70] According to these "fundamentalists," there should be no interaction between Christians and Jews absent the goal of winning souls for Christ.

In addition to making meetings less amiable, the divide over proselytization indicated the weakness in having a goodwill effort emerge from within an established Protestant organization. What was needed, said several Federal Council members sympathetic to the Goodwill Movement, was an organization of Protestants, Catholics, and Jews that stood apart from any doctrinal religious group and could have as its sole mission the promotion of interfaith goodwill.[71] Prominent members of the Federal Council, the Central Conference of American Rabbis, the Union of American Hebrew Congregations, the Archdiocese of New York, and other groups met to advance the idea.[72] In 1927 they created the National Conference of Jews and Christians (Protestant and Catholic), which began operations in 1928. In 1938, it changed its name to the National Conference of Christians and Jews (NCCJ) to minimize the appearance that the group was a front for Jewish causes and also to get rid of the parenthetical inclusion of Protestants and Catholics.

From the beginning, then, the NCCJ was a tri-faith enterprise. Its in-house historian wrote after interviewing several of the founders, "A need was felt for a structure in which American citizens could meet on a parity in conference, not with Protestants as hosts." As the NCCJ evolved, it attracted Protestants and Jews fairly easily, and a good number of Catholics as well. As early as 1928, the American Jewish Committee, the Anti-Defamation League of B'nai B'rith, the NCWC, the Knights of Columbus, and the Federal Council all sent representatives to NCCJ meetings, bolstering its emerging status as the nation's premier goodwill organization.

The NCCJ board also had the good sense to feature prominent leaders from each faith. When it named its first three co-chairs, it selected Roger Straus, a Jew and a prominent industrialist, Newton D. Baker, a Protestant and former secretary of war during World War I, and Carlton J. H. Hayes, a Catholic and a historian at Columbia University. The tri-faith tradition was set. The board also had the good sense to select as its president Presbyterian minister Everett R. Clinchy. A talented writer with a keen eye toward publicity, Clinchy was able to formulate and express a national vision that easily countered that of Hiram Wesley Evans. He was also just thirty-one when he became president, which allowed him to serve a long tenure as president and ended up giving the NCCJ institutional continuity. Along with Roger Straus, who remained the NCCJ's Jewish co-chair until the early 1950s, Clinchy was the ever-present organization man. His connection to the NCCJ allowed him to meet presidents, kings, and celebrated theologians. It also allowed him to travel the world to preach his message of tri-faith goodwill.[73]

From the beginning, the NCCJ sought to be an active promoter of a new kind of Americanism. Its first mission statement, drafted in 1935, set its purpose: "Believing in a spiritual interpretation of the universe and deriving its inspiration therefrom, The National Conference exists to promote justice, amity, understanding and cooperation among Jews, Catholics and Protestants in the United States, and to analyze, moderate and finally eliminate intergroup prejudices which disfigure and distort religious, business, social and political relations, with a view to the establishment of a social order in which the religious ideals of brotherhood and justice shall become the standards of human relationships."[74] Because the mission was centered on a vision of promoting goodwill between Protestants, Catholics, and Jews, it was, the NCCJ argued, all-inclusive. Its goal was national and ambitious: to develop a new "social order" centered on brotherhood and justice.

The NCCJ also hoped to be proactive, bringing together the three faiths before hostilities occurred. Its philosophy plainly acknowledged that "conflict between culture groups" was "a part of American life," and even "the essence of the national tradition and character." The NCCJ founders "would not have conjured [conflict] away if that were possible. [They] did not think it could be safely ignored," wrote one of the founders.[75] And conflicts regarding religion were inevitable. The Catholic claim of papal infallibility, the Jewish insistence on being the "chosen people" of the Old Testament and on preserving Jewish communalism, and the Protestant insistence on the supremacy of the Bible and on private judgment all posed irreconcilable theological problems. But there were commonalities as well. Each faith was premised on a personal God of righteousness and love. Each believed in the sacredness of all men as children of a common Heavenly Father. And each demanded a realization of God's will by practicing social justice and brotherhood. Promoting the commonalities while not dismissing the deep divisions was the guiding mission. Borrowing from earlier goodwill efforts, the NCCJ's ever-present slogan became "the brotherhood of man under the Fatherhood of God."

From the beginning, NCCJ members repeated tirelessly that they were not interested in making converts or in preaching some "vague sentiment of human brotherhood," as one founder put it. Their goal was to promote mutual understanding in order to prevent conflict from becoming violence, and they understood this as a way to make Protestants better Protestants, Catholics better Catholics, and Jews better Jews. This meant "not a denial or playing down of actual frictions, but rather a joint effort to recognize their origins and to prevent them from remaining (or becoming) occasions for animosity." In one of the first seminars held by the NCCJ, Catholic co-chair Carleton J. H. Hayes warned against "the assumption that strife and prejudice would disappear if only you could teach people to hew through the jungle of their diverse beliefs and attitudes to a common lowest denominator. On the contrary, what brought people together . . . was esteem and appreciation for the highest reaches of their respective culture."[76] The leaders thus "sought to dissect clashes resulting from differences in social or educational policy, not to hide them under much talk about tolerance and fairness."[77] The message was that, through education, cultural pluralism could work. In response to a Protestant lay leader's claim that "since no amount of palaver will lessen our religious differences, hadn't we better quit discussing them and confine our attention to cooperation in social work or civil affairs?" the NCCJ board responded: "We would be fooling ourselves if we did not state the fact that Protestants and Catholics and Jews each hold fundamentally opposing philosophies which, though they meet at many points, contain certain elements that are distinct and which cannot be fused. We must accept the fact of the existence of such incompatibilities and stop fretting about them. We shall never think exactly alike. We must find a meeting place on another plane than that on which we do our theological thinking. We must develop that high quality of respect for unlikeness which is the work of true cultivation of spirit. Cultural pluralism in America is not to be deprecated but welcomed."[78]

Catholics were the leeriest of the three faiths about joining goodwill efforts, partly because, since 1895, Catholics had been told by the Pope that, "unless by necessity to do otherwise, Catholics ought to prefer to associate with Catholics." In 1928, Pope Pius XI furthered this sentiment when he released an encyclical opposing religious interaction between Catholics and Protestants.[79] Furthermore, American Catholic communalism remained strong in the 1920s and 1930s. Shunned by most Protestants for the previous hundred years, they had created self-sufficient Catholic ghettos, Catholic professional organizations, Catholic welfare societies, and gigantic Gothic cathedrals that announced the Catholic presence and persistence in America. Taking papal dictates to their logical next step, many American bishops simply prohibited Catholics from participating in goodwill groups such as the NCCJ. The bishop of North Carolina, for example, believed that "this Brotherhood business would lead to some compromising of the Catholic belief or doctrine."[80]

Not all Catholics remained aloof. *Commonweal* and its editor, Michael Williams, led the charge for Catholic inclusion.[81] Former World War I chaplain Father Francis P. Duffy also became an advocate for the Goodwill Movement.[82] While the

NCCJ had more difficulty finding Catholic support compared to that from Protestants or Jews, it did have plenty of Catholic members, both lay people and clergy. Furthermore, Catholic participation was aided by the fact that there were three members in the tri-faith conception, not just two. One Catholic goodwill participant told the Episcopal bishop in his town, where goodwill efforts had been successful, "The absence of friction and the presence of such a high degree of Catholic cooperation is partly due to the fact that in all cooperative efforts all three—not only two of the faiths—have been called in. This has pleased Roman Catholics because they then could cooperate on a broad religious basis without being lured into any exclusively Christian line-up with Protestants, where their own interpretation might be compromised."[83]

One other thing that helped ease Catholic reticence was that when the NCCJ was founded, it had an immediate opportunity to prove its pro-Catholic credentials by defending Al Smith against the anti-Catholic diatribes that emerged during his bid to become president in 1928. Utilizing its philosophy of open engagement, the NCCJ invited discussions about Smith's Catholicism among leaders of the three faiths, and after the election it organized a conference in which a priest displayed his collection of anti-Catholic handbills that were produced during Smith's campaign.[84] Despite the lack of evidence for any more substantive protest against the visceral anti-Catholicism that emerged, the NCCJ would forever use its defense of Al Smith as an early assertion of its Catholic bona fides.

Latter-day publicity materials would also lionize the group's very early efforts to publicize and protest European antisemitism.[85] Beginning as early as 1931, the NCCJ published articles with titles such as "The Anti-Semitic Menace in Germany."[86] Its *Information Bulletin* reported on the issue regularly. "The present situation in the world regarding anti-Semitism deserves some attention and warrants educational measures on the part of non-Jews," wrote Clinchy in 1931. He cited antisemitic parades in Mexico City and the rise of National Socialism in Germany.[87] Clinchy also urged major Protestant denominations to speak out against antisemitism.[88] In May 1933, the NCCJ organized a drive to have twelve hundred Christian ministers sign a letter drafted by Harry Emerson Fosdick, perhaps the nation's most prominent liberal Protestant, that denounced Hitler's treatment of Germany's Jews. "We, a group of Christian ministers, are profoundly disturbed by the plight of our Jewish brethren in Germany," it read. "That no doubt may exist anywhere concerning our Christian conscience in the matter, we are constrained, alike with sorrow and indignation, to voice our protests against the present ruthless persecution of the Jews under Herr Hitler's regime." In the press, the NCCJ rightly got credit for orchestrating the gesture.[89]

Beyond Protestants, Catholics, and Jews, other religions were not included in the NCCJ's message of brotherhood. This was mainly because they were not present on the mean streets of industrial America (there was not a single mosque in the United States until 1915, for example). Early on, though, one NCCJ board member, Bruno Lasker, raised the question of whether the NCCJ should be more inclusive. "When I first brought up this matter in the NCCY [*sic*] . . . this body could not expand the scope of its concern," Lasker wrote in 1953. "And so American popular prejudice against the peoples of the Middle East, among others, based as it largely is on false concepts of their religious beliefs and institutions, is now as serious a factor in American foreign policy as anti-Catholicism was a generation ago."[90] There seemed to be only three "culture groups" in America—Protestant, Catholic, and Jew—and they remained the focus of the NCCJ.

Despite its public prominence, the NCCJ remained a small organization until World War II. Funds evaporated with the Great Depression. "Every time we issued a check," said one of the office workers, "we had to add our balance three or four times to make sure it wouldn't bounce."[91] Its office on 42nd Street in New York City had to be closed almost as soon as it opened, forcing the tiny NCCJ staff to move into the offices of the Federal Council.

There were several achievements, though. The NCCJ had consolidated the goodwill efforts of each of the three faiths in order to protest resurgent nativism. It had incorporated the American Jewish Committee and the Anti-Defamation League, which were protecting the rights of Jews in the face of rising antisemitism. It worked with the NCWC and the Knights of Columbus to consolidate a Catholic counterattack to the Klan. And it incorporated the weightiness of the Protestant perspective, which made its vision more authentically national. One early member said it "gave expression to a vision few saw, and fewer acted on in the late 1920's: universal relatedness among all believers."[92] But its work was only beginning. It needed to promote its vision more broadly. This was where Everett Clinchy would excel.

EVANGELISTS OF TRI-FAITH AMERICA

On the morning of Tuesday, October 31, 1933, a priest, a rabbi, and a minister boarded an airplane at what was then called Newark Municipal Airport. Before walking up the steps of the airplane, Everett Clinchy, Rabbi Morris S. Lazaron, and Father John Elliot Ross grinned for a few publicity shots and chatted with a reporter from Paramount Publix Corporation, who was toting along a camera crew. The resulting film short—which a few days later appeared in theaters across the country—said the three men were embarking on an "all American tour, taking them to thirty-eight cities in twenty-one states, from coast to coast, in the interest of justice, amity and understanding between Protestants, Catholics and Jews." They were doing so free of charge, under the auspices of the NCCJ.[93] Flashing a big smile, Clinchy said, "You see we are giving a practical demonstration that a Roman Catholic priest, a rabbi of the synagogue, and [a] Protestant cleric can live together harmoniously in a suitcase for seven weeks. If there is one word which character-izes our endeavor, it is good sportsmanship in American intergroup relations." Next, Father Ross announced, "I am going on this tour not only as a Catholic priest but as an American citizen. Religious liberty was made in America, and we must keep it safe from Old World jealousies and hates." Then Rabbi Lazaron dramatically took off his glasses and said: "As representative of the mother religion whose fol-lowers have been here since colonial days and who have stood shoulder to shoulder with our fellow citizens in the struggles of war and peace, I deem it a privilege to participate in this pilgrimage to ensure and maintain the American ideal of reli-gious liberty and human brotherhood."[94]

And then they were off. The three men traveled to Baltimore, then Washington, D.C., Cleveland, Columbus, and on and on, through thirty-eight cities and count-less discussions over a month and a half, making appearances and doing radio interviews. This ambitious publicity effort helped enshrine the tri-faith image in 1930s America. *Time* magazine, one of the many major media outlets covering the journey, called them the "Tolerance Trio."[95]

Before the trio began their journey, Protestants had written Clinchy chastising him for selling out to Catholics and Jews. Why should the Protestant majority compromise its place atop the social, cultural, political, and economic hierarchy? Why accommodate aggressive Jews and smug Catholics? Some Jews, meanwhile, wrote Lazaron wondering if Catholics were using the Tolerance Trio to promote Catholic political ambitions. In letters to Ross, some Catholics thought Jews were behind the whole thing, using the moral weight of a priest and minister to stem American antisemitism. Other Catholics warned Father Ross against playing poker on the trip, because "the Rabbi would end up with all the money!"[96]

As they toured the country, the trio used these complaints as starting points for their public discussions. Onstage or in the radio booth, the men developed a for-mat that allowed one member of the trio to ask questions of the others, allowing a full response before beginning with a new line of inquiry. They always tackled the thorny issues of Catholic political ambition and Jewish greed, which emerged as prominent reasons for distrust at every stop. They discussed why Protestants were alarmed by the idea of having a Catholic in the White House. They discussed whether Jews really constituted an economic power in the United States. Over

"New York — A minister, a priest and a rabbi unite against intolerance! Goodwill trio to preach gospel of amity and fellowship throughout the United States."

Paramount Newsreel Magazine

After returning from a trip to Germany in 1933, Everett Clinchy thought he'd have to go on the road to promote his vision of tri-faith tolerance. The result was a seven-week journey through thirty-eight cities where he engaged in frank discussion about divisions among Protestants, Catholics, and Jews, while accompanied by a priest and a rabbi. Here, the "Tolerance Trio," as *Time* dubbed them, prepare to disembark. The first trio was (left to right) Rev. Everett R. Clinchy, Father John Elliott Ross, and Rabbi Morris S. Lazaron. Used by permission of the Social Welfare History Archives, University of Minnesota Libraries.

time, they concluded, "the emotions vividly evident during the period turned in wholesome directions."[97]

Three men of faith in full religious garb traveling and speaking together was newsworthy in 1933 America. Through radio, local newspapers, and newsreels, the trio become widely recognized nearly everywhere they went. On November 11, just twelve days after their initial departure, a Chicago hotel clerk immediately recognized them from the Paramount newsreel he had seen in a theater a few days earlier. The hotel manager then came down and "insisted" the three men move from their inexpensive rooms to more spacious accommodations. As they toured the Chicago World's Fair, bystanders pointed them out. And when they dined at Chicago's famous Old Heidelberg restaurant, the headwaiter greeted them with gifts.[98]

At the end of the seven-week journey, they had reached 54,000 people in 129 different meetings, not counting those who had heard them on their twenty-one radio broadcasts or seen them in the various newsreels. In their wake, they left behind thirty-four different local organizations charged with promoting goodwill among Protestants, Catholics, and Jews. For a small, financially beleaguered organization, this was heady fruit.[99]

By the early 1930s, Tolerance Trios were not the only promotional tools in the NCCJ's arsenal. It had hosted a series of seminars, or Institutes of Human Relations, which were, in effect, local conferences of Protestant, Catholic, and Jewish leaders discussing prominent misunderstandings between the three groups. At its first institute, held at Columbia University, one conferee asked a Catholic priest, "Must I, a Methodist, go to hell?" The priest joked: "That's up to you!" which got laughs. He then added: "In Catholic theology God in His infinite wisdom allows freedom of conscience. I would hope that you should become a Catholic. But as long as your reason and conscience truly lead you to do otherwise, you have as good a chance to get to heaven as any Catholic."[100] While this was a bit theologically soft regarding the Catholic position on salvation outside the faith, it did serve as a palliative to members of other faiths and, in fact, embodied a position that was becoming increasingly common within American Catholic thinking. Later NCCJ institutes carried themes such as public opinion in a democracy, minority rights, and the common ground the three faiths shared. Leaders of the various religious civil organizations often played pivotal roles in the institutes. The American Jewish Committee, the NCWC, and the Federal Council often had a prominent member in highly visible leadership roles in the seminars. Some contingencies of each faith abstained, including Orthodox Jews and conservative Protestants, but for the most part the NCCJ did not have trouble finding conferees from each of the three faiths.[101]

In addition to the institutes, NCCJ fieldworkers also organized roundtables across the country, which brought together community leaders from each of the three faiths to discuss informally what they called the "rubs" in that particular community. NCCJ leaders hoped the roundtables would become permanent local organizations affiliated with the NCCJ, and often they did. It was an easy way to develop a national presence without having to invest significant resources.[102]

Both of these methods were successful in promoting the idea of interfaith good-will, but by far the most visible efforts were the Tolerance Trios. The idea was Everett Clinchy's, and his inspiration was the Nazi storm troopers he saw while visiting Germany in 1932–33. To ensure there was no anti-tolerance insurgency in the United States, Clinchy believed the NCCJ would have to go to the people, dispelling myths directly. "This kind of 'storm-trooping,'" wrote Clinchy, "is intended as a characteristically American 'mission,' in sharp contrast to Nazi precept and procedure."[103]

After Clinchy's first triumph, sending Tolerance Trios across the nation became an NCCJ staple. The NCCJ even coined a word to describe their discussions: "tria-logue." And Clinchy was keenly aware that the three men in the first trio were easily interchangeable. In fact, the more evangelists for goodwill he had, the better off he would be. And so throughout the 1930s the NCCJ recruited religious leaders to continue the journey. A variety of priests, rabbis, and ministers, as well as prominent laymen of each faith, came on board.[104] Before being sent throughout the country, the trios were given a long script they might follow. Somewhat shock-ingly, the script began with a stunning, unreferenced use of Booker T. Washing-ton's Atlanta Compromise speech, from Father Ross: "In all things religious we Protestants, Catholics, and Jews can be as separate as the fingers of a man's out-stretched hand; in all things civic and American we can be as united as a man's clenched fist."[105]

This paraphrasing of Booker T. Washington's theory of segregation went with-out comment in the NCCJ script. W. E. B. Du Bois had written strongly against Washington's metaphor three decades earlier, and in the 1960s it would be deni-grated for giving the appearance of acquiescence to racial segregation, but Wash-ington's metaphor served the NCCJ cause perfectly. The NCCJ had to be on guard against the appearance of proselytizing, so affirming a desire to remain as separate as the fingers on an outstretched hand was an ideal parallel for their vision of rela-tions between Protestants, Catholics, and Jews. But of course the use of the phrase also suggests a lack of concern about drawing parallels between racial minorities and religious ones, highlighting the fact that the pluralism advocated by the NCCJ was never explicitly inclusive of race. To borrow the phrase, then, was both insen-sitive and revealing of what was absent from the NCCJ agenda.[106]

After the unreferenced Washington metaphor, the script went on to reveal the truly stunning goal of the NCCJ: national unity under the banner of religious goodwill. Clinchy discussed the "two ways by which we may achieve national unity . . . the way of the demagogue . . . [or] the way of mutual appreciation." The nation consisted of and would thrive as a nation of believers unified not in faith, but in what undergirded their respective faiths. If religious bigotry could be made to go away, the nation would then recognize its common ideological core.

After the first tour, tens if not hundreds of other trios emerged. Touring through the South, Rabbi Philip S. Bernstein of Rochester recalled receiving a surprise invitation to address the Alabama state legislature. "We also got into little Southern towns where they had never seen a priest or a rabbi before," he said.[107] Father Michael J. Ahern, S.J., a Jesuit professor at Weston College in Massachusetts, participated in several different trios and estimated that over a period of fifteen years he spoke on more than twenty-five hundred occasions and traveled more than fifty thousand miles for the NCCJ cause.[108] A local Des Moines team, which was first organized in the wake of the original trio in 1933, traveled more than eleven thousand miles through Iowa, Kansas, and Illinois. They were called "a religious minstrel show" and earned the nickname "Corn Belt Crusaders."[109] In 1939 alone, Protestant, Catholic, and Jewish speakers appeared together at ten thousand meetings in two thousand communities in all forty-eight states.[110] They were a hot ticket during the Great Depression, when the theme of working together in order to honor individual dignity resonated loudly throughout the nation.

Two decades later, many in the NCCJ were somewhat embarrassed by the trios, thinking the potted performances were facile appeals to emotion. They took greater pride in the social scientific work on prejudice the NCCJ encouraged in later decades. They were, however, heartened to hear the 1955 testimony of Archbishop Gerald Bergan, who claimed the trios had fundamentally changed the culture in Iowa, where his diocese was. Because of the trios, Bergan wrote, the state had moved from a culture of "fear, mistrust and isolation, to understanding, good will and cooperation." Coming from a Catholic priest in what had been a stronghold for the Ku Klux Klan, Bergan's words were reassuring.[111]

In performing this work, the trios became new symbols of American moral righteousness, focused on confronting problems directly, being honest, and promoting the Golden Rule. They also put on display a new image of national unity. In a 1940 essay called "Satan, Be Warned," the *Saturday Evening Post* wrote of the tri-faith vision: "A united moral front is in the making. Such an alliance is the first of its kind. If what has already come to pass in hundreds of American communities is a portent, it may prove to be one of the most remarkable forces that ever ganged up on the devil." The essay mentioned how the NCCJ mission was seeping into the nation. New Jersey's state legislature authorized an official Good-Will Commission in 1938, consisting of five Protestants, five Catholics, and five Jews. Catholics had invited Protestants and Jews to work on the Church's Commission on American Citizenship. Protestants and Catholics in Knoxville, Tennessee, agreed to match funds, dollar for dollar, raised during a Jewish appeal for European refugee relief.[112] In the wake of the trios, a new moral image was emerging, one centered on tri-faith unity. As an NCCJ annual report revealed: "Priests, rabbis and ministers speaking from single platforms on social affairs is becoming 'the usual thing.'"[113]

THE NEW USUAL

In 1941, the NCCJ commissioned a rising star in the world of academic sociology, Alfred McClung Lee of New York University, to conduct an internal examination of its programs. He was asked to assess how effective the organization was in promoting its mission and if it had challenged the definition of Americanism promoted by Hiram Wesley Evans and other post–World War I nativists. Lee's report was overwhelmingly positive. The NCCJ had established local roundtables on a permanent basis in more than two hundred cities. More than two thousand less formal committees also existed, often in smaller towns.[114] The various Institutes of Human Relations had brought together thousands of leaders from the three faiths to discuss big national issues, including the country's impending participation in World War II. While these men and women might have been interested in the NCCJ's work from afar, they were "'sold' on becoming active by what they saw" at the institutes and roundtables.[115] The trios, meanwhile, had been incredibly successful in engaging interfaith dialogue and helping dispel the myths each group might have about the others. "In the last twelve years it is estimated that Protestants, Catholics and Jews sat down together 250,000 times to consider their relations as American citizens belonging to differing religious beliefs," Lee wrote. "That is a social change which has permanent effects." He added: "Students of social and cultural change agree that such devices as trialogue are the most efficient way of impressing new patterns of thought upon a society. New patterns more readily become habitual and customary when they are linked to a dramatic event. The trialogue, wherever it is presented, is a dramatic event."[116]

These techniques had been so effective, Lee wrote, that they had spurred the creation of yet another major NCCJ venture, the Religious News Service (RNS). Begun in 1934, the Religious News Service wrote and distributed stories about the three faiths, making the stories available to subscribers the same way the

Associated Press did. By the end of 1934, RNS had more than 150 paying sub-scribers, rising to 323 secular and religious newspapers and radio stations by 1941. The RNS's fifteen-minute weekly radio program (sent out in script form) reached eighty-five stations every week, sending to Americans yet another form of its message of goodwill between the three "culture groups."[117]

Regarding the NCCJ's capacity to transform American culture, Lee was adamant that the NCCJ was beginning to fulfill Clinchy's hopes that it could change Ameri-can "folkways," its *way of life*.[118] "The fact that these last fourteen years have not witnessed a recurrence of powerfully organized intolerance is in part, probably in large part, a tribute to the Conference as a communication agency and a demon-stration of the value of the atmosphere of fair play that the Conference has nur-tured," he wrote. Some eight hundred organizations had emerged during the 1930s to promote intolerance, he said, and "none was able to make religious intolerance the basis of a broad and popular movement." Thanks "in large part" to the NCCJ, "the depression and the clouds of war in 1928–41 did not produce an integrated, 'financially successful,' intolerance movement like the Ku Klux Klan of the post-World-War-I period." Instead, the NCCJ had created "a mood new in the history of human relations in the United States."[119]

Between 1928 and 1941, then, the NCCJ had become a propagandist for a new kind of America. It was a pluralist vision, centered on the common foundation Protestants, Catholics, and Jews shared, and it was intended to be nationally all-inclusive. The tri-faith image of the nation was beginning to take hold. There were of course some who opposed the idea. Members of the Klan wanted to pre-serve Protestant hegemony. Some more thoughtful Protestants were equally wary of sharing the stage with Catholics and Jews, with one Protestant businessman saying he was "weary of going to hear us Protestants made 'the goat.' We are so anxious to make amends to the 'minority faiths' for what some Protestants have said or done that we refrain from referring to the bigoted or sectarian things Cath-olics or Jews are doing. We are too humble. We take the punishment lying down."[120] Many Catholics were similarly resistant to the tri-faith call. Not only were they suspicious of Protestant motives, but they also sought to preserve Catholic sepa-rateness. The first Tolerance Trio, for example, could not perform in Cincinnati and Chicago because the local Catholic bishop in each diocese would not allow Father Ross to share a stage with Lazaron and Clinchy.[121]

Despite these hiccups, the goodwill efforts of the interwar years were starting to create a new vision of America, one based on tri-faith pluralism, one grounded in something that was coming to be called "Judeo-Christianity." During World War II, that vision would take off.

2

Tri-Faith America as Standard Operating Procedure

IN EARLY 1942, just months after the bombing of Pearl Harbor, the NCCJ was desperately exploring ways it could assist the war effort. If it could not do that, "all
organizations like the Conference should fold up and cease operations for the dura-
tion of the war," said Charles Evans Hughes, the retired U.S. Supreme Court justice
and an NCCJ luminary.[1] After a few easily dismissed ideas, Andrew W. Gottschall,
the NCCJ's Southern Region director, proposed sending trios to every U.S. military
installation in the world. The idea was "not to speak once and then leave, but to stay
on the Camp grounds for several days speaking to as many troops as possible with
the Conference message of unity of effort, and to stress the great importance of the
moral, social and ethical values involved in the world-wide military conflict now and
for the post war era."[2]

The board liked the idea and asked Gottschall to see if his ambitious proposal
was remotely possible. Gottschall went to work, eager to see if his ambitious plan
to define "the moral, social and ethical values" for which American soldiers were
fighting had any legs. What he discovered was discouraging. In addition to being
ambitious, the plan was chock-full of bureaucratic obstacles, not the least of which
was getting access to the bases, which had been granted to only two civilian organizations, the Red Cross and the USO. After encountering immediate resistance
from military personnel, Gottschall just about gave up on the idea. But he tried
one last time, leading him down a path that would eventually put the NCCJ in
contact with nearly nine million Americans and allowing it to "accomplish in a year

or two what in ordinary times would require thirty."[3] Through Gottschall's Camp Program—more formally, its Commission on Programs in Army Camps, Naval and Air Bases—the NCCJ would provide "among the best interpretations of why we fight," and tri-faith America would be on its way to becoming standard operating procedure in the United States of America.[4]

THE NCCJ AT WAR

The official alignment of good Americanism with the tri-faith idea began even before Pearl Harbor. On April 8, 1941, President Roosevelt announced the creation of the United Services Organization (USO). Later famous for supplying overseas entertainment to American GIs, at its creation the USO was charged with operating more than three hundred recreational centers near military camps, navy yards, and army bases across the country, most of them brand-new facilities opened in antici-pation of war.[5] But the president had another purpose in mind as well. He wanted to avoid the friction, confusion, and duplication of effort between Protestant, Cath-olic, and Jewish service agencies that had arisen during World War I. So to consti-tute the USO, he called together six large agencies, each having either a Protestant, Catholic, or Jewish affiliation: the Young Men's Christian Association (YMCA), the Young Women's Christian Association (YWCA), the Travelers Aid Society (then still an offshoot of the YWCA), the Salvation Army, the Catholic Community Service, and the Jewish Welfare Board.[6] At the press conference announcing the USO's founding, Roosevelt said, "We have got all of these organizations in under the same tent—which is a perfectly magnificent thing."[7]

The USO affirmed the importance of the three faiths in American life, but it did not promote a message; that was not its mission. The NCCJ, on the other hand, had a message to convey, one of the brotherhood of man under the Fatherhood of God. It was going to attempt "to immunize our soldiers against the virus of hate," as Everett Clinchy put it. "Now is the time to build the dyke against the post-war hate movement," he wrote, just four days after Pearl Harbor.[8] Gottschall's Camp Program was a prominent part of the NCCJ's response, and once it conquered the logistical difficulties entailed in gaining access to the hundreds of national and international military bases, a feat accomplished by mid-1942, the program was immediately implemented. It expanded quickly, in part because of the tremendous response it received. Chaplains wrote other chaplains speaking highly of the pro-gram's contribution to the war effort, calling it "a verification of our American Democracy," a step in promoting "the spirit of tolerance and good will."[9] Funds poured in from donors. The military offered free travel from one base to the next.

Brigadier General D. V. Gaffney wrote, "The effect of this united front, together with the very agreeable friendship between the individuals [in the trio], have had very gratifying results." With government endorsement, the idea of a tri-faith nation spread quickly from the NCCJ to hundreds of military bases across the nation and across the world.[10]

What were the trios saying that was so gratifying? On one hand, they were making bland pronouncements about the unity demanded by war. "Within the framework of the undivided political loyalty to the flag, and the country it represents, there is a place for religious and cultural diversity," read one report called "What Do Speakers Say?" "This religious and cultural freedom, so essentially a part of the American tradition and our dream of the Good Society, must be maintained and made secure through mutual understanding, appreciation, cooperation and the elimination of hate, prejudice and discrimination in human relations."[11] This was fairly boilerplate language during World War II, although coming from a trio of a Catholic, Protestant, and Jew, the message perhaps carried more weight.

More detailed outlines of the trio's talks suggest another goal as well. These outlines suggest the trios were tying together religion and democracy, suggesting democracy could not survive without a deeply felt religious faith, especially one premised on individual human dignity. The natural conclusion of this argument was, of course, that the United States could not survive as a democracy unless it reified its religious principles. "Religion is the foundation of democracy," read one bullet-pointed script. "Watch out for corruption and disintegration right within Judaism, Catholicism and Protestantism. [Stress the need] for awakening of spirituality of the entire citizenry, in terms of clean citizenship, unselfish dedication to great causes, etc."[12] While ensuring the trialogues "have a spontaneity and freshness that will save it from dragging," the three speakers were to align the survival of democracy with a tri-faith religious revival. The nation would survive only by honoring and embracing the common features of Protestantism, Catholicism, and Judaism—a personal God of righteousness and love, the sacredness of all men as children of a common Heavenly Father, and a realization of God's will by practicing social justice and brotherhood. Affirming these principles was by definition opposing Hitler. The trios were, in effect, trying to give concreteness to the vague ideal of "the American way of life," a concreteness centered on tri-faith religiosity.

By the end of the war trios had visited 778 different U.S. military installations. They had gone abroad to Alaska and the Canal Zone and were planning to appear in Europe and the Pacific just before the end of hostilities.[13] They had spoken to more than nine million men and women. Their reach proved beyond what Gottschall and the NCCJ ever could have hoped for. Enlisted men seemed to react to

MAY, 1943.

Soldiers hear NCCJ Trio

NATIONAL CONFERENCE OF CHRISTIANS AND JEWS

During World War II, the NCCJ gained access to a variety of U.S. Army and Navy installations where they convened meetings of chaplains, spoke to large groups of soldiers, and provided millions of pieces of literature, including tri-faith prayer cards and explanations of "why we fight." The NCCJ tried to fashion the war as one to save democracy and the Judeo-Christian religion that democracy was supposedly premised on. They spoke to more than nine million soldiers. Used by permission of the Social Welfare History Archives, University of Minnesota Libraries.

the dual message of national and spiritual unity. One said, "I agree with the chairman that there is a higher purpose in life, and I have made a new resolve to be more loyal to my faith and to be an advocate of goodwill and cooperation. More power to your organization in its army program. There is more and more anti this and anti that in our ranks, especially in regard to Negroes and Jews. Unless something is done to check it, we will be acting like Hitlerites here in America." Preventing Hitlerites in America was exactly the NCCJ's purpose. Another enlisted man said: "I was very impressed that, at last, Catholics, Jews and Protestants have found some common ground." Still another said, "It was an intelligent and clear presentation of the basic moral and personal reasons for our participation in this war."[14] Still another commented, "We thought it was swell, the best program we have listened to. The boys said you told us so we could understand what it was all about, and you were funny, too."[15]

One enlisted man approached one of the chaplains after a camp performance. The soldier was of Greek origin and was born Greek Orthodox but had not attended church "for a long time" and had grown cynical, thinking "there was too much that was farce" in religion. He had been persecuted for his faith too and he had, in turn, "persecuted the colored race and looked down upon other groups." But at one of the Camp Program meetings, "a miracle happened to me there. . . . As Rabbi Goldstein was speaking I was standing beside a colored soldier. All at once a new feeling came over me. I looked up to the heavens and thought that in spite of the inequalities of life and all the troubles of the world there was something great and good worth fighting for and dying for, if need be. Chaplain," the young man said, "my religion is going to mean something to me from now on."[16]

This sentiment was not unusual. Justifying the fight in cosmic terms, giving the very real possibility of death some meaning, and advancing a religious justification for national goals like tolerance and unity must have been compelling during a vicious war. "The three speakers, Catholic priest, Protestant minister, Jewish Rabbi, had those 36,000 men on their feet cheering, applauding, whistling, yelling—one of the most tremendous ovations I have ever seen given to men in my life, but they deserved it, they were tremendous themselves," was one NCCJ member's reaction to a Camp Program performance.[17]

Beyond the Camp Program, the NCCJ distributed a wide variety of books and pamphlets to millions of soldiers. To prepare materials, it gathered sixteen religious leaders—Protestants, Catholics, and Jews—to draft manuscripts, invited several army and navy chaplains to assess them, and then submitted materials to the War Department's Office of Public Relations. By the end of the war, the NCCJ had distributed more than eight million pieces of literature to base chaplains in batches of ten thousand. Their four-page pamphlets carried titles such as "The

Shield of Faith," "A Faith for Young Men in the Armed Forces," "The Growth of Good Will," "Why Suffering?" "What Makes Life Worth Living?" and "Why We Are at War."[18]

The most popular NCCJ literature was its "Why We Fight" series. The NCCJ defined the series as "brief statements prepared by Protestant, Catholic and Jewish leaders on the moral and spiritual issues in the present world struggle." In one such pamphlet, "When the Boys Come Home," intended for chaplains, the NCCJ stressed the opportunities presented by war, a chance to "bring about what may prove to be the most worthy social change of the 20th century—a deeply imbedded tradition of friendly understanding and civic cooperation among Protestants, Catholics and Jews." The pamphlet warned, "Of the 2.5 million Americans who joined the Ku Klux Klan in the early 1920s, a considerable proportion were ex-soldiers."[19] Another pamphlet, "Consolidating Victory!" said, "Twenty-five years ago we won a war but in the years that followed we lost the peace. Now this generation of youth has a war to win all over again and on a vaster scale." It pointed out: "Protestant, Catholic and Jew must work shoulder to shoulder to solve the tough economic, social and political problems of the world beyond war."[20]

The NCCJ also developed, printed, and distributed a tri-faith "prayer card," which went to every single American soldier. The card was the brainchild of Colonel Earle Weed, chief army chaplain for the Western Coast Defense Command. On his base, Weed had designed a half sheet containing a Catholic prayer (the Act of Contrition), a Protestant prayer from the Book of Common Prayer, and a Jewish prayer selected by a rabbi on the base. Weed wanted the card distributed widely, but the army could not perform such a task. When he showed the half sheet to Gottschall, Gottschall used NCCJ funds to print the cards the size of a folded-over business card, "small enough to be slipped into a soldier's or sailor's wallet, to be carried wherever he goes," Gottschall wrote. "If a man is wounded and cannot be reached by his chaplain, he will have at hand the prayer appropriate to his faith. This he may read to himself, or a buddy may read it for him."[21] Chaplains demanded the cards by the thousands. By the end of the war, the NCCJ had printed five million copies.[22]

The NCCJ also made a seventeen-minute film called *The World We Want to Live In*, which showed a variety of "men of goodwill" "vigorously attacking bigotry." The film told of "how suspicion and hate are used to undermine democracy." It displayed "shameful chapters" in American history and told of discrimination "in employment, in fraternities, in social standards." Then the picture showed Charles Evans Hughes (Protestant), Alfred E. Smith (Catholic), and Eddie Cantor (Jew) together expressing "the hope and the conviction that this country will maintain its freedoms throughout the war and in the days to come when the war is won."[23]

When chaplains and information and education officers requested it, Gottschall brought the film with him to camps and hospitals. Toward the end of hostilities, the Signal Corps purchased 250 copies of the film so "it could be shown to service people around the world." By the end of the war, Gottschall estimated that more than ten million service men and women had viewed it.[24]

Supported by the federal government, then, the NCCJ had become one of the most extensive propagandists for what it was the nation was fighting for. Its reach had been both broad and deep. By the end of the war, nearly every American soldier had touched a piece of NCCJ literature, watched an NCCJ film, or gone to an NCCJ Camp Program meeting. And in each of these ventures, the NCCJ put forward the notion that the United States was a tri-faith nation and that the tri-faith character of the United States was vitally important to the sustenance of American democracy. Tolerance between the three faiths became sacrosanct, and the NCCJ, along with the federal government, had made the tri-faith arrangement America's standard operating procedure. With the government's help, Clinchy's long-desired new "folkway" was coming to fruition. Clinchy was slow to take too much credit for the transition, saying, "In Rostand's play 'Chanticleer' a rooster came to believe that he brought the dawn because the rising sun coincided with his crowing. The National Conference does not claim to have brought the new day in the relationships among Christians and Jews." But he quickly added, "It is accurate, however, to consider your work as a Board of Trustees [of the NCCJ] to be an instrument of the Lord in giving shape, direction and extension to this developing folkway of friendliness in intergroup relations."[25]

Gottschall's favorite story regarding the NCCJ's deep penetration into the American war effort and its success in aligning the tri-faith vision with good Americanism concerned the marching band at Fort Benning, Georgia. After one of the base's intramural football games, a voice over the loudspeaker announced, "Our [band's] next number is in honor of the National Conference of Christians and Jews, whose representatives have been on the post for the past week speaking to the personnel of the various commands." The band then marched in order, forming a giant Star of David and playing "Ein Keloheinu," an ancient Jewish prayer about the uniqueness of God. Once "Ein Keloheinu" was completed, the band marched in order again, this time forming a giant cross and playing "Onward Christian Soldiers," the nineteenth-century hymn given new meaning during World War II after British prime minister Winston Churchill adopted it as his semi-official battle song. "The trio was thrilled by the band but what brought lumps to their throats was the tremendous emotional response of these thousands of American fighters for freedom," recalled Gottschall. "The massed thousands cheered wildly and warm-heartedly this gesture of good will."[26]

Gottschall certainly had a rosy view of what he had helped accomplish, but even given his partiality, the NCCJ had in fact gone to 778 military installations and spoken directly to nine million Americans. It had distributed more than ten million pieces of literature that aligned the NCCJ cause with that of the nation. Its film helped define "the world we want to live in" for more than ten million American soldiers. The NCCJ tried to define the war as a battle for the soul of humankind, a battle to safeguard differences (religious and otherwise), and a battle to defend the righteousness of "the three faiths of democracy." "The conference has demonstrated what the American way of life is," said Rabbi William F. Rosenblum, a member of one of the wartime trios. "It has demonstrated that you can accomplish the same object in different ways. Every man is trying to reach God in his own way. And we want the world to be the kind of place where you don't have to have regimentation to have peace."[27] Aligning "good Americanism" and "the American way of life" with a tri-faith pluralist vision was a considerable start.

RELIGION, NOT RACE

There were hundreds of organizations promoting tolerance and goodwill during the war, none of which had the reach of the NCCJ. There were two primary reasons for the NCCJ's success. The first was that the organization had hewed close to its central mission of religious goodwill, opting not to delve into other areas where tolerance might be preached, such as racial equality, which might have invited controversy and limited its reach. This was a conscious decision but not a foregone conclusion. Countless other organizations had broadened their mission during the war. The American Jewish Committee, the American Jewish Congress, and the Anti-Defamation League of B'nai B'rith (ADL) all expanded their mission beyond Jewish causes during the early 1940s, targeting all varieties of American intolerance. In 1940, for example, the ADL launched a "Lest We Forget" campaign promoting a vision of America as a heterogeneous society that had grown to near perfection through the contributions of countless minority groups, religious, racial, and ethnic. The American Jewish Committee, meanwhile, funded anthropologist Franz Boaz's anti-racialist research.[28]

In addition to these older groups with new missions, literally hundreds of groups were founded between 1938 and 1945 to promote a wildly inclusive vision of Americanism. The Common Council for American Unity was incorporated in November 1939 "to help create among the American people the unity and mutual understanding resulting from a common citizenship, a common belief in democracy and the ideals of liberty, . . . and the acceptance . . . of all citizens, whatever their national or racial origins."[29] The Council Against Intolerance in America, founded in 1938, distributed to schoolchildren pamphlets promoting the vision spelled out in its name. The League of Fair Play, the American Council Against Nazi Propaganda, the Friends of Democracy, the Committee for National Morale, the Institute for Propaganda Analysis, and the Council for Democracy were some of the groups to emerge during this broad "war on intolerance."[30]

Even more compelling was a transition in Americans' dominant conception of social justice, which was becoming increasingly defined in terms of protecting members of minority groups, specifically religious and racial minority groups, rather than redistributing wealth and ensuring the common health and wealth of the nation. This new vision of social justice was first enshrined in law in two places, almost simultaneously. In 1938, United States Supreme Court justice Harlan Fiske Stone identified the triad of "race, religion, and national origin" in footnote 4 of his decision in *Carolene Products v. the United States*, a case about the legality of dairy products crossing state lines. In the footnote, Stone announced that the Court would be vigilant in scrutinizing legislation passed by majorities, especially when that legislation curtailed political participation by "religious . . . or national . . . or racial minorities." If the majority could not control itself, "judicial inquiry" would intervene to protect "discrete and insular" minorities, minorities such as those bound by race, religion, or national origin.[31]

The day after the Court made the decision public, Stone wrote to New York judge Irving Lehman, "I have been deeply concerned about the increasing racial and religious intolerance which seems to bedevil the world, and which I greatly fear may be augmented in this country. For that reason I was greatly disturbed by the attacks on the Court and the Constitution last year [during Roosevelt's failed courtpacking scheme] for one consequence of the program of 'judicial reform' might well result in breaking down the guaranties of individual liberty." To protect those guarantees, Stone wrote what has been called "perhaps the most renowned footnote in constitutional law."[32] Instead of viewing class-based discriminations as those worth monitoring, as they had been doing throughout the Great Depression and New Deal, the courts suddenly deemed discrimination based on minority status as more threatening.

The second enshrinement of the new vision of social justice appeared in Section 11 of the newly revised Bill of Rights of the New York State Constitution, which declared: "No person shall, because of race, color, creed or religion, be subjected to any discrimination in his civil rights."[33] U.S. senator Robert Wagner was the amendment's strongest advocate. A German immigrant who came to New York before he was ten, he had a short career as a lawyer, and then entered politics. He became a perpetual proponent of liberal legislation, including the National Labor

Relations Act of 1935, commonly known as the Wagner Act, which protected the right of most workers to organize unions, engage in collective bargaining, and strike. A few years later his focus had shifted. At the New York State convention in 1938, Wagner introduced Section 11 with a riveting twenty-minute late-night speech. He directly attributed Section 11 to the "racial vandalism and political gangsterism" in Europe, "where the prospect of life without hope . . . has driven countless thousands to self-destruction." He then asserted that protecting "the integrity and civil liberties of minority races and groups" was now "the essential governmental problem of our time," thereby demoting questions of economic redistribution. He spoke of how antisemitism was "prevalent at home," and of prejudice against African Americans, a "prejudice so deep-seated as to be taken for granted by the community at large." Each of these hatreds, he declared, was "foreign to the American ideal and subversive to Americans' democratic faith."[34]

Section 11 passed easily at the convention. New York governor Herbert Lehman commented: "One of the splendid provisions in the new Constitution forbids discrimination against any person in his civil rights on the ground of race, color or creed. The equal protection of the laws is the greatest blessing that can be conferred by a democracy upon its citizens." The citizens of New York agreed, ratifying the constitution in the following months.

A new definition of social justice was coalescing—one premised on America's engagement with totalitarianism, one that prioritized the protection of minorities defined by race or religion, and sometimes by national origin. As the African American activist Roy Wilkins put it: "Hitler jammed our white people into their logically untenable position. Forced to oppose him for the sake of the life of the nation, they were jockeyed into declaring against his racial theories."[35] Thurgood Marshall put it slightly differently in 1944: "Distinctions based on color and ancestry are utterly inconsistent with our traditions and ideals. They are at variance with the principles for which we are now waging war. We cannot close our eyes to the fact that for centuries the Old World has been torn by racial and religious conflicts and has suffered the worst kind of anguish because of inequality of treatment for different groups."[36] This broad ideal spilled into the mission statements of nearly all the tolerance organizations formed during the late 1930s and early 1940s.

Unlike many groups, the NCCJ did not expand its mission or embrace the broad new definition of American social justice. It remained focused on religious goodwill. The trustees made the decision consciously. On December 22, 1941, the NCCJ trustees asked Clinchy to solicit opinions from American leaders sympathetic to the NCCJ as to what the organization could do to help the war effort.[37] Opinion was split. Some said the NCCJ should broaden its reach and be more inclusive, that it should utilize its position as one of the premier goodwill organizations in the country to lead what was coming to look like a war against intolerance. The prominent Episcopal bishop Henry W. Hobson said: "Nothing is more important than an educational program which will emphasize the relationship between various religious groups, and between members of the different races, which will make it possible for all to work together in building a better world. The National Conference of Christians and Jews is splendidly fitted to carry on part of this educational program."[38] Howard Coonley, chairman of the National Association of Manufactures, told Clinchy, "We are defending the hope of humanity for peace and freedom," and the NCCJ should focus on fulfilling that broad mission.[39] Norman Thomas, America's leading socialist, also suggested broadening the mission: "If anything, the kind of work the National Conference of Christian and Jews does becomes more, not less, necessary and without it the reaction which I have feared will be much worse."[40] Walter White of the NAACP, Clarence E. Pickett of the American Friends Service Committee, and Alfred M. Landon, the Republican politician, made similar comments.[41]

Others thought the NCCJ should "keep before the nation the values for which the American people are fighting," and those values were religious. E. R. Stettinius Jr., at the time the administrator of the Lend-Lease program, said: "With the world in turmoil and upheaval, the importance of the influence of religious organizations on people everywhere can not be over estimated. Anything that can be done to strengthen that influence is of tremendous importance." Henry Sloane Coffin, one the nation's foremost Protestant ministers and president of Union Theological Seminary, said: "We are at war with a people claiming to be 'a lordly race.' We must hold fast our national unity by insisting that all men have one heavenly Father who wills His Children to honor and serve one another as brethren."[42]

The range of respondents demonstrates the broad appeal of the NCCJ in 1941. Republicans and Democrats, liberals and conservatives, industrialists and civil rights advocates, all supported the NCCJ cause. Unity in religious terms was something everyone could get behind, from the nation's leading socialist to the chairman of the National Association of Manufacturers.[43]

Following the poll, the NCCJ board had two vision statements drafted, one by a staff member (a certain Mrs. Klein) that suggested broad changes, the other by Clinchy, a response that offered guesses as to what would happen if the NCCJ maintained its religious mission. Klein's report argued that a more expansive mission including "all minority groups" would simply be a "speeding up of an evolutionary process already at work." The NCCJ was already engaged in addressing racial inequality, working with fair-employment agencies, and fighting race-based housing discrimination in Chicago. Clinchy himself had even used the typical language of post-1938 tolerance several times, as when he spoke of ensuring there is "in America complete equity with regard to color, creed," and when he advised the National Congress of Parents and Teachers to "develop your activities so that the mothers of all children, whatever their religion, race or color will have a part and place in the program."[44] Furthermore, the NCCJ risked becoming outflanked if it did not "actively campaign against discrimination on all fronts." After all, following World War I, there were "anti-Semitic, anti-Negro, anti-Catholic, and anti-alien movements." As late as 1941, the Klein report said, there were campaigns to foster antisemitism among African Americans in Harlem. There was an "anti-Negro" Klan movement in Detroit, "which is also anti-Catholic." The Red Cross was in the process of creating a separate blood bank for black people. And there was a growing distrust of "loyal Americans of Axis descent." For the NCCJ to relate "to national effort in America at war," it should consider "a wider definition of prejudice." The "ideal of interracial, interfaith cooperation would not be lost sight of but would rather be all the more clear because worked out in action."[45]

Clinchy's response was unequivocal. If the NCCJ was to remain solvent, it needed to remember "that it has a definitely theistic basis." If it did not retain its religious focus, it would become "a kind of 'General League Against All Intolerance' of which the number already is legion." The NCCJ "has been one organization, in which the Negro, the Oriental, the alien and individuals of any persecuted bodies may confer *as a Christian or a Jew*. [Klein's] report proposes that we, like the Urban League or the N.A.A.C.P. become an anti-defamation society to fight prejudice against Negroes and aliens." To do so would transform the NCCJ from an organization "founded on religious teaching, appealing to religious motives, and supported by people who believe in religion, to a secular philosophy, disregarding ecclesiastical structure and ecclesiastical sensibilities and procedures." It would, he feared, be the death of the NCCJ.[46]

During the general discussion that followed, sentiments were mixed, but most supported Clinchy's argument. Mildred McAfee, president of Wellesley College and soon to be director of the U.S. Navy's WAVES program, said: "If we take as the specific area of this Conference the relations between the three religious faiths, a contribution to the solution of problems in that area will contribute to an understanding of other forms of prejudice. Start with religious prejudice and you may come out anywhere." George N. Shuster, a prominent Catholic intellectual associated with *Commonweal*, believed the NCCJ had survived "because it has stuck to its task of developing the common idealism of members of the Catholic, the Protestant and the Jewish faiths." If it broadened its mission to include groups it knew little about, it ran "the risk of disappearing, because of a lack of organizational unity. It would end up in a free-for-all which would accelerate intolerance."[47]

There was also an underlying fear about what would happen to religious goodwill if racial groups were included in a newly expanded mission. While nearly everyone on the board could be counted as a racial liberal, they also had to be cautious about how far they pushed the NCCJ. "I feel that we should stick rather closely to our original purpose," said Carlton Hayes, the NCCJ's Catholic co-chairman. "The field of intolerance is very wide. . . . On our staff throughout the country we use religious minded people who know the religious field." He advocated "a long term educational campaign carried on to teach tolerance among Protestants, Catholics and Jews, of each group of whom it is an accepted principle in their religious teaching. In 1943, 1944, and in 2043 and 2044 there will be a job to do to get Catholics, Protestants and Jews to live up to their implications of their faith in relationships across faith lines."[48] Ultimately, the NCCJ decided to retain its religious mission.

The NCCJ was not alone in demoting racial civil rights in favor of religious goodwill. Frank Sinatra and the executives at RKO studios made a similar decision in 1944. Throughout the war, Sinatra had added an epilogue to nearly every one of his weekly performances on CBS's *Old Gold* radio show. He gave a brief lecture on a "very, very important subject known as tolerance." Sinatra would describe a situation where some form of "intolerance" was on display in America, usually through a fictional scenario involving a child being persecuted because of his or her race or religion. Sinatra concluded his lectures explaining why this kind of intolerance was wrong. "Religion doesn't make any real difference, except to a Nazi or a dope," he said in one episode. Of the show, Sinatra claimed, "I have never believed in anything so zealously in all my life."[49]

In 1944, executives at RKO Pictures shrewdly sought to capitalize on the popularity of Sinatra's theme. They depicted one of the Sinatra's fictional radio scenarios on the silver screen, creating an eleven-minute short about a group of kids set on beating up another kid because he was a Jew. The kids see the error of their ways after Sinatra lectures (and sings) to them about tolerance and the war. One verse from the title song went: "The children in the playground, the faces that I see; all races, all religions, that's America to me."[50] The movie was a hit. It helped that RKO offered the film free of charge to movie houses nationwide. A *Cue* review gushed, "The picture's message is Tolerance" and the film "packs more power, punch and solid substance than most of the features ground each year out of Hollywood." The Academy of Motion Picture Arts and Sciences awarded the film a special Oscar in 1946, "for tolerance—short subject."[51]

There was, however, one adaptation made by RKO executives when it brought Sinatra's tolerance story to the silver screen: race was excised. First, they adopted a song called "The House I Live In" to use as Sinatra's aural vehicle, and then they removed its remarks about race. The song, which gave the film its name, was written in 1942 by the leftist songwriting team Earl Robinson and Abel Meeropol (aka Lewis Allen), and its lyrics demonstrated unequivocal support for racial equality. It spoke of harmony between "my neighbors white and black," and "the people who just came here, or from generations back." It spoke of economic equality and the development of American society with its "tasks that still remain." Yet RKO eliminated race almost entirely, with the single exception of the line "all races, all religions, that's America to me." Meanwhile, the film featured no black kids and, most remarkably, it even discussed the generosity of the tormented Jewish boy's father, who gave blood to the Red Cross without regard to whether a Catholic or Protestant or Jew received it. This was an odd statement considering there was never any consideration of dividing blood by religion, while the Red Cross famously segregated blood from black donors.[52] It is possible the producers adapted the film in reaction to a spate of violence against Jewish children in the Boston area in 1944, part of a wave of urban violence against Jews.[53] Or the producers may have decided the film would have broader reach and be less controversial if it did not press racial inclusion too far.

Meanwhile, organizations that promoted racial equality too strongly met with resistance throughout the war. In 1943, the Columbia University anthropologists Ruth Benedict and Gene Weltfish wrote a small pamphlet called *The Races of Mankind*. The pamphlet denied all biological differences between races, declaring racial distinctions "nonessentials." People of all colors had one of four blood types. They had the same number of molars. In war, the United States had to "clean its own house" and end racial discrimination. "The races of mankind are what the Bible says they are—brothers. In their bodies is the record of their brotherhood," wrote Benedict and Weltfish. The pamphlet stands as a milestone in asserting the biological irrelevance of race.[54]

And yet while *The Races of Mankind* had a long and vigorous life, it did not do so through the armed services. The pamphlet was forty-six pages long and designed to fit into a serviceman's pocket. The Public Affairs Committee, Inc., one of a number of newly formed organizations in the "war on intolerance," sponsored the pamphlet with the idea of selling them to servicemen at USO installations for ten cents apiece. But the booklet met immediate resistance. USO president Chester Irving Barnard, a prominent management expert, banned its sale. The pamphlet would disrupt unity, not promote it, he argued.[55] The War Department, after initially ordering several thousand copies, seconded Barnard's decision, banning the pamphlet at the urging of the U.S. Congress, which claimed the pamphlet provoked "racial antagonism," especially a section showing that World War I intelligence tests demonstrated that African Americans from the North had scored higher than white Southerners.[56]

The Races of Mankind debate had the misfortune of occurring during the 1943 race riots, which badly affected its reception. Spurred by competition for wartime jobs and housing near those jobs, violent racial conflict bubbled up in Detroit, Dearborn, Chicago, Baltimore, New York City, and dozens more cities in the summer of 1943. In Los Angeles, white rioters targeted both African Americans and Mexican Americans in what became known as the "Zoot Suit Riots." Later that year, African Americans in Harlem attacked white-owned shops without any discernable provocation. "I get the impression," wrote Ralph Ellison, who witnessed the event in Harlem, "that they were giving way to resentment over the price of food and other necessities, police brutality and the general indignities borne by Negro soldiers."[57]

By sticking to its "theistic basis," the NCCJ was able to avoid the controversy surrounding racial equality. Nobody in the NCCJ was blind to the contradiction of advocating the brotherhood of man under the Fatherhood of God while choosing not to take a stand against racial discrimination. Some even demanded the organization get more involved. Board member Theodore Speers said, "I do not see how an organization which has gone on record, as the National Conference has, as an opponent of prejudice among racial groups, can beg the question of the Negro and his relationship to the community, and, in addition, the relationship between other colored races in this country and the so-called white race," adding, "I suspect that the Negro problem alone will overshadow in significance and acuteness the inter-religious relationships of Catholics, Jews, and Protestants." He even blasted the NCCJ for making the tri-faith conception an entirely white conception, even though it did not have to be. "I judge that neither Catholics, nor Jews, nor Protestants are free from taint in this regard," he said.[58]

The NCCJ had to respond, but did so tepidly. It requested racially integrated audiences hear the Camp Program trios, but only "wherever possible."[59] It also frequently included language about racial goodwill in many of its materials, such as in one pamphlet on the Camp Program: "Through this vigorous nation-wide program breaking down racial and religious prejudice among millions of men in uniform . . . the N.C.C.J. is making a definite contribution to victory."[60] But it had no African American clergymen in any of its trios, and never contemplated sending a more inclusive panel. It also never produced materials specifically addressing interracial goodwill. To do so would belie the NCCJ mission, and perhaps derail it too.

JUDEO-CHRISTIANITY AND THE THREE FAITHS OF DEMOCRACY

Along with deliberately sidestepping race, the second reason the NCCJ succeeded in promoting its tri-faith vision during the war was because the organization embodied something called the "Judeo-Christian tradition." A phrase first used in 1899, it was adopted broadly in the late 1930s, when a variety of intellectuals were searching for an inclusive ideal to counter fascism and its cynical alignment with Protestantism and Christianity. "Judeo-Christian" was a perfect salve. The phrase was religious, inclusive, and untainted. It became a "tradition" most Americans were eager to embrace.[61]

The phrase also had an obvious organizational midwife in the NCCJ. Being an organization of Christians and Jews, and having a history of locating common ground between the three faiths, the phrase and the organization could not have aligned more perfectly. Beginning as early as 1938, Clinchy began using the phrase in nearly all his talks. He left no doubt that the "tradition" embraced "unity without uniformity," a single civic and spiritual tradition containing three diverse strands.[62] It was also, of course, a perfect foil to European totalitarianism. As Clinchy wrote: "Political party machines, led by Nazi Hitler, Communist Stalin, and Fascist Mussolini alike, deny the sovereignty of God above all else, pour contempt on the spiritual values of the Judaeo-Christian tradition, and refuse to recognize those natural rights of freedom of conscience, freedom of church press, of pulpit, and of religious organizational work. . . . Never before in history have Protestants, Catholics and Jews been as aware of each other's suffering and as willing to mobilize spiritual forces as American citizens." After all, he concluded, the "Judaeo-Christian tradition" was the foundation of "the American Way of life."[63]

To demonstrate what was at risk in the battle against totalitarianism, in September 1941, while visiting London with a priest and a rabbi, Clinchy spoke on nationwide radio to American listeners. "Night is falling in London," he said darkly. "Firewardens check the air-raid sandbags and water-pails in every building. Women smother each window with black curtain. Traffic along the Strand, Piccadilly, the East End, slows up. Britain is blacked-out." To prevent this from happening in America, the nation needed to reassess basic principles, affirming its unity without uniformity. It needed to know "there will be no Judaeo-Christian religion if the Nazis win." Without that, it was unclear whether democracy could survive.[64] In its "Why We Fight" series of pamphlets, the NCCJ portrayed the conflict as a "war of ideas between Totalitarian Dictatorship and the essentials in our Judaeo-Christian tradition."[65]

Buoyed by NCCJ marketing, "Judeo-Christianity" was in vogue throughout the war. Presidents and intellectuals employed the term, as did Protestant, Catholic, and Jewish leaders. Military men used it. Whatever else it might mean, the phrase was intended to serve as a unifying religious tradition that had somehow helped establish freedom of thought, speech, and religion in the Western world. That "tradition" was useful to an America at war.

The phrase did, however, acquire two distinct meanings during the war. The first was theological, pointing to the common texts shared by each of the three faiths, basically the Old Testament. Emerging from a common theological core, the three faiths were bound to have some values in common. "Spiritually, we are all Semites," said Pope Pius XI in 1938, a quotation the NCCJ used as propaganda for the next decade.[66] The Jewish Welfare Board's *Book of Jewish Thoughts* tied Judaism to Americanism via the theological version of the Judeo-Christian tradition as well. The book, distributed to Jewish GIs throughout the war, said the "common faiths" within the "tradition" consisted of a belief in a supernatural power and in the brotherhood of man, seeing each individual as a child of God with a shared "belief in the existence of positive ethical standards of right and wrong that exist apart from the will of any man."[67] Not everyone agreed with this broad theological interpretation, especially Catholics, who had been taught to see other religions as fundamentally wrong, and some Jews, who wondered how Jesus fit into this. During the war, however, theological distinctions were usually quieted in favor of national unity; afterward they would more fully return.

The second meaning of Judeo-Christianity was more civic, a broad arrangement where Protestants, Catholics, and Jews could all participate in the American project without losing their religious identities or having to accommodate to a Protestant cultural hegemony. American democracy had certain principles—inalienable individual rights, principles of brotherhood, negative liberty, freedom of expression—that did not contradict Protestant, Catholic, or Jewish religious claims and, better still, often aligned with them. The groups should each lessen their frustrations with one another in order to focus on civic good. They should celebrate that which they shared rather than that which divided them. This was a less demanding and controversial meaning of Judeo-Christianity, one without a theological core, but one that might more easily promote civic harmony.

The NCCJ was aware of the distinctions: a vibrant theological tradition animating social ideals versus a softer civic agreement where social and theological differences were demoted in the name of peace. During the war it wanted desperately to ground Judeo-Christianity in theology, demonstrating that democracy could not survive without Judeo-Christian faith. But if that could not be done, the NCCJ would settle for civility. At a minimum, it did not want the return of nativism, but at best, it wanted a new spiritual grounding for American life.[68]

In an effort to champion the first meaning, the NCCJ tried several times to align overtly the religious values of Protestants, Catholics, and Jews with good Americanism. In one effort, in 1941, the NCCJ published a short book called *The Religions of Democracy: Judaism, Catholicism, and Protestantism in Creed and Life*. With the title, the authors meant "the belief in the worth and rights of the individual which characterizes all three of the faiths with which it deals . . . [and is] at the foundation of all true democracy." The book was composed of three parts: "The

Beliefs and Practices of Judaism," by Louis Finkelstein of the Jewish Theological Seminary in America; "The Roman Catholic Religion in Creed and Life," by Father John Elliot Ross; and "Protestantism in Creed and Life," by the Protestant ecumenist William Adams Brown. It argued not only that ignorance bred prejudice but also that democracy thrived in the presence of Judeo-Christianity. The two were mutually beneficial.[69]

The broadest attempt to put theological meat on the bones of "Judeo-Christianity" came in 1942, when the NCCJ brought together several of the nation's leading clergymen to draft a Declaration of Fundamental Religious Beliefs Held in Common by Catholics, Protestants, and Jews. The NCCJ claimed the document, demonstrating "the 'oneness' of aims among the three faiths," was the first of its kind in the United States. It was intended to be the Bible of Tri-Faith America with its foundation in "the Judeo-Christian tradition."[70]

The declaration, made public via hundreds of simultaneous celebrations throughout the country, argued that the United States was more or less composed of members of the three faiths, which therefore meant that all Americans possessed a common theological foundation based on monotheism and the notion that God had made man in His image.[71] Because of this common foundation, those within the Judeo-Christian tradition had to acknowledge that human beings were not only creatures of God, subservient to His will, but also brothers under His rule. And brotherhood meant that it was presumptuous to interfere with another's form of peaceful worship. Therefore, an acknowledgment of brotherhood led to freedom, which of course was the basis for democracy. The declaration concluded by directly tying together democracy and faith: "We believe that recognition of man's dependence upon God is essential to the progress of true civilization; that nations, as well as individuals are bound to acknowledge this; and that educational or social theories which would state man's duties, standards, and happiness without reference to God are doomed to failure." More specific to the United States, the declaration read: "We believe the republican form of government to be the most desirable for our nation and for countries of similarly democratic traditions." Americans only had to look to their history to find the "moral and religious principles" necessary for "liberty and happiness." The United States, founded on "Judeo-Christian" principles, was one exemplar of the "Judeo-Christian tradition," and was fighting to continue as such.

The Declaration of Fundamental Religious Beliefs was neither a profound code nor a very original one. But it synthesized the meanings of "Judeo-Christianity" for the NCCJ. And once defined, the language of Judeo-Christianity and its American origins emerged everywhere in NCCJ's wartime materials. One "Why We Fight" pamphlet read: "Our Founding Fathers said that 'all men are created free and equal.' Our rights, they said, come from God and man's relation to God." It added: "We Americans are not afraid to render public thanks to God on Thanksgiving Day, to open sessions of Congress with a prayer. Our form of government is primarily religious and moral. We strive to wed political power to moral purpose."[72] In a speech to the National Congress of Parents and Teachers, Clinchy tied together the "American Way" with "the Judeo-Christian tradition," saying, "The totalitarian nations of Europe differ profoundly from all that we sum up as 'The American Way'. . . . [In the United States] the religious affirmation of the worth and the rights of the individual lies at the foundation of democracy." Clinchy then specified that it was not just "religion" that was important to preserve, but specifically Judeo-Christian religion: "Behind the guns, the tanks, aeroplanes and the marching men of the present war there is a challenge of a spiritual kind which is directed against not only the very existence of democracy in general, but against Protestants, Jews and Catholic in particular. . . . [They] must rally together to their defense. They must seek to understand and appreciate one another, and learn to cooperate with each other more than they have ever done in the past." If the country refused to honor its Judeo-Christian tradition, "we would submit to the same forces of tyranny and despotism which have engulfed so many of the formerly free nations of the world."[73]

The NCCJ's most controversial and ultimately unsupportable claim that American democracy owed its origins to and depended for its survival on religion emerged in the prospect of a history book about the faith of America's founders, "to present an interpretation of early American history in respect to the religious assumptions underlying the great writings of the Founding Fathers." Carlton J. Hayes, NCCJ's Catholic co-chair and a historian at Columbia, thought such a project was doomed because no reasonable historian had located any such unified religious underpinning.[74] But those in the NCCJ advocating the program wanted to "make a ripple on the conventional interpretation of the Colonial and early Federal periods of our history."[75] F. Ernest Johnson of the Federal Council was the most eager author, proposing that the book describe the "natural theology of the Declaration of Independence and the Constitution as constituting the common religious platform generally accepted by our citizens." He was attempting to stretch America's Judeo-Christian tradition back to the Founding Fathers, rather than see its origins in the struggle against twentieth-century totalitarianism.[76] After a few initial meetings, the other interested authors, Father Moorhouse Millar of Fordham University and Louis Finkelstein of the Jewish Theological Seminary, quickly became "aghast at its ambitiousness and the formidability of the task." Lowering their expectations, they thought about producing a book that explored the religious assumptions of the founding documents. A book

highlighting these assumptions would lay "a foundation of sympathetic understanding" for those within the Judeo-Christian tradition.[77] The tri-faith authors
met regularly to discuss the project, and in 1943, they met with the American
Council of Educators to discover what kind of book might be useful for teachers.[78]
But in the end, it seems, they simply gave up on the idea, discarding it as too
ambitious and, perhaps, unsustainable.

THE REACH OF THE TRI-FAITH IDEA DURING THE WAR

If the more religious meaning of Judeo-Christianity reached only so far during
World War II, the civic version seemed to have limitless possibilities. The U.S. armed
forces, for instance, made the tri-faith arrangement its standard operating procedure.[79] Chaplains were identified by one of the three faiths. So were soldiers' dog
tags. Jews were asked to perform camp duties on Christian holidays. Christians
reciprocated. Army commanders asked priests and ministers to perform Jewish
services in places where there were no Jewish chaplains. The army requested
monthly reports that included a question on what chaplains were doing for men not
of their faith. Stretched thin by war, men of the cloth had to be flexible. Tensions
arose, especially from Catholics declining to participate in interfaith services and
from Jews afraid they were bending too much. But the wartime experience did
bring members of the various faiths closer together. A wartime essay called "The
Army Way," by Major General Frederick E. Uhl, commanding general of the Fourth
Service Command, argued, "Throughout the years, it has been army practice for
Protestant, Catholic and Jewish chaplains to serve in the same chapels. Services
vary, of course, according to faiths. With a Catholic chaplain in charge, Protestant
and Jew work harmoniously together. Or, in a reverse situation, the Catholic may
work under Jewish or Protestant direction. The point is: these men of different
faiths are not cramped by army creed nor army prejudice. Each follows the tenets of
his church without conflict, for the simple reason that the purpose is not to convert
or to destroy one another, but to live and help live, to provide the spiritual sustenance and comfort of religion for all soldiers." He also saw the war as an opportunity to exploit wartime demands in the name of goodwill, "to eliminate the last
vestiges of religious bigotries and hatred . . . Now the way was open for Judaism,
Protestantism and Catholicism to stand shoulder to shoulder before our swiftly
expanding armed forces." While this view certainly downplayed many of the tensions that arose between the three faiths during the war effort, with this perspective it was perhaps unsurprising that Major General Uhl became a friend of the
NCCJ during the war.[80]

Outside the service, war brought almost all Americans into the fold of civic Judeo-Christianity. Even the nation's most famous Catholic, Father Fulton Sheen, began preaching brotherhood. In October 1940, Sheen gave a sermon "calling for peace between Jews, Protestants and Catholics" in the face of war.[81] He occasionally slipped into Catholic triumphalism, as when, in 1942, he said American soldiers were "fighting because they believe in Christian ideals, in liberty and the survival of spiritual values."[82] But by the end of the war he had firmly broadened his view. In a national radio broadcast in 1945, he said: "Men of goodwill: unite! Unite because the new enemy is, as the Holy Father calls it, a 'common danger.' It is common to Jews, Protestants, and Catholics. It makes no distinction among them. . . . We are all in the same boat because all men of goodwill are afloat on the sea of moral love."[83]

For a Catholic of Sheen's stature to argue on behalf of a common "sea of moral love" was a coup for proponents of Judeo-Christianity. Indeed, throughout the war, the NCCJ was struck by "the new Catholic attitude of cooperation with non-Catholics," as it titled a 1942 report. Before the war, every bishop had his own policy toward goodwill, as the first Tolerance Trio had discovered. During the war, however, the NCCJ noticed such a dramatic new openness that "it is now possible to believe that the Vatican itself has given a directive which not only enables Catholics to cooperate with non-Catholics, but encourages them to do so."[84] Louis Minsky, author of the report, pointed to John Courtney Murray, S.J.'s 1942 essay in *Theological Studies*, which proclaimed: "There is no doubt about the fact that His Holiness desires co-operation." Minsky similarly cited the Jesuit weekly *America*'s 1942 editorial on the "substantial agreement" reached between Catholics and non-Catholics on wartime aims and postwar ideals. The archbishop of Philadelphia, who had been "uncompromisingly opposed to cooperation" before the war, now announced his support for goodwill efforts. For the first time, Protestants began receiving invitations to local Catholic conferences. Antisemitism disappeared from most Catholic newspapers, replaced with sympathetic appeals to fight Jewish persecution in Europe. Leading bishops sent expressions of sympathy to the Synagogue Council of America once the direness of the Holocaust became apparent. Even "the visit of Myron Taylor [the unofficial American ambassador to Rome] to the Vatican did not raise the usual Protestant outcry," wrote Minsky. Relations were not always smooth, but this was improvement. There remained "the usual rubs," concluded Minsky. "But these rubs are outweighed by the growing recognition of the common peril which confronts them, of the common stake which they have in the future development of society, and by the increasing disposition to cooperate where such cooperation is possible."[85]

During World War II, the NCCJ was not alone in promoting the idea that American tolerance and unity were best exemplified by the coming together of Protestants, Catholics, and Jews. In fact, tri-faith unity became the easiest way to demonstrate American freedom in the face of fascism abroad. At this 1944 Times Square rally are (left to right) Rabbi William Rosenblum, Rt. Rev. Joseph H. McCaffrey, Mary Frances Lehnerts, Mayor Fiorello La Guardia, Rev. John H. Johnson, Rev. William C. Kernan, and P.M. Philip Sneider. Photo by Hulton Archive/Getty Images.

All was not always well, though. The NCCJ monitored a rise in antisemitism throughout 1943. "Every regional office records more talk against Jews, more conspicuous attitudes and acts on the anti-Semitic line," the trustees noted in late 1943. "Those who hate the New Deal more than Hitler are more openly identifying

Roosevelt with Jewish policy makers, law writers, and economic theorists." The report also noted: "These are times when those brakes *are off* which normally curb loose talk and restrain our animal impulses." It pointed to the "white-Negro riots, the natives versus zoot suit Mexicans, and the anti-Japanese hysteria on the west coast" as proof.[86]

But this rising xenophobia now met stern resistance. "If it is true that there never before has been as much anti-Semitism in the United States as today, it is also true that there never have been as many individuals and agencies willing to work against it," wrote the NCCJ in 1943.[87] Carey McWilliams, the leftist writer, agreed. A peerless monitor of racial and religious persecution in America, McWilliams counted at least 250 local and national tolerance organizations founded in the aftermath of the 1943 riots.[88]

Hewing to its task of promoting religious goodwill, the NCCJ continued to find new ways to fight its crusade, to make its cause nationwide. This was no more evident than during Brotherhood Week, another NCCJ event begun in the 1930s. The idea was to have a holiday like Christmas, Yom Kippur, or the Fourth of July in order to celebrate the brotherhood of man under the Fatherhood of God. It traced its origins to a 1929 Denver roundtable, when Father Hugh McMenamin proposed a week where pulpit emphases on Friday and Sunday focused on goodwill. The local communities could also hold activities to demonstrate good interfaith relations, he suggested. The idea took shape immediately after the Tolerance Trio concluded its first tour, and the NCCJ held the first Brotherhood Day in 1934. The following year the date was changed to align with George Washington's birthday, thus connecting the ideal of brotherhood to that of good Americanism.[89] In 1939, Brotherhood Day was transformed into a weeklong celebration because "a day would no longer encompass the vast variety of activities which came to be associated with the event." The rise of European totalitarianism had increased the importance of American brotherhood, lionizing most of all amity between Protestants, Catholics, and Jews.[90]

After Pearl Harbor, Brotherhood Week became a national event. During Brotherhood Week 1942, "reports from the field indicate that press and radio publicity, as well as the number of meetings held, showed a fifty percent increase over the previous year. Practically every major press service in the country carried Brotherhood Week articles to dailies and weeklies. One article alone, by Wendell L. Willkie, warning against complacency toward intolerance in wartime, was syndicated to 700 newspapers."[91] In 1943, President Roosevelt served as honorary chairman of the event, commenting that Brotherhood Week "reminds us of the basic religious faith from which democracy has grown—that all men are children of one Father and brothers in the human family . . . [I]t is good for us to pledge renewed devotion to the fundamentals upon which this nation has been built." Capitalizing on Roosevelt's theme, the NCCJ adopted "Brotherhood or Chaos" as the theme of Brotherhood Week 1944.[92] That year, Clinchy wrote, Brotherhood Week "was virtually taken over by the nation. Schools, churches, colleges, government agencies, civic institutions, radio, press and almost every other opinion-making organization now count Brotherhood Week as a national event in the calendar year."[93]

In the buildup to Brotherhood Week 1946, promotional materials showed the faces of three soldiers who had died during the war: Arthur J. King (Protestant), William R. Sorensen (Catholic), and Jerry Neumann (Jewish). The men "died together in a common cause," read the flyer. The living now had "an opportunity to salute their unselfish patriotism during American Brotherhood Week." Protestant, Catholic, Jew: as martyrs, they were Americans all.[94]

The image of men of the three faiths dying in common cause became another component of NCCJ propaganda during the war. It even emerged in a short comic book, titled *Three Pals*. Based on the "true story of three heroic and brave Americans"—Gershon Ross (Jew), Blaine Kehoe (Catholic), and George Foster (Protestant)—the book told the story of the three men from the time they starred together on the 1939 Swampscott (Massachusetts) High School football team,

Civic leaders make plans for Brotherhood Day observance. Albert D. Lasker, Judge John D. McGoorty, and General Charles G. Dawes.

The Amusement World Does Its Bit. Lawrence Tibbett, Andre Kostelanetz and George M. Cohan take part in a Brotherhood Day program.

During the buildup to World War II, the NCCJ's Brotherhood Day was expanded to a weeklong celebration. During the war, Brotherhood Week "was virtually taken over by the nation. Schools, churches, colleges, government agencies, civic institutions, radio, press and almost every other opinion-making organization now count Brotherhood Week as a national event in the calendar year." This 1938 image shows the United States filled with Protestants, Catholics, and Jews, while the NCCJ is busy "making America safe for differences." Used by permission of the Social Welfare History Archives, University of Minnesota Libraries.

each a running back in a three-pronged offensive powerhouse. They evidently socialized together too, with Foster's comic book character saying he loved Gershon's mother's Jewish cooking and Kehoe's figure asking if fish would be served at dinner, because it was Friday. After Pearl Harbor, the "three pals" phoned one another from their respective colleges and jobs. They agreed to enlist, one in the navy, another in the army, the third in the marines. Shortly thereafter, one died in Saipan, the other in Cape Gloucester, the third in a submarine-monitoring blimp over the Atlantic. "The three pals will never meet on earth again," concluded the comic book, "but they have done their job gallantly and well; and their spirits mingle as in days of old, Catholic, Protestant, Jew. They died, as they lived, in true brotherhood . . . Americans All!"[95]

This of course echoed the celebrations of the Four Chaplains. Together as one, Protestants, Catholics, and Jews were emblems of American unity and symbols of a new national image. By the end of the war, it was not just the NCCJ promoting interfaith martyrdom as a symbol of perfect Americanism. The tri-faith idea had spread.

3

Tri-Faith America in the Early Cold War

IN EARLY 1946, shortly after the hostilities of World War II had ended, the Advertising Council of America was looking for programs to boost. It was desperate too. Begun in the first months of the war, after ad executives became afraid of wartime regulations the federal government might impose on their industry, the War Advertising Council, as it was then called, started as a nonprofit organization composed of Madison Avenue's best and brightest who donated time and material to help the federal government "sell" governmental programs to the American public. During the four years of fighting, it had churned out iconic campaigns including Rosie the Riveter, Smokey Bear and his slogan "Only You Can Prevent Forest Fires" (in response to fears that the Japanese would start forest fires in the Pacific Northwest), and "Loose Lips Sink Ships," which was so effective in warning people away from spreading rumors that the council had to tone down the advertisements for fear of sparking violence.

After the war, the ad executives wanted to preserve the Ad Council and the enormous goodwill it had generated among the public and in the federal government. But they expressed concern about it becoming part of any state propaganda machine. At a meeting shortly after the end of hostilities, several executives discussed incorporating nongovernmental causes to its slate of free advertising campaigns and rebranding the organization as, simply, the Advertising Council. The newly composed council would possess a Public Advisory Board of "15 to 20 outstanding leaders of public opinion" and prioritize only projects that were "in the best interests of the public as a whole."[1]

When the newly composed Ad Council put out its first call for proposals in 1946, the NCCJ saw a tremendous opportunity. The Ad Council had already helped promote the 1946 Brotherhood Week, which it retitled *American* Brotherhood Week and promoted like a national holiday. Because of this experience, the NCCJ knew of the council's desired emphasis on postwar unity. Sensing the opportunity to harness the power of millions of dollars of free advertising to promote its tri-faith agenda, the NCCJ's application to the Ad Council presented the NCCJ as an established leader in the wartime tolerance movement. It stressed the history of the NCCJ (conceived "the year Al Smith was so defamed because he was a Catholic running for the presidency"). It said its past successes were based on the group's "responsible leadership and sponsorship," thus proving the NCCJ's nonradical credentials. It mentioned that two of its three chairmen were prominent businessmen (Roger Straus and the newly tapped Thomas E. Braniff, a Catholic and president of Braniff Airways). And it quoted business-friendly language of national unity: "Intolerance and suspicion prevent our working together as a team to win the victories of peace." The application requested aid in order to extend its efforts "in the field of education in inter-group relations."[2]

When the Ad Council finally unveiled its list of successful applications, only three causes appeared: atomic energy, world trade, and the NCCJ's vision of Tri-Faith America.[3] Unlike other applicants, such as the United Negro College Fund (UNCF), the NCCJ seemed the most effective way for the Ad Council to champion unity and brotherhood without engaging too overtly in the rough waters of racial equality.[4]

Within days of the decision, Ad Council representatives visited NCCJ headquarters to craft a plan of action.[5] They selected the high-profile Lee Bristol, vice president of advertising at Bristol-Myers Company, to coordinate the campaign. After dubbing the campaign "United America," they petitioned seventeen advertising agencies to participate. Twelve sent ads. "Ordinarily we ask one advertising agency to do the creative work in any campaign, but, in this instance, knowing how many advertising agency people are interested in the subject, we are asking a number of agencies to cooperate in the preparation of material," said the council's invitation.[6] One executive called the campaign "one of the most important that the Council has ever undertaken."[7] Catholics and Jews within the advertising industry were particularly eager to participate, putting on display a transformation the industry had undergone during the previous decade and a half, when Catholics and Jews first entered advertising in significant numbers. Thomas D'Arcy Brophy, president of Kenyon & Eckhardt and one of the nation's leading postwar advertising men, had attended Catholic schools and had helped start the tri-faith USO during World War II. It was natural he would play a role in "United America."[8] Samuel Dalsimer, who managed the creative side of "United America," was a Jew active in the Anti-Defamation League.[9] The council set an aggressive schedule and hoped for a broad, nationwide campaign that would perpetuate the unity forged during the war.[10]

They were not disappointed. The campaign lasted six years, from 1946 to 1952. During its first quarter alone, "United America" made 293 million listener impressions on radio broadcasts across the country.[11] That quadrupled to 831 million listener impressions in 1947, and more than 1 billion in 1949. "United America" ads appeared in dozens of shows, including *The Abbott and Costello Show*, *The Jack Benny Program*, *The George Burns and Gracie Allen Show*, and Drew Pearson's *Washington Merry-Go-Round*.[12] Print ads appeared in magazines and newspapers. One 1949 ad showed a Pilgrim coming ashore in 1620, with an upset Native American saying, "Ugh! . . . foreigners!"— highlighting the non-native origins of almost all Americans.[13] Another ad, showing a young white kid in a baseball uniform defending his pitcher, an African American, saying, "What's his race or religion got to do with it—he can pitch!"[14] Another ad, from 1951, showed a bird nailing up a sign above his nest: "No Catholics, Jews, Protestants." A neighbor bird came over to point out that "only silly humans do that!" The ad concluded: "Remember . . . Brotherhood is something that makes freedom possible—and freedom is a mighty valuable thing these days."[15]

In general, the ads lionized brotherhood more than equality, emphasizing amity and goodwill rather than specific instances of abuse. Throughout the six-year campaign, its central theme was "Judge others on their individual worth!" The ads urged Americans, "Speak up, wherever we are, against prejudice, and work for better understanding. Remember that's being a good American." The ads easily made the transition from the anti-Fascism of the immediate postwar period to Cold War anti-Communism, simply substituting the enemy. One 1950 ad stated, "Communism thrives on dissention—Management against Labor—Christian against Jew—White against Negro."[16]

But the NCCJ quickly learned that there was a cost to the Ad Council's support. During the first year of the campaign, it became apparent that the Ad Council was leery of any prophetic religious commitment to brotherhood. True brotherhood might prove too disruptive, too demanding. In a letter to the big three religious organizations of midcentury America—the Federal Council of Churches, the National Catholic Welfare Conference, and the Synagogue Council of America—Douglas Meldrum, the Ad Council's chief administrator for "United America," listed the reasons why it had undertaken the campaign in the first

Seeking to maintain the goodwill it had won during the war, the Advertising Council in America chose to promote a handful of programs "in the best interests of the public as a whole." One of the first campaigns it embraced was "United America," proposed by the NCCJ. This 1951 ad challenges residential discrimination against Protestants, Catholics, and Jews. Courtesy Ad Council Archives, University of Illinois Archives, RS 13/2/207.

place, citing the council's desire to minimize antagonisms like those that had emerged "in offices, shops, mines, factories, and constantly threaten[ed] to break out into open acts of destructive violence" following World War I. Meldrum also said, "Division in the United States creates an impression throughout the world that America is weak and our country's position and prestige is thereby lowered in world affairs."[17] While practical, these arguments were hardly stunning endorsements of the ideal of the brotherhood of man under the Fatherhood of God. Meanwhile, and more troubling, the Ad Council perpetually kept the three religious organizations at arm's length. At one closed meeting, the directors expressed concerns that "these people would be almost bound to put in the religious aspect of this question very strongly and in spite of any indoctrination we might give them before the meeting."[18]

Perhaps the Ad Council was afraid of interfaith squabbles. Some Catholics had objected to "United America" from the beginning, fearing "that the more publicity that is given to a thing of this sort [intolerance] the more active it becomes" and that such a campaign might turn into "special pleading" by a single group, the unnamed group being American Jews.[19] More likely, however, Ad Council executives were afraid that a stern religious commitment to goodwill might push the campaign in uncomfortable directions, particularly toward promoting equality. In their eyes, unity took priority over equality.

For those in the NCCJ, demoting the prophetic nature of goodwill was a tough pill to swallow. When the Ad Council came to the NCCJ asking for money to continue the campaign beyond its first year, the NCCJ dragged its feet for months. Only after multiple requests and after other prominent religious organizations contributed did the NCCJ feel comfortable supporting the venture.[20]

Matters concerning race were equally thorny. For instance, although the initial NCCJ application stressed the need to improve "intergroup relations," the early correspondence from the Ad Council almost always mentioned the "program on inter-faith tolerance and understanding" or "the Interfaith program," placing emphasis on religion rather than anything broader.[21] Meanwhile, those advocating racial equality saw themselves quickly relegated to the sidelines. In late 1946, the American Council on Race Relations sent a note to Ted A. Repplier, head of the Ad Council Advisory Board, requesting that Repplier attend its conference "as the first step in securing more effective joint thinking and action with respect to public information in the field of human relations."[22] Repplier declined the invitation, but receiving it made him realize that this major organization in intergroup causes had never been sent information on "United America."[23] Similarly, when members of the NAACP, the Council for Democracy, and the American Jewish Committee discussed setting up their own panel to promote greater radio activity "on the subject of inter-race and inter-faith understanding," the Ad Council discouraged them, pointing out "the great dangers that might arise if this matter was handled without a great deal of knowledge both of the radio industry and of the Council operation."[24] The Ad Council wanted control of the message about tolerance and did not want racial equality to play too prominent a role. Indeed, in 1948, the council suspended the "United America" campaign during the four months leading up to the presidential election because President Truman's sweeping civil rights plank and Strom Thurmond's subsequent defection from the Democratic Party to create a pro-segregationist State's Rights Party had made racial equality a prominent campaign issue. "United America has been kept off the air," said one committee member, ". . . because the problem of interracial equality has become a political issue."[25]

"United America" did not entirely ignore race. Among other acquisitions, it purchased several of Bill Mauldin's cartoons on postwar race relations. In one 1951 advertisement, an African American factory worker walks behind several of his white co-workers, one of whom is about to whisper something to another, who instead raises his hand and says, "Don't give me that stuff . . . around this plant we judge a guy by what he does."[26] Despite a handful of instances, though, to the Ad Council, it was safer to promote unity rather than equality, and when the two clashed, the whole project seemed to derail.

Chafe as they might about compromises, the NCCJ still took the free advertising in order to promote Judeo-Christian brotherhood. Pluralism was becoming the normative way to think about the United States, and that pluralism was safely centered on tri-faith religion. The cost of this success was that the prophetic component of the vision—the one demanding a vitality of faith and a life based on the gospel—sometimes seemed to be nothing more than rhetoric. But, ironically, this might have been the result of compromises made by the NCCJ itself.

CHURCHES AS CITADELS OF AMERICA'S "RELIGIOUS TRIANGLE"

Despite the limits of postwar tolerance, Judeo-Christianity and the tri-faith idea it embodied experienced few boundaries during the Cold War. Being engaged with an enemy that basked in godlessness made America's religious character seem all the more vital. As President-elect Dwight D. Eisenhower said in 1952, "Our form of government, has no sense unless it is founded in a deeply felt religious faith, and I don't care what it is. With us of course it is the Judeo-Christian concept."[27] Judeo-Christianity, however interpreted, served as the moral backbone for midcentury America, and it counted among its members Protestants, Catholics, and Jews.[28]

The Cold War was not the only reason for the embrace of the tri-faith idea. The social dislocations of suburbia, the anxieties of the atomic age, and aggressive marketing from various religious groups were also contributing factors. "The many new churches and synagogues being built on every side in this country, the religious weeks conducted in almost every large university of the land, the frequent professions of religious faith made by our political leaders, the religious advertisements in the bus, subway and trolley, are all eloquent testimonies to an upsurge of religious interest in America," said the Reverend Gustave Weigel, a Jesuit priest and forthright critic of American society. "There may have been moments when religion was more intensive in the United States," he added, "but never a time when it was so extensive." He titled his 1955 essay "Americans Believe That Religion Is a Good Thing."[29]

Statistics bear him out. In 1952, 75 percent of Americans polled said religion was "very important" in their personal lives, an all-time high. In 1957, 81 percent said religion could answer "the problems of the day," also an all-time high. Eighty-six percent said religion was increasing its influence on the United States. Nearly half of all Americans said they attended a religious service every week, and all the major religious indicators reached all-time highs during the decade.[30] In August 1957, the monthly *Presbyterian Life* topped one million subscribers for the first time, claiming to reach the largest number of Christians assembled on one list since the birth of Jesus. The Methodist-sponsored *Together* passed a million subscribers that fall.[31] In 1954, the Reverend Norman Vincent Peale visited a bookstore to see how his pastoral book *The Power of Positive Thinking* (1952) was selling compared to the recently released Kinsey Report, *Sexual Behavior in the Human Female* (1953). The bookstore clerk revealed that Peale's book was way ahead, adding, "Religion is much more popular than sex this year."[32]

Politicians were perhaps the quickest to proclaim the importance of tri-faith religion in Cold War America. They recognized that tri-faith proclamations were easy ways not only to distinguish the United States from the Soviet Union but also to build national unity. In 1955, Eisenhower launched the annual "Back to God" campaign, sponsored by the American Legion, saying: "Without God there could be no American form of government nor an American way of life." Speaking on national radio, he added: "Recognition of the Supreme Being is the first—the most basic—expression of Americanism. Thus the Founding Fathers saw it, and thus, with God's help, it will continue to be."[33] Eisenhower often spoke of God but hardly mentioned Jesus, keeping his rhetoric coolly Judeo-Christian. Under his administration, Congress added "under God" to the nation's Pledge of Allegiance (1954) and "In God we trust" became the national motto (1956), formally replacing *E pluribus unum*, which was first placed on the Great Seal of the United States in

1792. Advocating these changes, Eisenhower said (during another "Back to God" campaign speech): "Whatever our individual church, whatever our personal creed, our common faith in God is a common bond among us. In our fundamental faith, we are all one. Together we thank the Power that has made and preserved us a nation. By the millions, we speak prayers, we sing hymns—and no matter what their words may be, their spirit is the same—'In God is our trust.'"[34]

Even Harry S. Truman, less publicly religious than Eisenhower, made strong claims about the religious sources of American democracy. In 1950, shortly after the terms of the Cold War had shifted from the progressive, freedom-declaring definition of Americanism that lasted into 1949 to the witch hunts targeting progressives, homosexuals, and suspected Communists in the early 1950s, Truman said in his annual Brotherhood Week address, "The only sure bedrock of human brotherhood is the knowledge that God is the Father of mankind." Turning to the Soviets, he said, "In the history of the world, there have been some movements inspired by a desire for brotherhood and greater justice among men which have denied or forgotten the religious foundation of those ideals. Sooner or later these movements have wavered and lost their way. They have become self-centered; they have set up their own interests as the only standard of right and wrong, and they have degenerated from movements of liberation into movements of tyranny and oppression." Truman concluded: "We can succeed in achieving brotherhood only if we acknowledge that the ideal of brotherhood is something outside us and above us, something by which we in our turn will also be judged."[35]

The following year, Truman's Brotherhood Week announcement (every president between FDR and Lyndon Johnson served as honorary chairman of the event) proclaimed: "Until the world accepts the principle of Brotherhood of Man under the Fatherhood of God, it will be compelled to live under a day-in day-out alert with the dread of deadly explosions always imminent."[36] In 1952, Truman also signed into law the National Day of Prayer, a holiday now celebrated the first Thursday of May. Both houses of Congress passed the law quickly, after the Reverend Billy Graham, the nation's most visible Protestant minister, urged them to do so.

More expressively than Truman, Eisenhower's secretary of state, John Foster Dulles, told the entire world that the Cold War was essentially a battle between those who believed in the moral laws of the Judeo-Christian tradition and those who found value in materialist secularism. In an address to the United Nations in September 1953, Dulles was certain these differences could be overcome, but only if the Soviet Union recognized some inherent truths: "Our hope is that the Soviet Communist leaders, before it is too late, will recognize that love of God, love of country, and sense of human dignity, always survive. Repressive measures inevitably lead to resentment and bitterness and perhaps something more. That does not come about through artificial stimulation. It comes about because the Creator endowed all human beings with the spark of spiritual life."[37]

For these politicians, faith was armor in the worldwide struggle against Communism. It was the way Americans could be strong in the face of the Soviet opposition but benevolent toward one another. It enhanced one's power by adding humility and kindness. If one was true to one's faith—if a Protestant was a better Protestant, a Catholic a better Catholic, a Jew a better Jew—one would also be a better American.

The NCCJ helped Eisenhower make this claim overt. During the summer of 1953, J. B. Matthews, executive director for the Senate Permanent Subcommittee on Investigations (Senator Joseph McCarthy's subcommittee) and a former Methodist minister and missionary, penned an article in *American Mercury* titled "Reds and Our Churches." The essay's inflammatory first sentence claimed: "The largest single group supporting the Communist apparatus in the United States is composed of Protestant clergyman." He listed by name 102 clerics who "threatened the nation," although his proof was merely that they had signed a petition protesting the McCarran (Internal Security) Act.[38]

Religious leaders closed ranks against Matthews. The *Christian Century* called Matthews "venomous." The *Christian Advocate*, official organ of the Methodist Church, said the charges were "of the degree of stupidity and misrepresentation that can be reached only in an atmosphere of suspicion, distrust, and fear." *America* and *Commonweal* made formal protests in their editorial pages too.[39]

Within days of the release of the Matthews article, the NCCJ filed a protest with the president. After first checking with the White House, the NCCJ sent a telegram to Eisenhower asserting, "We fully recognize the right of Congress to investigate the loyalty of any citizen regardless of the office he may occupy, ecclesiastical or otherwise. But destroying trust in the leaders of Protestantism, Catholicism or Judaism by wholesale condemnation is to weaken the greatest American bulwark against atheistic materialism and Communism." The NCCJ had stood behind Al Smith in 1928 and protested antisemitism in the 1930s; "now, with Protestant loyalty and integrity under attack, Catholics and Jews regrouped for the mutual defense of the third side of America's religious triangle."[40]

Within two hours of receiving the NCCJ telegram, Eisenhower issued a public reply. "Generalized and irresponsible attacks that sweepingly condemn the whole of any group of citizens are alien to America," he wrote. "Such attacks betray contempt for the principles of freedom and decency. And when these attacks—whatever their professed purpose be—condemn such a vast portion of the churches or clergy as to create doubt in the loyalty of all, the damage to our nation is multiplied." In a stirring affirmation of the importance of the nation's spiritual center, he declared: "The churches of America are citadels of our faith in individual freedom and human dignity. This faith is the living source of all our spiritual strength. And this strength is our matchless armor in our worldwide struggle against the forces of godless tyranny and oppression."[41]

Such a militaristic description of American religiosity was hardly alien to the NCCJ. For more than a decade, it had argued that faith was needed for democracy to survive. "Today we are engaged in a deadly world struggle between the forces of atheistic Communism and the forces for good, for 'the brotherhood of man under the Fatherhood of God,'" read its 1954 annual report. The report (tellingly titled "One Nation Under God") contrasted this new anti-Communist, nation-building mission with the group's earlier mission of "rallying Catholics, Protestants, and Jews to the common defense of any group under un-American attack." While the NCCJ claimed success for its "important part in making organized bigotry an unpopular cause in this country," the nation now needed something more potent: "The extent to which we *make real* our ideal of 'one nation under God' may very well determine whether the teeming millions of Europe and Asia will cast their lot with the free world or succumb to the lures of the Moscow hate merchants." Tweaking its World War II rhetoric, the report concluded: "The most stirring idea throughout the world today is the great assertion of the Declaration of Independence that God has endowed *every* person with unalienable rights to life, liberty and the pursuit of happiness."[42] A 1958 self-evaluation affirmed, "The Conference holds firmly to the basic values implicit in the Judeo-Christian and American traditions. Among these are: the God-given dignity and worth of all persons; the Brotherhood of man under the Fatherhood of God; and the ideals of brotherhood and justice as the standards of human relationships."[43]

In addition to being a perfect weapon in the Cold War, tri-faith Judeo-Christianity also filled a moral void at the center of midcentury American liberalism. For decades, leading liberal thinkers had struggled to develop a secular intellectual orientation for liberal ideas that did not culminate in Communism or Fascism. John Dewey's *A Common Faith* (1934) and his *Liberalism and Social Action* (1935) were the foremost attempts to describe such a secular construct, but Joseph Wood Krutch, Walter Lippmann, and Sidney Hook proffered others. Dewey and his ilk were baffled that liberalism—based on the idea that human reason was superior to supernatural understanding—did not necessarily lead to higher morality. In fact, it did not seem to possess any clear morality at all. Thus, liberalism, with its emphases on human freedom and individual rights, had unleashed democracy and capitalism but proved incapable of providing a moral compass that could constrain the worst abuses of its progeny, such as demagoguery and extreme economic disparity. By 1949, Lionel Trilling was writing somberly in *The Liberal Imagination* that the politics of the postwar

In Cold War America, the NCCJ embraced the nation's new slogan, "One Nation Under God." It became the theme of its 1954 Brotherhood Week and, the NCCJ hoped, helped demonstrate the vital connection between religion and democracy. Used by permission of the Social Welfare History Archives, University of Minnesota Libraries.

world required the capturing of the popular imagination, and liberalism, with its bland proclamations on behalf of individualism and human reason, was wildly uninspiring, especially when compared to conservative allegiances to tradition and nationalism. Trilling tried to recapture the "variousness and possibility" that had led to liberalism's triumph in the eighteenth and nineteenth centuries, but he was never certain he had accomplished his mission. Secular liberalism had done a better job creating democracy and capitalism than it had in controlling and regulating them.[44]

Within this vacuum, America's Judeo-Christian "tradition" was a salve. It was tolerant but grounded. It was tough but, in its civic guise, not too demanding. It highlighted individual dignity but did not force a confrontation with race directly. In the postwar period, it was useful in animating American social justice. Sidney Hook and other secular liberals persisted in chiding the religious faith implied in Judeo-Christianity, with Hook famously lambasting his fellow intellectuals for their "failure of nerve." Despite the protests, though, Judeo-Christianity became the faith that underpinned postwar liberalism. When congressmen were debating the addition of "under God" to the nation's Pledge of Allegiance, many reported they had never received so much supportive mail.[45] In 1952 Budd Schulberg wrote that the greedy protagonist of his 1941 bestseller, *What Makes Sammy Run?*, "in throwing over the way of his father without learning any sense of obligation to the Judeo-Christian-democratic pattern, . . . had nothing except naked self-interest to guide himself."[46] Well-known historian H. Stuart Hughes said:

> Ten or fifteen years ago, no self-respecting "enlightened" intellectual would have been caught dead with a religious interpretation of anything. Only the Catholics thought in these terms—plus a scattering of Protestants, whom we dismissed as harmless eccentrics. We were either "idealistic" socialist-radicals or skeptical, hard-boiled Freudian-Paretans. Any other attitude would have been considered a betrayal of the avant-garde. . . . [Now t]he avant-garde is becoming old-fashioned; religion is now the latest thing.[47]

The Judeo-Christian ideal helped bring together a loose coalition of seekers for social justice under the guise of religious faith. While materialist ideas had served as the animating impulse of activists in the 1930s, now the religious idea of individual dignity premised on the brotherhood of man under the Fatherhood of God took on the mantle. Religious narratives were employed to make the case for improving the lives of Americans. Biblical stories were referred to frequently. This transition did not always alter the demands made in the name of justice, but class-based calls for equality were traded for calls made in the name of individual dignity under the watchful eye of God. The flexibility of the term "Judeo-Christian" better served this need. It could propel hope, joy, and redemption, but it could also possess irony, complexity, and contingency if that better fit the circumstances. With liberalism adrift in the late 1940s, the Judeo-Christian tradition emerged as solid ground.[48]

The NCCJ made the most of the connection. "What we today call the American Way of Life," said a 1954 report, emerged from both "freedom and faith . . . the two basic spiritual foundations of our American heritage—the warp and woof of the loom which finally built a nation." While "exactly what that Way of Life is can never be adequately defined," one central component was "the Bible with the religious and ethical traditions based on it." The report added, "The basic respect for the freedom and dignity of all human beings and the principles of equal justice and opportunity for all, regardless of race, color, creed or position, have deep roots in the Biblical conception of Man created in the image of his Maker and therefore endowed with a divine, creative spark."

Pluralism and tolerance were components of the American way of life too, and they were also grounded in religion. "Our very love of freedom and truth," the report said, "also led the Founding Fathers to insist that prescribing religion of any kind is not the business of government." The report then went on to compare quotations from the Bible and from "our great national documents" in order to show "the moral and spiritual resources in our heritage in a way that no historical summary can approximate." The report concluded: "Our great religious faiths are thus . . . the fountainhead of our moral and spiritual values."[49] With the three faiths of democracy active and engaged, America was emboldened.

THREE FAITHS UBIQUITOUS

Within this faith in faith, there were always three prongs. "Protestant, Catholic and Jew are united in the religious idea that forms the conceptual basis for the *unity in diversity* that characterize our American heritage," said the NCCJ.[50] In an Ad Council–supported venture called "Religion in American Life" (RIAL), a nationwide campaign "to increase worship attendance at churches and synagogues as a significant contribution to the deepening of American morals and spiritual life," Protestants, Catholics, and Jews were always prominently featured. In 1959, for instance, Francis Cardinal Spellman, archbishop of New York, Rabbi Max D. Davidson, president of the Synagogue Council of America, and Eugene Carson Blake, past president of the National Council of Churches, all came together to praise the RIAL campaign as "vital" for the life of the nation.[51]

A common feature of Washington, D.C., political life during the 1950s was the prayer breakfast, typically presided over by a priest, a rabbi, and a minister, who provided "a sort of ecclesiastical garnish to all manner of secular dishes."[52] A member of each of the three faiths almost always offered a prayer to open all the major political conventions of the decade, becoming a "traditional and somewhat theatrical custom" by 1960.[53] At a rally to support federal aid abroad, with the president in attendance, Bishop Fulton Sheen joined the president of the National Council of Churches and the president of the Synagogue Council of America to lend support.[54] Representatives of all three faiths were asked to be onstage at the decade's various presidential inaugurations as well. A Catholic priest, a Protestant clergyman, and a Jewish rabbi were the keynote speakers at New York City's celebration of I Am an American Day in 1946, at which half a million people congregated.[55] Thomas D'Arcy Brophy of the Ad Council worked the trio into a proposal he made for a "super-radio program" on good Americanism in 1946.[56]

Meanwhile, President Truman's 1948 Committee on Civil Rights, which produced the famous volume *To Secure These Rights*, included Rabbi Roland B. Gittelsohn, the Reverend Francis J. Haas, a Catholic, and the Reverend Henry Knox Sherril, the presiding bishop of the Episcopal Church and soon to be president of the National Council of Churches. Having all three on the committee not only demonstrated a commitment to pluralism but also gave it broad moral authority. When the Episcopal Church's National Council thought it could expedite the liberation of people behind the Iron Curtain through prayer, it enlisted priests, ministers, and rabbis for the cause. The Voice of America and Radio Free Europe picked up the story, assuring those in Communist countries "that the crusade of prayer was on."[57]

During these years, *Time* could say that a book such as *The Questioning Child and Religion* is directed to "all conscientious parents—Catholic, Protestant and Jew— living in the U.S., where children who play the same games might pray quite differently."[58] The magazine later described John F. Kennedy's cabinet thusly: "six Protestants, two Jews, one Roman Catholic and one Mormon or—to put it another way—three Governors, two businessmen, two lawyers, two State Department hands and a Congressman."[59]

The image of the three faiths working harmoniously became ubiquitous. In 1948, the spirited but implausible film *Big City* told the story of a baby abandoned in a wicker bassinet on a cold winter day in New York City. The child is found by three friends, a Protestant minister, a Jewish cantor, and a Catholic policeman. The men decide the girl cannot stay out in the cold. After allowing her to stay a short time in the house of the police officer (whose Catholic mother would "know what to do with it"), the three men shockingly decide to adopt the baby, move in together, and raise her, producing a wonderful, well-adjusted child. Unhappiness finds her only several years later, when the Catholic police officer finds a potential bride who wants to adopt the girl. By now the "wee lass" has become a small woman with well-honed diplomatic skills who brokers a deal to keep the interfaith trio together. At the end of the lighthearted saga, the cantor of this unconventional "family" treats the audience to a selection of Jewish songs, including a rousing version of the popular and solemn Jewish prayer song "Kol Nidre," which is sung, in Hebrew, by the entire cast. In *Big City*, Catholics, Jews, and bighearted Protestants became paragons of American moral authority.[60]

In education, similar tri-faith images emerged. In 1955, the Ad Council and the United States Information Agency crafted a "People's Capitalism" exhibit that toured the world to promote economic differences between the United States and the Soviet Union. The text of the exhibit said American society was founded on "a belief in God," a conviction that "all men are created equal," and a philosophy that

"It's a little baby... why not take it up to my mother? She knows how to take care of it!"

Big City, produced by Metro-Goldwyn-Meyer in 1948, told the story of a Protestant minister, a Jewish cantor, and a Catholic policeman who together decide to adopt a baby they find abandoned on the street. In *Big City*, Catholics, Jews, and bighearted Protestants became paragons of American moral authority, perfect symbols of American unity in the late 1940s. *Big City* © Turner Entertainment Co., a Warner Bros. Entertainment Company. All rights reserved.

"the state exists only to serve the individual, not the reverse." President Eisenhower said he loved the exhibit but requested greater emphasis on America's three great faiths by showing pictures of "Catholic, Protestant and Jewish places of worship side by side."[61]

Eisenhower might have seen something similar at Brandeis University. Brandeis, the nation's first Jewish-sponsored nonsectarian university, devoted an entire section of its campus to a picturesque pond bordered by three chapels, one Protestant, one Catholic, and one Jewish. The chapels "marked a bold departure from U.S. campus tradition, which prescribes either a single, nondenominational chapel or a variety of structures built over a period of time for different faiths," wrote *Life* in its coverage of the tri-faith dedication. The university celebrated the opening of the chapels by granting three honorary degrees, one to a member of each faith. Brandeis president Abram Sachar said, "Here at Brandeis, please God, we shall each respect our own faith . . . and carry this respect with pride in the presence of each other."[62]

Brandeis was not alone among universities in demonstrating the efficacy of the idea of Tri-Faith America. In 1953, Seton Hall University, one of the country's largest Catholic institutions, started the nation's first Judeo-Christian studies program, led by the Reverend John M. Oesterreicher, an Austrian-born Jew who converted to Catholicism. As Cold War Christians became increasingly interested in the teachings of the Old Testament, especially its focus on the faulty nature of man (a vibrant subject in the atomic age),[63] Oesterreicher received support from numerous Catholic intellectuals, who penned articles, gave papers, and offered financial support. Jews, who were increasingly adopting Jesus as a symbol of an ideal Jewish teacher, were similarly interested in the intellectual cross-fertilization.[64] To them, it also must have been comforting to have a Catholic priest point out (as several did) that a proper reading of the Gospel of John does not name "the Jews" as Christ's killers; rather, the text says, "It is I who am the sinner; it is we, all of us, who are the crucifiers of Jesus." In 1956, the program published *The Bridge: A Yearbook of Judeao-Christian Studies*, a collection of essays about connections between Christians and Jews in history, the arts, and philosophy. *The Bridge* was the program's effort to put substance into the phrase "Judeo-Christian," to "show the unity of God's design as it leads from the Law to the Gospel—the unbroken economy of salvation." While Jews might not have been entirely happy to be on the early, unevolved end of "God's design," many Jewish participants perceived this to be a momentary rhetorical lapse rather than a dismissive comment. Besides, the gesture of Catholic goodwill was too hard to pass up.[65]

Even Harvard University, a bastion of blue-blooded Protestantism and founded to train Puritan ministers, acquiesced to the tri-faith order. In 1958, it appointed

British historian Christopher Dawson to be its first professor of Roman Catholic studies. Dawson sat alongside Harry A. Wolfson, Harvard's first professor of Jewish literature and philosophy (a chair it had established in 1925).[66]

Those outside the fold of the three faiths hardly seemed to exist. In a 1960 book, *Housing Choices and Housing Constraints*, the sociologist Nelson N. Foote referred to those without "religious identification" as "today's bohemians and eggheads." Everyone else was either a Protestant, Catholic, or Jew.[67] "An atheistic American is a contradiction in terms," said the Reverend George M. Docherty while arguing for the addition of "under God" in the Pledge of Allegiance.[68] Similar points were made throughout Tri-Faith America by the Census Bureau, within residential communities, and on numerous school boards.[69]

The tri-faith image even entered the world of elite manners. In 1952, Amy Vanderbilt published the first edition of her *Complete Guide to Etiquette*. The guide included directives on the proper way to address a letter, draft formal invitations, and hold forth during dinner parties. But it unexpectedly included an entire chapter, "Interfaith Courtesy and Understanding," that among other things explained Jewish holidays and Catholic rituals.[70] This was a first in the etiquette business. Vanderbilt's main competitor, Emily Post, had offered directives on the proper way to address a rabbi or a priest in 1945, and she had also included a small section on the do's and don'ts of certain religious ceremonies, including the correct procedure at Reform and Orthodox Jewish weddings. The book's solitary footnote attested to Post's unfamiliarity with these kinds of events: "The Author is indebted for the following material to Rabbi Nathan Krass of Temple Emanu-El, New York."[71]

But Vanderbilt's inclusion of an entire chapter was something new. Vanderbilt's readers learned there were more high holidays than Christmas and Easter. Jews had different burial customs than Christians too, along with a host of dietary restrictions and unique traditions for weddings and circumcisions. Catholics had different rituals as well. They were, for instance, supposed to raise their hat every time they passed a cathedral. A good host should be aware of such things, for in midcentury America it was not beyond reasonable doubt that a Catholic or a Jew might appear at one's dinner table. She concluded: "As America grows we'll need, more and more, to use courtesy in our community life."[72] She then tackled some of the thornier questions that might arise along these pluralist lines, such as whether a Christian should send a Christmas card to a Jewish friend (yes, but not one detailing Christ or the nativity) and which of the various dietary laws of Catholics and Jews should be respected when one hosts a dinner party (none, although a variety of options should be made available).[73]

By 1965, Emily Post's book (now operationally run by Post's daughter-in-law, Elizabeth) had done substantial catching up. It advised on the proper etiquette for

Roman Catholic weddings and how one should behave if one had an audience with the Pope. In a section on "forbidden ground" for party conversation, Post's 1965 book warned: "Certain subjects, even though you are very sure of the ground upon which you are standing, had best be shunned; for example, criticism of a religious creed or disagreement with another's political conviction. . . . The tactful person keeps his prejudices to himself." In the few decades following World War II, inter-faith courtesies had become part of the accepted terms of American living.[74]

The most lasting claims about the tri-faith character of the postwar nation came from sociologists, who noticed not only the anti-Communist component of post-war faith but also its significance in American society. The most famous of these commentators was Will Herberg, whose 1955 book *Protestant-Catholic-Jew* served as the benchmark for descriptions of America's religious sociology for the next decade. The book affirmed the arrival of Tri-Faith America but also exposed cer-tain weaknesses within it, particularly the triumph of the civic version of Judeo-Christianity at the expense of the prophetic one.

In *Protestant-Catholic-Jew*, Herberg made two big arguments, one dealing with America's spirituality, the other with its sociology. Spiritually, Herberg, a devout Jew, channeled Jeremiah. His book argued that despite the dramatic and lavish displays of religiosity during the Cold War, Americans had little genuine belief in or fear of God. They lacked knowledge of or even interest in the dynamic transfor-mative capacities of faith. Religion, he argued, had become captive to a civic faith, to the American way of life, which was the real god most Americans worshiped:

> The religiousness characteristic of America today is very often a religiousness without religion, a religiousness with almost any kind of content or none, a way of sociability or "belonging" rather than a way of reorienting life to God. It is thus frequently a religiousness without serious commitment, without real inner conviction, without genuine existential decision. What should reach down to the core of existence, shattering and renewing, merely skims the surface of life, and yet succeeds in generating the sincere feeling of being religious. Religion thus becomes a kind of protection the self throws up against the radical demand of faith.[75]

While this very well may have been true, this vision of spiritual emptiness also aligns with Herberg's life as a lonely searcher. He never earned his Ph.D. and was never trained formally as a sociologist, so he had constant reservations about his academic qualifications to be a professor. He came to study religious sociology via theology. A socialist in the 1920s and 1930s, Herberg experienced something of an existential crisis in 1938, after his Bolshevik hero, Nikolai Bukharin, was tried and executed in Stalinist Russia. Searching for a new nonmaterialist mode of under-standing, Herberg became a disciple of Reinhold Niebuhr, the nation's foremost Protestant theologian, during World War II. Niebuhr discouraged Herberg from becoming a Christian, saying Herberg had to become a better Jew before he could ever be a good Christian. So Herberg returned to the faith of his parents. By the late 1940s he was writing dense treatises on Jewish philosophy, including a huge book in 1951 called *Judaism and Modern Man*.

Only then did he turn to religious sociology. He penned a series of essays on the civic battles between Protestants, Catholics, and Jews and became increasingly frustrated with the secular direction of Jewish American social thought, seeing it as being overly accommodating rather than a staunch component of a religiously plural society.[76] Alone among his co-religionists, Herberg advocated on behalf of granting public monies to Catholic parochial schools, thus making him something of a perennial outlier, a Jew not fully accepted by the Jewish community, an aca-demic accused of being overly theological. This wasn't helped by the fact his aca-demic position was at Methodist-sponsored Drew University, in rural New Jersey.

Herberg's cynicism ran deep through *Protestant-Catholic-Jew*. All the religious proclamations of the postwar era, he said, emerged not out of a profound search for divine guidance but because of "the social necessity of 'belonging.'"[77] Borrowing heavily from David Riesman's *The Lonely Crowd*, Herberg noted how important it was to be "recognized" in society, to have a "brand name," in Riesman's words. This was how one advanced in an "outer-directed society" that judged a person by app-earance.[78] Transposing religion onto Riesman's analysis, Herberg concluded that religious identities were the "brand name" midcentury Americans depended on. "Not to identify oneself and be identified as . . . a Protestant, a Catholic, or a Jew is somehow not to be an American," he wrote. Atheists and agnostics were un-American. Buddhists and Muslims were foreign. Seeing "pervasive secularism amid mounting religiosity" and broad but shallow religious interest, he diagnosed America as suffering from secularization but grabbing on to religious identities nonetheless.[79]

Despite the lack of belief backing up the social posturing, the three faiths had nevertheless become "the primary context of self-identification and social loca-tion" in postwar America.[80] "When an American asks of a new family in town, . . . 'What *are* they?', he means to what religious community they belong, and the answer is in such terms as: 'They're Catholic (or Protestant, or Jewish),'" Herberg wrote.[81] Reflecting on the important social identifiers in postwar American life, Herberg said it had become "virtually mandatory for the American to place himself in one or another of these groups. It is not external pressure but inner necessity that compels him. For being a Protestant, a Catholic, or a Jew is understood as the specific way, and increasingly perhaps the only way, of being an American and locating oneself in American society. . . . Not to be a Catholic, a Protestant, or a Jew today is, for increasing numbers of American people, not to be anything, not to have a *name*."[82] He finished by telling the story of an army sergeant who, when confronted by a theologically astute recruit who insisted he was neither Catholic, Protestant, nor Jewish, said in exasperation: "Well, if you're not Catholic, or Protestant, or Jewish, what in blazes *are* you?"[83]

Herberg provided plenty of evidence for the importance of tri-faith religious identification within American society. He claimed that "American Protestants experience no difficulty in passing from one denomination to another when social or personal convenience requires, nor are there ever any real difficulties in intermarriage."[84] A general decline in Protestant denominationalism was seen in the fact that only about 7 percent of Protestants belonged to "exceptional" sects such as the Pentecostal, Holiness, and millennial groups.[85] Stressing the process of unification, socially and institutionally, Herberg failed to see the split between evangelical and mainline sects that was on the horizon. Protestants, more unified than ever before, were one of the largest social groups in American life.

As for Catholics, Herberg pointed to the incredible number of institutions designed solely for them. There were Catholic recreational baseball teams, sewing circles, bowling leagues, hospitals, orphanages, welfare agencies, Boy Scout troops, and war veterans associations. There were associations of Catholic doctors, lawyers, teachers, students, and philosophers. There were Catholic leagues of policemen, firemen, and sanitary workers. And there was the Catholic educational system, which boasted nearly five million students at the time—more than half of all Catholic elementary-school-age children. Taken together, this Catholic "system" constituted "at one and the same time a self-contained Catholic world."[86] Herberg also pointed to the increasing number of marriages between Irish and Italian Catholics, a union that at one time had been taboo.[87] Herberg showed that even though Catholics could be said to be "Americanizing" by losing their ethnic affiliations, they were still perpetuating an intact Catholic community.[88]

Among Jews, Herberg found a similar unity and a similar desire to maintain a touch of uncompromised particularism. He cited a survey of an eastern city of 127,000 inhabitants that found that every single Jew, young and old, sought to retain his or her Jewish identity, a conscious decision preventing both assimilation and intermarriage. Almost 100 percent of Jewish adolescents in the sample thought of Jews in religious terms rather than racial or ethnic ones, meaning they no longer saw in themselves the Eastern European ethnic immigrant; now they opted to define themselves religiously.[89] Jewish Sunday schools had become overtly religious and increasingly popular.[90] Jewish holidays were celebrated lavishly. One poll found that 50 percent of American Jews replied affirmatively to a question about being an active member of a synagogue. The traditional distance between the three major Jewish denominations was decreasing as well, Herberg argued, with the vast majority of the Jewish population falling into the mold of the Reform movement, although nominally choosing to claim Conservatism as their home.[91] American Jews too, then, were increasing in unity and showing no sign of willingly assimilating into a broader Anglo-Protestant identity.

Despite the occasionally somber tone in Herberg's book, reviewers loved it. Major media outlets treated it as an important intervention, and forty reviews appeared in its first year. The reviews often left aside the book's jeremiad, focusing instead on its sociological claims about Tri-Faith America. *Protestant-Catholic-Jew*, Reinhold Niebuhr said in the pages of the *New York Times*, provided "the most fascinating essay on the religious sociology of America that has appeared in decades."[92]

Perhaps one reason reviewers did not challenge Herberg's tri-faith thesis too much was because Herberg had effectively simplified and popularized a theory sociologists had been describing for years. In 1952, for example, eminent sociologist August B. Hollingshead concluded that "two social worlds have evolved—a Negro world and a white world. The white world is divided by ethnic origin and religion into Catholic, Protestant, and Jewish contingents." Although Hollingshead's description was more complicated than Herberg's (in addition to race and religion, it included ethnicity, class, and occupation), his fundamental assumption was that white Americans were divided into three faiths.[93]

Ruby Jo Kennedy, a sociologist interested in the retention of cultural inheritances, conveyed similar findings in a wartime article. In 1944, while studying intermarriage trends from 1870 to 1940 in New Haven, Connecticut, Kennedy found that "the large nationality groups in New Haven represent a triple division on religious grounds: Jewish, Protestant (British-American, German, and Scandinavian), and Catholic (Irish, Italian, and Polish)." During their first years in the United States each national group tended toward endogamy, but each also began to marry outside of its nationality group. By 1940, "while strict ethnic endogamy is loosening, religious endogamy is persisting." Catholics married Catholics more than 85 percent of the time, Protestants married Protestants nearly 80 percent of the time, and Jews married Jews more than 94 percent of the time. She concluded: "The traditional 'single melting pot' idea must be abandoned, and a new conception, which we term the 'triple melting pot' theory of American assimilation, will take its place, as the true expression of what is happening to the various nationality groups in the United States."[94] Kennedy was not the first to propose the tripartite melting pot theory, but once she put forward her thesis in 1944, numerous social analysts began to rely on religious divisions to describe the physical, social, and psychological divisions within American communities.[95]

Herberg was the most famous of the bunch, and for those writing after Herberg, *Protestant-Catholic-Jew* was the primary point of embarkation. Bennett M. Berger's 1960 study of autoworkers in California used Herberg's tripartite formulation to test the depth of religious commitment in his sample.[96] Martin E. Marty, associate editor of *Christian Century*, used Herberg's argument as the jumping-off point for his 1958 series of essays, "The New Shape of American Religion." Marty's articles (and the book they developed into) are usually remembered for his claims about the triumph of "religion-in-general" in America, but he began his series by accepting Herberg's theory of a religious tripod, adding a fourth "partner" to the vision—secular humanism.[97] John Courtney Murray, S.J., the nation's foremost Catholic social theorist, agreed with Marty in his 1960 book, *We Hold These Truths*. Murray suggested the four "conspiracies" were "at war intelligibly" in American society.[98] (Incidentally, Herberg disputed the addition of secular humanism to his tripartite description, saying, "Practically nobody in this country fails to identify himself as Protestant, Catholic or Jew" and that "the fourth group is really the mass of the three groups, cutting horizontally, in different ways." There was no group of self-identifying "secular humanists," he added, but secularism was pervasive to those who identified as Protestant, Catholic, or Jew.)[99] As late as 1970, Charles H. Anderson cited Herberg in the first footnote of his book *White Protestant Americans*, which was subtitled, significantly, *From National Origins to Religious Group*.[100]

DISCOMFORT, DISSENT, AND DIFFERENCE

Despite the unity implied by the tri-faith understanding of the nation, each of the three faiths encountered the postwar world dramatically differently. These differences shaped the debates of the postwar years, ensuring that, despite the claim that "religion-in-general" had triumphed in Cold War America, each of the three faiths had different goals in mind and different problems to solve.

The Cold War was one major line of distinction. In the battle against Communism, the Catholic Church had long-standing credentials. It vowed to fight Communism at all costs. The Church supported the right-wing dictator Francisco Franco instead of the Communist opposition during the Spanish Civil War of the late 1930s. It was critical of the Soviet Union during World War II, when the United States and the Soviet Union were allies. But the Church's staunch anti-Communism came into vogue during the Cold War. Bishop Fulton Sheen, America's best-known Catholic, was the most effusive in criticizing Communism, publishing anti-Communist books, giving blunt anti-Soviet speeches, and making anti-Communism a key part of his radio and television programs. His vociferousness won him plaudits from some of the most visible anti-Communists in the United States, such as FBI director J. Edgar Hoover. As a service to Sheen, the FBI began checking the loyalty of many of Sheen's employees and all his prospective converts.[101] In 1952, Sheen won an award from the Freedoms Foundation of Valley Forge, Pennsylvania, presented by Vice President Richard Nixon, for his "outstanding contributions to a better understanding of the American way of life."[102]

For postwar Catholics, then, opposing Communism was second nature. Cardinal Spellman organized huge anti-Soviet rallies at venues as large as New York's Polo Grounds. When Whittaker Chambers accused Alger Hiss, a blue-blooded Protestant New Deal administrator, of selling secrets to the Soviets, American Catholics took pride that their loyalty was no longer in question. Instead, a member of the Protestant social elite was having to defend himself.[103]

There were risks associated with this easy kind of politics, risks exposed by Senator Joseph McCarthy, who stoked nationwide fears that Communists had infiltrated the American government and American society in general. Throughout McCarthy's period of prominence, from 1952 to 1954, Catholics supported him more than any other group, especially Catholic intellectuals.[104] Even in disgrace, during the televised trial where Senator Joseph N. Welch famously asked McCarthy if he had any decency, McCarthy still won Catholic plaudits. While the trial was ongoing, Cardinal Spellman shook McCarthy's hand at a Holy Name Society mass as six thousand Catholic policemen cheered.[105] Throughout the Cold War, Catholic loyalty was difficult to question, but the accusation that Catholic anti-Communism was just another unthinking action by a group eager to assert its newfound patriotic credentials was equally prevalent.

There were Catholic theological dissidents to the tri-faith idea as well. For generations, Catholics had been taught that tolerating other faiths meant tolerating error and therefore were to be discouraged. Some Catholics even opposed offering use of their nonsanctified buildings to non-Catholics in need. The Very Reverend Francis J. Connell wrote in the *American Ecclesiastical Review*, a monthly magazine for clergy, that a Catholic fraternal organization had acted wrongly when it offered use of its building to a Protestant congregation whose church burned down. "According to the ideas of 'intercredal fellowship and brotherhood' current in the United States, and accepted by many Catholics, the Catholic organization performed a commendable deed," Connell wrote. "[But] some scandal was surely present in the fostering of the erroneous belief that all religions are good and should be aided. . . . However much we may esteem our non-Catholic brethren personally, and admire their sincerity and fervor in the practice of their religion, we must remember that their religion is false and that its practice is opposed to the commandment of Jesus Christ that all men profess the one religion which He established."[106]

Connell was not alone among Catholics in this kind of thinking. Even John Courtney Murray, Catholicism's primary advocate for religious pluralism, said the amity implied by Judeo-Christianity was too easily granted. To him, "creeds at war intelligibly" was as good as interfaith relations should get.[107]

This sentiment carried weight because American Catholics saw little need to accommodate. Catholic creed and practice had been stable for a century, and the Church in America was growing. The number of Roman Catholics in the United States had increased nearly 48 percent between 1949 and 1959, totaling nearly forty million people. In 1959, the church reported more than a hundred thousand adult converts.[108] Catholic parishes appeared solid. Many Catholic children went to parochial schools throughout their youth, then to a Catholic university or into a job where they worked alongside other Catholics.

There were sizeable but largely unnoticed cracks in the apparent solidity of postwar Catholicism, cracks first identified in Father John Thomas's 1956 book *The American Catholic Family*. Thomas argued that, despite all the appearances of Catholic strength, old ethnic units were breaking down and outmarriage was on the rise. Thomas charted a decline in the need for pastoral counseling as American Catholics adopted a less religious interpretation of the good life, leading them to look to secular cures for modern psychological woes. Meanwhile, widespread access to contraception was beginning to erode the link between sexual pleasure and personal responsibility. "We cannot simply assume that physical union restricted to mutual gratification produces the same stabilizing and unifying effects as normal intercourse," Thomas wrote. In addition, Catholics were beginning to view marriage as other Americans did, as primarily a private affair. This was leading to increasing numbers of divorces. The American system of constant achievement, toward which Catholics were moving, also robbed Catholics of a secure understanding of what the good life should be, leading to alienation, disaffection, and troubled family lives. Thomas put the burden on priests to ease the Catholic transition into mainstream American life without giving up religious principles. If priests could explain the importance of going to Mass every Sunday and of eating fish on Friday, they could explain why "objectionable practices in the dominant culture" were objectionable from the Catholic point of view.[109] Thomas's critiques would later be borne out, but during the 1950s this was the minority perspective. At the time, parish life seemed vibrant, churches appeared solid, and coffers were full.[110]

For Jews, the Cold War presented greater challenges. Since the turn of the twentieth century, many American Jews had embraced liberal politics. Some had been sympathetic to Soviet Communism, and Jews became easy targets in Communist witch hunts. Quite simply, their religion made their patriotism suspect. In the film *Three Brave Men* (1956), adapted from a series of Pulitzer Prize–winning articles by Anthony Lewis, the navy suspends a Jewish civil servant named Bernie Goldsmith (the character was based on the real-life Abraham Chasanow) who worked in intelligence during and after World War II. Goldsmith's only offense is past connections to a few liberal organizations (membership in the National Lawyers Guild and a subscription twenty years earlier to a publication put out by the journalist George Seldes, who was blacklisted in the 1950s), while a few shadowy unnamed characters say they somehow know he is a Communist. As seeming proof, they point to Goldsmith's attempts to insert a clause into the community's housing regulations prohibiting discrimination against "race, color, or creed." Under this cloud of suspicion, the neighborhood shuns Goldsmith until a kind Protestant minister, who notices that Goldsmith's rabbi is ill and therefore unavailable, fights back. At the request of the minister, a Catholic neighbor comes to Goldsmith's aid, assuring the minister that he is not afraid to associate with Goldsmith because no one would ever believe a Catholic could be sympathetic to Communism. In the end, when the navy puts Goldsmith on trial for disloyalty, all the principal witnesses either recant or devolve into over-the-top antisemitic tirades about Jewish bankers controlling entire industries or about Goldsmith being part of a Jewish-Communist conspiracy. The navy reinstates Goldsmith, and the film ends triumphantly. But the point was clear: being a Jew and having liberal politics opened one up to accusations of Communism. In the real trial of Abraham Chasanow, the government interrogator, Roy Cohn (also a Jew), alleged that Chasanow had connections to other Communists, all of whom were Jewish.[111]

Jews knew they were prone to the accusation. They shuddered when Julius and Ethel Rosenberg, a Jewish couple, were convicted of and later executed for spying for the Soviet Union. In the shadow of the trial, Jews openly discussed methods of countering the image. The Jewish press aggressively asserted that the Rosenbergs were simultaneously anti-American and anti-Jewish, while Jewish civic organizations worked to minimize Jewish support for the couple during the trial. "As the leader of a great group of veterans of the Jewish faith," wrote Jesse Moss, national commander of the Jewish War Veterans, "I especially resent the efforts to make an issue of the religious identification of the defendants. We despise equally those who would callously use the Rosenbergs to injure the Jews and those who would callously use the Jews to help the Rosenbergs. No American can tolerate either."[112] Meanwhile, the major Jewish civic organizations took part in their own anti-Communist purge.[113] "Judaism and communism are utterly incompatible," said a member of the American Jewish Committee before the House Committee on Un-American Activities.[114]

One way American Jews assured others they were good Americans was to stress their faith. Judaism was, after all, a key part of Judeo-Christianity. "The mystery of the messianic idea has created a religious character which is common to both Jew and Christian," stressed the famous Yiddish novelist Sholem Asch in his 1945 book *One Destiny: An Epistle to the Christians*. "It created similar religious values in both faiths." On religious grounds, Asch argued, Jews and Christians were "equal partners . . . in spite of the fact that we belong to separate faiths."[115] Throughout the mid-1950s, *Commentary* ran a series of articles on "patterns American Jews are evolving in their community living and religious expression," finding a "return, in many aspects, to the practices of traditional Judaism." Morris Freedman's article on a Conservative suburban congregation in New York, for instance, concluded that the new congregation possessed "grandeur in the externals, undemanding informality and trial and error in substance." The display of one's Judaism was more important than following the letter of the law, perhaps, but the display was unabashed.[116]

Meanwhile, many Jews took interest in studying the Old Testament, reading and purchasing books such as Mortimer J. Cohen's *Pathways Through the Bible* (1946). By 1956, the Bible or books about the Bible constituted half of all books the Jewish Publication Society distributed and sold. This sparked a Jewish theological renaissance, with sales of books by Martin Buber and Franz Rosenzweig increasing throughout the decade.[117] Rabbi Joshua L. Liebman, meanwhile, dissociated Jews from secular politics in his 1946 bestseller, *Peace of Mind*. To Liebman, atheism meant "the inability of a man to utter an all-embracing 'yea' to existence. It is the denial of meaning in life. It is the distrust of the universe." Pushing the thesis to the extreme, Liebman asserted that believing secular philosophies was actually a mental illness, with atheists suffering from "lovelessness in early childhood, endocrine disturbances in adolescence, or a covertly hysterical fear of emotion in adulthood."[118] Promoting one's Jewish faith may have carried risks of being associated with radicals, but it also suggested that one was a God-fearing person who believed in the individual dignity of humankind and the brotherhood of man under the Fatherhood of God.

The Holocaust girded American Jews' commitment to their faith as well. During the war, Jewish soldiers who witnessed the opening of the concentration camps often committed themselves to defending their co-religionists and fighting any subsequent challenges to their faith.[119] After the war, American Jews fought to ensure that the country did not forget the events of the Holocaust and the challenges it presented to American Jewry. They built myriad memorials on American soil, in Yiddish, English, and Hebrew. They struggled to provide financial aid to the survivors. They sought to have Germany punished for its crimes. They lobbied for the U.N. Genocide Convention and on behalf of Israel. They campaigned to have the history of the atrocity taught to American schoolchildren.[120] If the exigencies of McCarthy's Cold War put American Jews in an uncomfortable position, promoting their faith suggested their shared commitment to individual dignity and common humanity, to the ideals of Tri-Faith America.

Even Protestants had a difficult time negotiating Cold War politics. The Alger Hiss case, for instance, cast suspicion on the Protestant elite, and what were in the 1930s realistic left-leaning political options now made one's patriotism suspect. And even clerics were not safe. As J. B. Matthews was accusing Protestant ministers of being Communist sympathizers in the pages of the *American Mercury*, Methodist bishop G. Bromley Oxnam, the face of American liberal Protestantism, had to defend his reputation before the House Committee on Un-American Activities. Representative Donald L. Jackson, a Republican from California, referred to Oxnam as being to Communism "what Man o' War was to thoroughbred racing," adding: "Having served God on Sunday and the Communist front for the balance of the week over such a long period [of] time, it is no wonder that the bishop sees an investigating committee in every vestry." Oxnam defended his reputation and gathered several prominent clergymen—Protestants, Catholics, and Jews—to shield his honor, and he was later acquitted of all charges. But the fact that a respected leader of mainline Protestantism had to defend his patriotism was suggestive of the difficult times.[121]

At the same time, many Protestants resisted the implication that all Protestants were the same in the tri-faith conception. Centuries of divisions, based on theology, liturgy, geography, race, ethnicity, and practice, seemed to have been muted in order to fit into the new American standard operating procedure. In 1957, for instance, several Protestant servicemen complained that the armed services were trying to mold all Protestant denominations into one "all-embracing religion for American soldiers" by designing a standardized worship for all Protestants. Mormons, Buddhists, and atheists were also lumped into this Protestant category, provoking many on both sides to complain. But they didn't complain too loudly. Any church that openly resisted found its quota of chaplains cut. "It is considered that the general Protestant religious education program provides for all Protestant groups," read a memo from Scott Air Force Base. "Separate denominations' religious education programs will not be conducted."[122] Even Protestants could not break the hold of the tripartite vision in Tri-Faith America.

A more substantive Protestant concern during the postwar years was the fear that Catholics were preparing, in the words of a 1949 *Christian Century* article, to "win America." The Catholic Church's vigorous growth and its authoritative position on the Cold War made many Protestants fearful of Catholic ambitions. And Catholics did not allay these fears, widely promoting its "Make America Catholic" movement and reporting a hundred thousand American converts annually. While Protestant churches were often full during the 1950s, they seemed to lack the vigor of their Catholic counterparts. "Protestantism in short has lost the initiative," wrote Will Herberg in 1952, "it has been thrown on the defensive, and what is worse, it has developed a defensive minority-group psychology in which it sees itself threatened on all sides."[123]

This led many postwar Protestants and Catholics to view one another as enemies. They differed on school funding issues, whether an American diplomat should be sent to the Vatican, how birth control should be distributed, how public culture should be censored, and numerous other social questions. Because of the underlying fears of a shifting hegemony, each saw the devil in the other. Catholics, with their obedience to their hierarchy, were prone to Fascism, said Protestants such as Paul Blanshard, whose 1949 book *American Freedom and Catholic Power* set the terms for public debate about American Catholicism. A group Blanshard helped found, Protestants and Other Americans United for the Separation of Church and State, devoted itself to ousting Catholic influence in American life. Protestants, meanwhile, were on the slippery slope to secularism, said Catholics.

By the late 1950s, tensions had cooled a bit, but they were still evident. At the annual convention of the Catholic Press Association in 1958, the Reverend Gustave Weigel told the audience that Catholics and Protestants were becoming less afraid of one another. In part, he said, Protestants were looking to Catholics for ways to counteract "the weakening hold of the Protestant churches on their members." Memberships might be up, but Protestant authority was down. "When the minister looked at his congregation of 60 middle-aged and old folk at his Sunday morning service in a church big enough for 300," Weigel generalized, "he could not help thinking of the Catholic church across the street where the building was filled five times every Sunday morning." For their part, Catholics had become increasingly secure in the United States and were "perfectly ready to associate with the Protestant with affection and trust."[124] There was more than a little snootiness in the essay, but Weigel was serious in his efforts to mitigate tensions. Weigel and Robert McAfee Brown co-authored *An American Dialogue* in 1961, a book subtitled *A Protestant Looks at Catholicism and a Catholic Looks at Protestantism*. The volume was "a convincing sign that we are really beginning to emerge out of the intellectual parochialism and self-isolation that has hitherto been so characteristic of American religious pluralism," wrote Will Herberg in the volume's foreword.[125] But by 1961 Protestant-Catholic tensions had already shaped much of the social discourse of Tri-Faith America.

Despite the critiques, complaints, and complications, the three faiths had become some of the most recognized communities in postwar American life. Catholics and Jews now resided comfortably alongside Protestants in America's spiritual and social triangle. As a pluralistic formulation, the tri-faith conception solved several problems. It allowed the United States to differentiate itself from the Soviet Union. It permitted the United States to claim a victory for pluralism without having to address the concerns of racial minorities. And it morally grounded postwar American liberalism.

But it provoked questions as well. The debates among the three groups about pluralism, about the proper course for America, and about the importance of group identities in American life would define postwar America. The next section of this book examines how divisions between Protestants, Catholics, and Jews shaped much of the public discourse in the postwar years and explores the intellectual heritage and historical precedent Tri-Faith America bequeathed to later generations.

PART TWO

Living in Tri-Faith America

4

Communalism in a Time of Consensus: Postwar Suburbia

DURING THE SECOND week of October 1958, the sociologist Herbert Gans and his wife moved to the new suburb of Levittown, New Jersey, joining twenty-five families who were the first to populate what had been farmland a year before. Gans's sole intention with the move was to study how midcentury suburbanites created communities. He had studied suburbs before, publishing a few articles on the development of the Jewish community in Park Forest, Illinois, but as a leading expert in the development and transformation of communities, Gans was frustrated that he had arrived several months after the Park Forest community was formed. He promised himself that if he ever had the chance to move into a brand-new suburb, he would.[1]

He got his chance in 1958. "I was there purely as a researcher," he later said. "I was trying to understand how a bunch of strangers made a community."[2] As a sociologist, Gans prided himself on debunking false images, and during the 1950s he had become increasingly disturbed by the image of the suburbs portrayed in fiction and journalism. The "suburban myth," as it came to be called, was that the suburbs were bland white melting pots with uniform houses, shallow conversations, and drab gray-suited men. Mom was in therapy, taking barbiturates to get through the dreary day of making peanut butter and jelly sandwiches and chauffeuring kids to and from their various activities. Dad was working long hours in the city, drinking several martinis at lunch, and sleeping with his younger secretary. Suburbanites were bored and lonely, alienated from the "real world" of the cities. Throughout the 1950s, the myth gained a life of its own: adultery, divorce, juvenile delinquency, mental illness, and absent fathers were all vital components. Mass-produced houses created mass-produced people with mass-produced problems.[3]

Gans believed the myth had sprung up as urban intellectuals and journalists began to feel cultural and political power slipping from cities to suburbs. It was aided by a touch of class snobbery too, because people who lived in places such as Levittown were lower in status and different in lifestyle than most journalists and cultural critics. "In the city," Gans said, these people "had been invisible." But not any longer.[4]

By the time Gans moved to Levittown, New Jersey, there were two other Levittowns already in existence, one on Long Island, begun in 1947, and one in Bucks County, Pennsylvania, established in 1951. Because of William Levitt's talent for self-promotion and his basic understanding of the principles of mass production, these Levittowns had come to epitomize suburbia and therefore gained notoriety for epitomizing the "suburban myth." "Hair-raising stories about the homogeneity of people and conformity of life in the first two Levittowns made it clear that if any of the evils described by the critics of suburbia actually existed, they would be found in a Levittown."[5] It was, Gans said, "a logical target" for debunking.[6]

Gans and his wife bought a plot of land two years before the community opened. They chose a plot in the middle of a block, so as not to miss any of the action. After moving in, Gans began taking notes and sending out surveys. He never hid his identity as a researcher, but he also refrained from taking notes in front of other Levittowners, and he had his surveys and written inquiries printed on stationery from the University of Pennsylvania, his employer. Three thousand more families arrived in the next eighteen months, and by 1964 there were about twenty-five thousand inhabitants. During the first few years, Gans was working sixteen-hour days attending meetings, going to youth sporting events, and generally observing Levittowners.[7]

The book that emerged from the research, *The Levittowners: Ways of Life and Politics in a New Suburban Community*, is widely regarded as the best sociological study of suburban life from the postwar period. More than any other study, it documented the conflicts that ensued when it came to creating a new American neighborhood. Levittowners had come from different classes, different religious backgrounds, and different political traditions. Most were happy in Levittown, and most struggled to resolve through consensus any disputes that emerged. But conflict was inevitable and, Gans wrote, a major shortcoming of Levittown was "the inability to deal with pluralism." He added, "People have not recognized the diversity of American society, and they are not able to accept other lifestyles."[8]

Gans zeroed in on two aspects of American diversity he saw as prominent. He was first fascinated by the class distinctions in Levittown. The inhabitants were overwhelmingly lower-middle-class, and Gans saw a struggle between residents who had come from working-class families and felt socially satisfied and those who had come from the upper middle class and had ambitions to one day move to higher-status suburbs. As he later recalled, "They were normal disagreements—the lower-income people wanted the cheapest schools because they couldn't afford higher taxes; the young professionals who were there until they made enough money to move to an upper-middle-class community wanted foreign languages and other 'fringes' in the school since they could afford the higher taxes. But," he said, "that's true everywhere and at all times."[9]

Another important division Gans noticed demonstrated the efficacy of the tri-faith conception in postwar suburbs. Gans found that Levittowners, across the spectrum of class, were "giving up ethnic and regional allegiances and are gradually moving toward the triple melting pot in religion. They are Protestants, Catholics, and Jews," he wrote, "who believe in an increasingly similar God, share an increasingly similar Judeo-Christian ethic, and worship in an increasingly similar way with similarly decreasing frequency."[10]

Religious divisions appeared almost as soon as the suburb was established. Some of Levittown's first organizations were defined by religion, a circumstance aided by the fact that William Levitt gave free land to any church or synagogue that applied for it, except for fundamentalist Protestant churches, which Levitt deemed outliers. Most of the state and national denominational offices planned the construction of houses of worship before the first residents arrived, often choosing a "starter" minister who, they hoped, would appeal to the town's residents. These ministers went door-to-door enrolling members. The Protestant denominations that had the most success paid little attention to the previous denomination of possible recruits, but tried to win them over with social services. They were neighborhood churches fulfilling not only spiritual needs but social ones as well.

Catholic Levittowners immediately requested their own parish and got the help of the overseeing Trenton diocese in building a parochial school even before the church was completed. Funds for these projects came from the diocese as well as the area's Catholics, who quickly located one another through the diligence of an insurance agent "who went from door to door and registered Catholic families even while he was trying to sell insurance." Meanwhile, disagreements between Conservative and Reform Jews led to the immediate creation of two separate Jewish congregations within the first year of the suburb's existence.[11]

But it wasn't the religious institutions that exacerbated tripartite social divisions so much as the residents, who felt committed to defend their social and religious identities as they moved into the newly developed suburb. During his two years in Levittown, Gans met many Catholics and Jews who felt alienated in Levittown, which didn't look like the ethnic neighborhoods from which they had moved. This led them to seek solace among their co-religionists. Within five weeks of first arriving in the new suburb, the twenty-six Jewish families had met to discuss the formation of a synagogue. Not a single Jewish family declined to send a representative to the initial meeting. A few days later, a mahjong club for Jewish women was formed. Cooperative babysitting exchanges were popular among Levittown's Jews, as were Jewish women's groups, including ORT. Jewish men, meanwhile, almost immediately formed a B'nai B'rith Lodge, a civil defense group, and a Jewish service fraternity. "The Jewish community organized almost immediately," wrote Gans, "because Jewish women found themselves ill at ease with their neighbors." Gans (a Jew himself) suggested that the 14 percent of Levittowners who were Jews "wanted to be Jews (and to be with Jews), and they wanted their children to learn Jewish culture patterns which parents themselves were neither willing nor able to teach them at home."[12]

Catholics, too, "differed from the evolving block culture," and they also began to meet, "partly in common defense against the middle-class [Protestant] ethos." Most of Levittown's Catholics had come from urban parishes with a strong culture of informal gatherings, female kibitzing, and separate spheres between men and women, and stand-up cocktail parties were not what they were accustomed to. Most helpful to the creation of Catholic community, however, was the fact that four Catholic families had happened to buy homes close to one another, creating a central location for lengthy kaffeeklatsches and Catholic self-awareness.

As this kind of religious social differentiation occurred, a Catholic political faction began to appear. Catholics constituted 37 percent of Levittown's residents, and a few "spokesmen" emerged, subsequently leading politicians to seek their counsel "on issues affecting their coreligionists." Predictably, Levittown's Catholics were often at odds with their neighbors on issues concerning schools, calling public schools too lax both morally and educationally. They enrolled their children in the neighborhood parochial school "as soon as it opened," leading Catholics to become an even more distinct subcommunity because, for the most part, their children only associated with other Catholics. They also voiced loud complaints during town hall discussions about raising taxes for the ballooning public school system. In Levittown's 1961 school board elections, the candidates opposing school taxes were simply called "the Catholic slate." Even President Kennedy, who visited Levittown just days before the school board election, could not persuade enough voters to leave the Catholic ticket for one made up of a coalition of Protestants and Jews.[13]

Similar struggles emerged in the Levittown Youth Sports Association, as "working-class Catholics," who made up a majority of the coaches, favored an aggressive and competitive playing style. Protestants, who "only wanted to enable their children to play softball," rejected this style. Tempers flared, and the Levittown Youth Sports Association almost had to be dissolved. To alleviate tensions, a parish priest wanted to create a Catholic Youth Organization, but instead confronted a rebellion from several

Protestant youths who were protesting Catholic control over the leagues and the Catholics' close supervision at the association's dances. Protestant parents, meanwhile, rebuked the Catholic coaches, "who, wanting urgently to win, began to question the decisions of the umpires." At the end of the season, the Catholic managers forced Protestants out of the athletic association. Competitively, it paid off. In 1964, a local team nearly won a world championship. But the battle created lasting tensions.[14]

Most of the area residents were Protestants. They had been suspicious of the Levittown residents "because rumors had it that many of the newcomers were Catholics leaving Philadelphia slums to escape Negroes, and some were Italians who carried knives." Yet 47 percent of Levittowners were Protestant. Almost immediately nearly all the secular organizations became either predominately Protestant, Catholic, or Jewish. Hoping to retain some voice of cultural authority, Protestants quickly realized that in order to have a strong voice in the community, they would have to either organize themselves or align with one of the neighborhood's Catholic or Jewish groups. In a diverse society, with group communalism persistent and connections between coreligionists strong, Protestants were a people apart as well, just one group of three.[15] Tri-Faith America forced Protestants to reevaluate the notion that their organizations were normative "American" organizations.

Multiple Protestant denominations competed for adherents. Gans recalled with humor how Episcopalian and Presbyterian ministers, the leaders of denominations often associated with the upper and upper middle classes, struggled to gain adherents among the lower- and middle-class Levittowners.[16] Meanwhile, the new town was initially a boon for small Protestant denominations, particularly the Dutch Reformed, the Evangelical United Brethren, and the Church of Christ, which had long been losing ground to the more mainline denominations.

But no Protestant denomination became dominant. After the initial competition for congregants, the Protestant ministers formed a unified ministerium, held joint events, and celebrated Reformation Sunday together. The handful of fundamentalist churches remained outside the ministerium, and they were considered outliers within the community, as they were elsewhere in postwar suburbia. Despite the initial institutional competition, Gans later recalled, "denominational differences didn't matter to many of the citizens; if the church was close and the minister friendly and the other worshippers not too dissimilar in religiosity, class, etc., and they let you bring your kids or set up childcare facilities for them, that's where you went. I assume that in all or most churches the denominationally loyal provided the base, but many or most Protestants were not loyal."[17]

For the most part, throughout Levittown theological disputes were uncommon and direct religious tensions short-lived. "The ministers and rabbis," Gans wrote, "tried to minimize differences between religions and worked actively to squelch community religious conflict the moment it appeared, fighting charges of anti-Catholicism and anti-Semitism that arose once or twice in political campaigns."[18]

This may have led Levittowners to dismiss the importance of religious identities in the sorting of Levittown's social groups. One Levittowner said, "Religious differences aren't important, as long as everyone practices what he preaches."[19] But they were a constant undercurrent throughout the community. They were important enough to help determine who one's friends were, where one chose to live, what groups one affiliated with, whom one let babysit one's children, where one sent one's kids to schools, which athletic league one's kids participated in and which clubs they joined, and more.

Gans was not alone in finding religious communalism at the heart of postwar American life, or that religious divisions animated much of the discussion about diversity and pluralism during these years. These were, in fact, the central findings of numerous contemporary studies of postwar America. Most of the studies noticed variations based on location. In New York City, strong ethnic allegiances remained within Irish, Italian, Jewish, and other communities.[20] In Boston, divisions remained fierce between Protestant blue-blooded Brahmins and Irish Catholics.[21] Furthermore, Catholics, Jews, and especially Protestants often lacked centralized unity within their own group. Irish and Italian Catholics often sparred for priority within various dioceses, Orthodox, Reform, and Conservative Jews differed in how they practiced their faith, and the variety of Protestant denominations made it difficult to demonstrate a unified Protestantism, despite numerous postwar attempts at ecumenism.

Nevertheless, in almost all contemporary studies of postwar American suburbs, religious identities were undeniably strong and the battles inherent to Tri-Faith America were particularly visible. In the end, what emerged from these interfaith debates was a persistent defense of communalism in a time of perceived conformism. Contrary to the suburban myth, postwar Catholics and Jews wanted to maintain group identity and were willing to conform only so much in order to fit in.

CIVIL RIGHTS LIBERALS AND POSTWAR CHALLENGES
TO HOUSING DISCRIMINATION

One irony of postwar religious communalism was that, for the most part, it was not forced by law or social circumstance but was chosen. And in fact, throughout the 1940s and 1950s, a collection of goodwill organizations and advocates, including Protestants, Catholics, and Jews, struggled to overturn the legal infrastructure supporting housing discrimination. The American Jewish Committee Field Advisory Committee, for instance, produced reports and publications detailing housing discrimination and lobbied legislatures. The American Jewish Congress crafted model anti-discrimination legislation that was submitted to numerous states and municipalities, and spent considerable legal and financial resources challenging housing laws. The Anti-Defamation League of B'nai B'rith also devoted time and resources to ending housing discrimination.

Jews worked alongside Protestant organizations, a handful of Catholic organizations, some African American groups, and a collection of other goodwill organizations throughout the 1940s and 1950s to fight discrimination in housing. In 1955, Cardinal Spellman testified before the federal Civil Rights Commission, saying, "Discrimination for any reason and disguised in any form is in violation of God's commandments and the Constitution upon which our free nation was built," thereby uniting flag and cross in the name of equality.[22] The prominent Catholic bishop of Chicago, Bernard J. Sheil, gave the keynote address at the Conference for the Elimination of Restrictive Covenants in Chicago in May 1946, saying housing restrictions were "diametrically and blatantly opposed to every concept of Christian ethics."[23] In 1953, the National Council of Churches adopted a resolution demanding the end of discrimination in housing.[24] Individual Congregational, Presbyterian, and Methodist churches produced outlines for community programs dealing with mixed housing. And the American Council on Race Relations maintained up-to-date reports on local problems. Together, these groups fighting housing discrimination might be called the civil rights liberals of the postwar years.

The religious groups among them—and even many of the nonreligious ones—justified their anti-discrimination stance using the rhetoric of Tri-Faith America. The NCCJ's Brotherhood Week publicity materials, for example, frequently showed cartoons of Uncle Sam "building brotherhood" brick by brick, with the bricks made of "freedom of worship," "housing for all," and "fair employment."[25] Cardinal Spellman was thus not alone in uniting faith and flag in the name of anti-discrimination.

In overturning legal housing restrictions, postwar civil rights liberals were somewhat successful, especially at the state and local levels. Between 1945 and 1951 they persuaded numerous states to outlaw various forms of residential segregation, covering more than two hundred local housing authorities.[26] In 1957, New York passed a law banning discrimination in the issuance of government-insured mortgages. Similar laws were introduced in fourteen states in 1957 and enacted in four the following year: Massachusetts, New Jersey, Oregon, and Washington.

In states that chose not to enact statewide measures, municipalities such as Cleveland, Philadelphia, San Francisco, and Hartford drafted their own laws. In 1957, New York City enacted the first law in the United States that banned discrimination in the sale or rental of private housing, even when such housing received no governmental aid or assistance. Most of these laws made it illegal to prevent someone from buying or renting a home or apartment based on race, religion, or national origin.[27] In Boston, Milwaukee, Seattle, and Los Angeles, either city or local housing authorities announced policies of nondiscrimination but did not legislate them. Meanwhile, judges found in favor of integrated housing numerous times—in Evansville, Toledo, Denver, Los Angeles, and elsewhere. In New York City, Wilmington, San Francisco, and other localities, city councils sought to end discrimination in publicly financed housing.

This all underscored the fact that during the postwar years, overt discrimination in housing was under attack. The biggest accomplishment by civil rights liberals, however, was the United States Supreme Court's decision in 1948 to outlaw restrictive covenants, or legal agreements between property owners preventing them from selling or renting their property to certain kinds of people, usually Catholics, Jews, African Americans, or Asians. Through these covenants, an apartment building, a block, or an entire neighborhood would disallow access to an offending minority. Such covenants were pervasive beginning at the turn of the twentieth century, and by the 1940s several Supreme Court judges had to recuse themselves from cases involving restrictive covenants because they lived in or owned property bound by one.

In 1948, declaring that judicial enforcement of restrictive covenants was a discriminatory act upheld by states and therefore in violation of the Fourteenth Amendment, the U.S. Supreme Court struck down their legality in the case of *Shelley v. Kraemer*. The Shelleys, a black family, were finally allowed to move into the St. Louis, Missouri, home they had purchased back in 1945. Demonstrating the breadth of those affected by the issue of restrictive covenants, amicus briefs were filed on behalf of the Shelleys by the Protestant Council of New York City, the General Council of Congregational Churches, the American Unitarian Association, the American Jewish Congress, the American Jewish Committee, the Anti-Defamation League of B'nai B'rith, the American Civil Liberties Union, the American Indian Citizens League of California, the Congress of Industrial Organizations, the American Federation of Labor, the American Association for the United Nations, and the Anti-Nazi League to Champion Human Rights.[28]

That a case about restrictive covenants would end up in front of the United States Supreme Court was never preordained. The constitutionality of restrictive covenants had been upheld numerous times, and they were declared legal as recently as 1945. But in the *Shelley* case, two important friends aided the civil rights liberals.

The first was Supreme Court justice Frank Murphy. A Roman Catholic, Murphy had been mayor of Detroit, governor-general and high commissioner of the Philippines, and governor of Michigan before moving to Washington, D.C., in 1939 to serve as U.S. attorney general. In 1940, President Roosevelt named him to serve as a justice on the United States Supreme Court. He was a quintessential New Dealer. As governor, he supported sit-down strikers in the General Motors factory in Flint, Michigan. As attorney general, he initiated several major anti-trust lawsuits. He was also an important part of the tolerance crusade of the 1930s, speaking on behalf of the freedoms of speech, religion, press, and assembly during the war years. And as a Supreme Court justice, he voted against Japanese internment during World War II. His most important contribution to American law was creating, in 1939, a special division within the Department of Justice devoted solely to the protection of civil rights.

Murphy saw his Catholicism as the key to his understanding of social justice. He often told colleagues he prayed for guidance on certain cases, and he unabashedly referred to his religion while on the bench. Indeed, his religion became something of a joke on the court. Murphy was appointed after President Roosevelt's court-packing scheme failed, and former attorney general Homer Cummings quipped that Murphy's nomination would fulfill Roosevelt's goal of increasing the size of the Court because Murphy would bring along with him the Father, the Son, and the Holy Ghost.

Murphy was the key in getting the court to hear a case on restrictive covenants. He had tried to steer his fellow justices to hear a case on the matter in 1945, but he could not acquire the four votes necessary. He tried again in 1947, and finally convinced Chief Justice Fred Vinson to approve a collection of four cases that came together under the banner of *Shelley v. Kraemer*.[29]

The other friend that civil rights liberals had was the first postwar president. President Truman took civil rights seriously, although more than once he frustrated civil rights liberals with his unwillingness to take political stances that would jeopardize his electoral viability or his political needs. Nevertheless, Truman ended segregation in the armed forces, was the first president to speak at a conference of the NAACP, convened several meetings with civil rights leaders, and commissioned reports studying prejudice in American life, the most famous of which was *To Secure These Rights*. After the Supreme Court agreed to hear the *Shelley* case in 1947, Truman authorized Attorney General Tom C. Clark to write an amicus brief for the case. Restrictive covenants, the brief said, "cannot be reconciled with the spirit of mutual tolerance and respect for the dignity and rights of the individual which give vitality to our democratic way of life."[30] The language was premised in Judeo-Christian morality.

With its 1948 decision, the U.S. Supreme Court, for the first time in American history, upheld the right of minority people to move where they wanted over the rights of private property holders to sell to whom they wanted. The Supreme Court buttressed the *Shelley* decision in 1953 with *Barrows v. Jackson*, in which the Court held that someone who sold his or her house to a minority could not be financially liable for breaching the now-illegal restrictive covenants, regardless of whether the sale substantially reduced the value of other properties in the neighborhood. By denying the ability of a neighbor to be reimbursed for the decline in value that an unwanted neighbor might bring, the legal bulwarks of restrictive covenants were finally removed.[31]

Despite their significance, the decisions of course did not eradicate discrimination. In 1960, for example, a group of prospective buyers sued a homeowners association in Grosse Pointe, Michigan, for having an alleged "point system." As the case gained publicity, reporters learned that the Grosse Pointe Property Owners Association had hired detectives to examine the ethnic, racial, and religious background of all prospective homebuyers, with investigators asked to determine how "swarthy" the prospective buyers were, whether or not they could be "Americanized," and what both the outside and inside of their current house looked like. The investigators then gave the information to a committee of real estate brokers, who converted the findings into "scores" between 1 and 100 and informed the Grosse Pointe Property Owners Association. "Passing grades" (meaning a family was allowed to move into the neighborhood) depended on the family's race, religion, and ethnicity. While racial groups such as African Americans were summarily left out, Poles could pass with a score of 55. Southern Europeans, who were mostly Catholic, passed with a score of 75. Jews needed a score of 85 to gain entrance, although by the middle 1950s, the association developed a special "blue form" for Jews because so many of them were achieving the target score due to high incomes and prestigious professions. The system was dismantled after the intense public exposure brought on by the lawsuit, although it may have been simply replaced by a more discreet system of discrimination.[32]

Grosse Pointe was just one example of covert discrimination in housing. In Bronxville, New York, a new covenant trying to work around the *Shelley* and *Barrows* decisions required a prospective purchaser to get the support of the four nearest neighbors in order to be approved. Other communities formed "improvement societies" to control the listings of real estate agents.[33] As late as 1959, the ADL estimated that twenty-seven million Americans—nearly one-sixth of the nation—did not have complete freedom to choose the neighborhood in which they would live.[34] And some of these twenty-seven million were religious minorities. In 1959, Washington, D.C., had at least fourteen neighborhoods that restricted Jews.[35] In 1963, Dr. Dan W. Dodson, a Protestant minister, remarked, "Jesus Christ—himself a Jew—would not be a welcome citizen of communities such as Grosse Pointe, Michigan or Bronxville, New York."[36]

But of course no one would equate housing discrimination against religious minorities with "the far more widespread and pressing problem facing Negro Americans," as a report of the U.S. Commission on Civil Rights put it in 1959.[37] Despite the Grosse Pointes and Bronxvilles, a vast majority of the twenty-seven million Americans denied the freedom to live where they wished were racial minorities, usually African Americans. After a 1957 Levittown, Pennsylvania, riot prevented an African American family from moving into that suburb, a white resident of Levittown told the *Pittsburgh Courier* that when he purchased his home he was told that there could be no assurance that his next-door neighbor would not be a "Jew, Protestant, or Catholic" but he "could be assured that he would not be obliged to live next door to blacks."[38] Another suburbanite cited the decline in property values during the foreseeable "white flight" as his reason for rejecting racial inclusion, saying, somewhat remarkably: "We just can't afford to be democratic."[39]

For Catholics and Jews, however, access was usually granted. "The suburban Jew is usually accepted as a full member of his community," said one social planner in 1955. "He can live where he wants to, join community groups, run for local office and participate in parent-teacher associations, rotary clubs and civic improvement associations with little concern over his Jewishness."[40] Catholics had similar freedoms. The idea of living in such proximity to one another was something new, however, as was the idea of building a community together. So, as Gans and others wondered, how would postwar communities form? How would pluralism work? How would different religious groups, often long-standing adversaries, build neighborhoods in Tri-Faith America?

THE SOCIAL AND PSYCHOLOGICAL LINES OF RELIGIOUS COMMUNALISM

The answer, as Gans and many others found, was not in the creation of anonymous and bland suburbs, but rather in a process of accommodation whereby religious minorities and the Protestant majority made concessions to allow the persistence of groups and group identities. Taken as a whole, the evidence from postwar suburbia demonstrates that religion was a persistent social marker throughout the 1950s, as important as race, and in some instances more important, in animating discussion and debate. While race was often too contentious to create anything but fireworks, religious differences sparked vigorous conversations about the meaning of pluralism in American life.

In "Westwood," for example, a pseudonym for a midwestern, mostly Irish suburb, Catholic sociologist Andrew Greeley found what he called "two 'invisible' ghettos" that had formed since World War II. The neighborhood was made up of fairly wealthy people, mostly middle-aged business professionals who golfed a lot, voted conservatively, and were concerned about the well-being of their children. According to Greeley, outsiders looking at Westwood would see a contented, homogenous community. Yet although they "dressed alike, earned the same kind of income, lived in the same homes, rode the same commuter trains," people in Westwood "occupied two very different worlds."[41]

By the 1950s, Westwood was 45 percent Catholic, and these Catholics had developed a social and political world all their own. Catholic and Protestant parents did not socialize at cocktail parties, they did not play bridge together, they swam at opposite ends of the community pool, and they surely did not exchange partners at the local dances. Studying the starting cards at the local country club's golf course revealed that Catholics played golf with each other about seven times more than they would in a random sample. "The present situation," Greeley suggested, "is one in which the invisible walls of the ghetto cut across the fairways of Westwood Country Club instead of being coterminous with its fences."[42]

The construction of Westwood's first parochial school brought interfaith bitterness to the surface. Protestant and Catholic students hardly saw each other, rarely exchanging greetings and never mingling on their separate playgrounds. For the remainder of their adolescence, the kids would "continue to be unaware of each other's existence—except as part of the scenery."

Greeley's hunch was that "as the Catholic population of the [suburbs] grew in size and in structural integration [after the war], opportunities for contact with non-Catholics decreased." Catholics increasingly felt they could sustain a viable community without having to outsource for social and business partners. Religious intermarriage data for Westwood showed that from 1936 to 1955 (before large numbers of Catholics moved in) 20 percent of marriages that took place in the Catholic Church were religiously mixed, but from 1955 to 1965 that figure had dropped to just 3 percent. This showed an increased self-consciousness among Catholics, with a priority placed on remaining true to one's coreligionists. For Catholics in Westwood, the sense they were different from their Protestant neighbors spurred their sense of Catholic identity.[43]

Greeley also noticed it was infrequent for the two groups to exchange direct hostilities, favoring instead a form of peaceful coexistence. When the ecumenical movement finally did make it to Westwood, in the mid-1960s following the Second Vatican Council, long-hidden tensions appeared. In the buildup to the first interfaith meeting between Westwood's Catholic and Protestant clergy, Protestant phone lines "were burning up" to discuss strategy. Planning the event was plagued by questions about whether Catholics could offer cocktails to Protestants. On the day of the event neither side said anything productive for the first twenty minutes until someone jokingly prodded the meeting to life by saying they were not out to resolve the tensions born during the Reformation; rather, they just wanted to make things more pleasant in Westwood. In Westwood, if property lines could not differentiate between Protestant and Catholic, social and psychological lines did.[44]

These distinctions were not unique to Westwood. As one suburban Catholic woman recalled, "You'd better believe that the conversation about differences was pretty intense. . . . The nuns announced regularly that all Protestants went to hell and the Protestants had quite a bit to say about Catholic ignorance and idolatry."[45] Meanwhile, as Garry Wills recalled, midcentury Catholicism "was first experienced by us as a vast set of intermeshed childhood habits" that led Catholics to believe "we grew up different . . . It was a ghetto, undeniably. But not a bad ghetto to grow up in."[46] Intermarriage outside the faith was sneered at, although not completely unknown. August Hollingshead found Catholics married other Catholics nearly 94 percent of the time in New Haven, Connecticut, where "Catholics are becoming a mixture of Irish, Polish, and Italian as a result of intermarriage between these groups."[47] In Detroit, the intra-Catholic marriage rate was 81 percent.[48] For postwar Catholics in the Northeast and the Midwest, the reality resembled the 1955 Academy Award–winning film *Marty*, in which the two protagonists disregard their ethnic differences (one is Italian American, the other has an Irish background), focusing instead on their shared Catholicism.[49]

Leaving the Church was even more despised. As one Catholic Detroiter put it, "I'd get hung" if he changed his faith, especially if he did so in order to marry a non-Catholic.[50] "Losing one's faith," recalled Garry Wills, was a "betrayal, not only a betrayal of grace, of God's gift, but of others—parents, children, all those woven up in the same cocoon. . . . To leave such a shelter was to fall forever in uncharitable darkness."[51]

If Greeley's Westwood displayed a prominent Protestant-Catholic divide, Benjamin Ringer, Marshall Sklare, and Joseph Greenblum's "Lakeville" typified the Jewish-Gentile one. As in Westwood, there was superficial homogeneity in Lakeville, a suburb north of Chicago that had been predominantly Protestant before World War II. After the war, Jews and Gentiles lived in similar houses, went to the same grocers, and attended the same schools. Yet here too sociologists detected a pattern of social and psychological segregation. Jews associated "almost overwhelmingly" with other Jews, with 42 percent saying that their circle of close friends was completely Jewish and an additional 49 percent saying it was majority Jewish, making the total percentage of Jews who associated mostly with other Jews 91 percent. Intermarriage was actively discouraged, and those who did risked ostracism. Jews, according to Lakeville Jews, were supposed to socialize with other Jews, even if their neighbors were Protestant. Preserving the community was sacred.[52]

This persistent communalism was relatively new in Lakeville. Over the course of the 1950s, the area's Jewish population grew so much that the authors could legitimately call it a "subcommunity," one large enough to establish "a network of clique associations" that would later develop formal institutional structures. Jews, numerous enough to constitute an influential "subgroup," acted as one. The opinion of Jewish leaders became important for Lakeville politicians. Organizers at all levels had to consider "Jewish opinion." And Jewish children grew up a part of a self-conscious Jewish community, albeit one that had to converse with the larger, non-Jewish community.[53]

Jews had moved into Lakeville so rapidly that a host of negative stereotypes became attached to them. The Protestant majority thought Lakeville's Jews were "trying to wield their newly obtained wealth to acquire social and even political power in the community." They accused the Jews of "clannishness, of lacking dignity and taste, of not knowing how to use their money, and of exaggerating its importance in their own lives and in their relations with others."[54] For their part, Jews felt "attacked from all sides."[55] The authors suggested that many Protestants and Jews lived in a middle ground, where intermingling occurred mostly for business reasons or for some other social necessity, but hardly ever for leisure. Interfaith tolerance of the "passive 'live and let live' variety" was the norm. As a college-educated Jewish woman put it at the time, "Today . . . Jews and Gentiles have much in common. But somehow a social barrier exists."[56]

While traditional religious adherence was somewhat limited in Lakeville, there was a flurry of secular and civic associationalism along religious lines. More than 70 percent of Lakeville Jews belonged to non-synagogue-related Jewish organizations. Eight in ten Jewish women belonged to a Jewish organization, 40 percent to ORT and 26 percent to Hadassah. Thirty-seven percent of Lakeville's Jewish men participated in B'nai B'rith. Although more orthodox Jews were skeptical of the role played by these organizations in preserving Judaism, the authors nevertheless concluded, "The importance of Jewish organizations derives as much from the explicit or implicit contributions they make to Jewish survival as from their specific aims and accomplishments. With family and neighborhood ties far weaker than they once were, membership in Jewish organizations has become important as a way of belonging to the Jewish community."[57]

Numerous other studies affirmed both the perpetuation of religious communalism in postwar America and the rise in awareness of it. Catholics commented on how the "endless round of fund-raising events" demanded to build all the new parish buildings cemented social ties within new Catholic communities.[58] Priests were fund-raisers, not just moral and religious leaders. Rabbi Albert I. Gordon's 1959 study *Jews in Suburbia*, meanwhile, examined eighty-nine suburban communities in ten states representing both coasts and the Midwest, noting a "vexing tendency toward ghettoism" among Jews.[59] He quoted one suburban Jewish woman describing Jewish-Gentile relationships:

> Our husbands do business with them [Christians]. We see them in the town's shopping area. It's always a very pleasant, "Hello, how are you?" kind of superficial conversation. We may even meet at a meeting some afternoon or even perhaps at a PTA school affair, but it is seldom more than that. It is a kind of "9 to 5" arrangement. The ghetto gates, real or imagined, close at 5:00 p.m. "Five o'clock shadow" sets in at sundown. Jews and Christians do not meet socially even in suburbia. If we do, you bet that it is to help promote some cause or organization where they think we Jews may be helpful. But after five o'clock there is no social contact, no parties, no home visits, no golf clubs—no nothing!

"This is not," concluded Gordon, "an isolated opinion expressed by an unhappy and unaccepted Jewish person. On the contrary, it is the most representative comment made by Jews and is generally confirmed by Jews in suburban communities all through America."[60] Another more colorful assessment was that the Jews in the shtetls of Europe "were in closer contact with non-Jews than are today's Jews in suburbia."[61]

Like Catholics, Jews were seeking other Jews for comfort and community. Harry Gersh, writing in *Commentary* in 1954, quoted a suburban rabbi saying, "Most of my new congregation are new to synagogue experience. . . . In the city it takes an effort to become a member. . . . But out here it's the path of least resistance." Harry Golden, dean of southern Jewry in the 1950s, joked that newly arrived Jews in the South would immediately turn down an invitation to join the synagogue, only later to recognize the centrality of the synagogue in Jewish communal life. A month later, "Mr. Newcomer is pulling all sorts of wires to become a director of the Temple, and his wife is knee-deep in rummage sales with the ladies of the auxiliary."[62] "Religious institutions," said Nathan Glazer in 1958, "have responded to the needs of these 'returning Jews.' . . . It is the social needs of the individual Jew, and the communal needs of the entire community, that the synagogue has met."[63] A nationwide survey of 1961 from the American Jewish Committee concluded that most suburban Jews "appear to engage in most of their activities exclusively in association with other Jews."[64]

As Gans and others had recognized, this persistent communalism was largely a matter of the minority groups' choice. As an American Jewish Committee report from 1955 put it, "The identification of the Jew with other Jews . . . is a matter of his own choosing," and "the extent of that identification seems to be consider-able."[65] This chosen anti-assimilationist tendency was most clearly revealed in par-ents' attitudes about intermarriage. Only 2 percent of Lakeville's Jews said they would be "somewhat happy" or "very happy" if their child were to marry a non-Jew. "I'm not an assimilationist," said one mother tellingly, "and an intermarriage means a loss. They slip away."[66] Another mother said, "I want enough Jews [living around me] to create an atmosphere where I have my own identity."[67] They put considerable effort into not falling for the appeal of assimilation. As the authors of the Lakeville study concluded, the "desire for a religio-ethnic subcommunity which is simultaneously 'Jewish' as well as compatible with and integrated into the larger structure of Lakeville and American society is as much a fact of life in present-day Lakeville as is its Gentile past."[68]

REJECTING THE MELTING POT

Persistent religious communalism was not just a suburban phenomenon either; it had gone nationwide. In Philadelphia, Chicago, and New York, sociologist Nelson N. Foote and his team of researchers found glaring disparities between Protestants, Catholics, and Jews in where they chose to live and what kinds of houses they bought. Although the new urbanites they studied had similar characteristics—they were young college graduates buying either new apartments or older, rehabilitated homes—disparities emerged when Foote and his team looked at religious prefer-ences. In determining what kind of house one bought, Foote wrote, "of the three factors considered—education, place of birth, and religious identification—only religion proved significant." To a "startling" degree, "well-to-do Jews" preferred new apartments, while Protestants and Catholics preferred rehabilitated homes in older neighborhoods. Foote hypothesized that Jews "who have climbed the social struc-ture within one generation might prefer the obviously bright shiny status building over the often externally unimpressive rehabilitated house." Many Catholics, mean-while, opted to live in urban neighborhoods due to loyalty to a particular parish, which may have kept them in a specific part of town. Along similar lines, Catholic priests lobbied lay Catholics to purchase homes within a parish's boundaries, thus ensuring the continued solvency of the group.[69] Foote concluded that people moved where their friends were, that Jews wanted to live with other Jews, Catholics with Catholics, and Protestants with Protestants.[70]

Other major cities divided along similar lines. A large study of Detroit from 1957 by Gerhard Lenski, a sociologist from the University of North Carolina, con-firmed the importance of the "religious factor" in postwar American society, as communalism sharpened between Protestants, Catholics, and Jews. To his credit, Lenski included African Americans in his study, but he made a point to call them "Negro Protestants," thus assimilating them into the rhetoric of Tri-Faith America. But it wasn't racial distinctiveness that astounded Lenski. Detroit's Jews, Lenski found, had an incredibly high degree of social cohesion, with 96 percent of Detroit Jews saying that "all or nearly all" of their relatives were Jewish, and 77 percent reporting that all or nearly all of their close friends were Jewish."[71] Meanwhile, about 35 percent of Detroit's Catholics went to Catholic schools, a figure that increased throughout the 1950s.[72] Detroit's white Protestants saw this and began to feel suspicious of Jews' wealth and Catholics' power in city politics. Perhaps to secure their base, Lenski observed that "the denominational groups within Detroit Protestantism no longer constitute self-contained socio-religious groups to any great degree." They had intermeshed too much. In addition, Detroit Protestants regularly married and socialized between denominations, but not between faiths.[73]

Lenski differentiated between religion as a social category and a devotional one, concluding that the former was pervasive in midcentury Detroit. In fact, Lenski said, "the [devotional] scene in present-day Detroit is best described as generally placid and unexceptional." He went so far as to claim that the religion of some groups, particularly white Protestants and Jews, was "being transformed" into a "cultural faith" instead of a "transcendental faith."[74] Despite the rise in the sociological importance of religion and the decline of these theological components, Lenski nevertheless believed that differences among religious groups in Detroit were "*not* declining and are not likely to decline in the foreseeable future. They are, at the very least, as sharply drawn as ever."

Lenski also thought he could extend his analysis to the entire nation: religious divisions, he wrote, were "vigorous and influential in contemporary American society." Indeed, he found that religion was "constantly influencing the daily lives of the masses of men and women in the modern American metropolis" and that religious communalism has been "gaining in strength in recent years, and promises to gain in the foreseeable future." Although he said he was not a "religious determinist," he claimed that belonging to a particular faith predisposed individuals to accept or challenge certain aspects of the American way of life:

> Depending on the socio-religious group to which a person belongs, the probabilities are increased or decreased that he will enjoy his occupation, indulge in installment buying, save to achieve objectives far in the future, believe in the American Dream, vote Republican, favor the welfare state, take a liberal view on the issue of freedom of speech, oppose racial integration in the

schools, migrate to another community, maintain close ties with his family, develop a commitment to the principle of intellectual autonomy, have a large family, complete a given unit of education, or rise in the class system. These are only a few of the consequences which we have observed to be associated with differences in socio-religious group membership, and the position of individuals in these groups.[75]

Lenski worried that persistent religious communalism meant that "the old American ideal of a great melting pot out of which would someday emerge a new, unified nation seems to have been abandoned," and it was religious groups that had abandoned it. This was all the more troubling because the issues that propelled the change—suburbanization, internal migration of African Americans, changed modes of transportation and communication, the postwar housing boom—were "basically national in character." Thus, America was well on its way to becoming a pluralistic society, with religious groups serving as catalysts.

Lenski feared this would lead to what he called a "compartmentalized society" where "virtually all the major institutional systems are obliged to take account of socio-religious distinctions." Soon "political parties, families, sports teams, and even business establishments [would be] generally identified with one or another of the major groups." He worried that Americans would eventually have to acknowledge the persistence of group identities in American life, all because the "socio-religious" groups wouldn't willingly give up their communal identities. To the consternation of some, Tri-Faith America was threatening the great ideal of the American melting pot.[76]

It would be incorrect to say that some of the separatist walls between Protestants, Catholics, and Jews were not crumbling. Indeed, the very fact of continued contact between the three groups signified change. But the initial reaction to this change was not to assimilate willingly but rather to fall back on what was familiar, to emphasize commonalities with a few neighbors. As the Jewish writer Irving Howe said of his youth, "'Feeling Jewish' is something that occurs to people only when they already see some alternatives to being Jewish. . . . Growing up in the Bronx . . . I had no distinctive consciousness that there was any choice or alternative."[77] In the religiously mixed suburbs, on the other hand, Catholics began to feel particularly Catholic and Jews began to feel particularly Jewish. Intermarriage was a possibility, and thus its danger became a focal point for both Catholics and Jews. Socialization between groups was risky, and thus boundaries had to be guarded. In this atmosphere, postwar Catholics and Jews struggled and strove to maintain their particular communities. What they wanted most was an affirmation of the persistence of group identities, for it to be okay to be Jewish or Catholic while living in Levittown, or anywhere else in America. "Protestants are no longer the dominant majority," said Andrew Greeley, "but the majority experience is still fresh in their minds. It is possible to argue that, under such circumstances, the *absence* of a multiple melting pot situation would be surprising."[78] And multiple melting pots is what they got.

5.

A New Rationale for Separation: Public Schools

in Tri-Faith America

ON MAY 2, 1956, Salvatore Gangi, Gerald King, and Edward Doyle were elected to the school board of Levittown, New York, on Long Island. Together, the three men constituted what was called the "Catholic slate," and the campaign was unusually contentious for a school board election, mainly because the three Catholics vocally attacked the non-Catholic incumbents for raising taxes, acquiescing to the philosophy of "progressive" education, and generally increasing the godlessness in Levittown's schools. There was also some antisemitism involved, as when the Catholic slate sneeringly referred to the incumbents as "Stanley, Miltie, and Joey" (for Stanley A. Freedman, Milton Alpern, and Joseph Astman, two of whom were Jewish, the other Protestant). Despite Stanley, Miltie, and Joey's warnings about what the Catholics would do to the school district's budget and to its educational content, the Catholic slate's arguments were convincing to just enough voters: fewer than fifty votes out of nearly six thousand cast separated some of the candidates, but the Catholic slate carried the day.[1]

It did not take long for Stanley, Miltie, and Joey's fears to manifest themselves. At the beginning of the 1956–57 school year, the Catholic slate allowed one of the district's principals to send a letter reminding parents of the importance of religion in their children's education. "We would hope that your child will be given some religious training in the church of his choice so that he will understand the principles of honesty, obedience, truthfulness and respect for authority at all times," read the letter. While Jewish and Protestant members of the community may not necessarily have disagreed with the content of the message, they protested its tone and implication, and suggested that Levittown's Catholics were being deliberately provocative by injecting religion into the most delicate arena within the public sphere, the public schools. The dispute led to a near-riot at a later school board meetings, with tensions boiling over when the Catholic chairman asked "all those who are in favor of God" to please rise.[2]

Jewish frustrations increased when overtly Christian celebrations commenced during the 1956 holiday season, with "Silent Night," "The First Noel," and "What Child Is This?" all sung at one of Levittown's public celebrations. In the spring, the Catholic slate sought to remove from the classroom a ten-minute animated film called *The Story of Menstruation*, which had been shown annually to the district's fourth-, fifth-, and sixth-grade girls. The Catholics, whose church throughout the twentieth century had been famously conservative toward any notion of sexual liberalism, argued that the cartoon brought discussions of sexuality into the classroom when such discussions were best managed at home. Although Jewish organizations joined with civic unity groups such as the American Civil Liberties Union (ACLU) to protest the movie's removal, they were hesitant to plunge "the whole of Levittown into a religious war" and thus opted not to file a lawsuit.

Instead, they waited for the year to pass and then coordinated a political attack. They lobbied Protestants to vote against the Catholic slate in the springtime elections, and they mobilized Levittown's Jews. The following May, voters removed the Catholic majority from the school board. Despite the successful utilization of democratic methods to end public debate, the episode nevertheless "left a residue of bitter religious antagonism" between the two sides. Catholic and Jewish methods of creating pluralism were at odds, and no more so than when dealing with the question of how to educate their children.[3]

Similar debates occurred the same year in New Hyde Park, New York, and Newark, New Jersey, concerning the posting of a plaque of the Ten Commandments. In Ossining, New York, Catholics and Jews divided over the placement of a public crèche. There were tensions in Texas, California, and Illinois as well. Both Catholics and Jews were fighting for the recognition of America's religious pluralism, but it was quickly apparent that those visions often did not align.

The disputes frequently ended up in court, and from 1947 to 1963 the U. S. Supreme Court decided five landmark cases on matters of religion in public schools. In 1948, the Court declared in *McCollum v. Board of Education* that it was unconstitutional to release students from class so they could receive religious education. In 1952, it refined its view in *Zorach v. Clauson*, which allowed students to receive devotional religious education if the students left school grounds. Meanwhile, in the 1947 case of *Everson v. Board of Education*, the Court used language that sounded like a stirring endorsement of the separation between church and state, but then allowed public funds to be used for transporting students to Catholic parochial schools. Throughout the late 1940s and the 1950s, the Court's decisions did not offer any clear direction about the proper place of religion in schools or the proper role of the state in supporting religious education.

By the early 1960s, however, the direction of the Court became clearer. Tri-faith pluralism demanded state neutrality, especially at a time when each of "the three faiths of democracy" was thought to be integral to the national image. In 1962, after local communities had added numerous, seemingly innocuous prayers to the beginning of the school day in the 1940s and 1950s, the Court declared them all illegal in *Engel v. Vitale*. The state could not endorse any form of public prayer, especially in a public school setting. Then in 1963, in *Abington School District v. Schempp*, the Court outlawed devotional Bible reading in public schools. By the early 1960s, the U.S. Supreme Court effected what has come to be called "the second disestablishment" of religion in the United States, with devotional religion effectively wiped out of America's public schools and from many aspects of the public sphere more generally.[4]

Despite efforts of groups such as the NCCJ to produce amity, then, the years between 1947 and 1963 were notably divisive between Protestants, Catholics, and Jews. Not only did the courts have a difficult time deciding how church-and-state cases should be decided, but Protestants, Catholics, and Jews split over which positions to advocate and which to oppose. Protestants and Catholics attacked each other so vehemently over whether public funds could be used to transport students to parochial schools that prominent Jews proposed sitting the debate out. Other times Catholics and Protestants found common cause in opposing American Jews, as in 1948, when Jews were roundly blamed for the U.S. Supreme Court's decision outlawing the release of students from school for religious education. In one incident, the famous Jewish attorney Leo Pfeffer, a prominent advocate for a high wall of separation between church and state, had to be sneaked into Minneapolis in order to avoid a confrontation with Protestants and Catholics who associated him with a perceived rise of American godlessness.[5]

For the most part, however, Catholics and Jews opposed one another in debates about religion in the public sphere, as evidenced in the school board election in Levittown, New York. Each group blamed the other for inciting dangerous passions, and issued accusations that vital American ideals were being sacrificed in the name of self-promotion. As Will Herberg said, "The Catholic Church still remains in Jewish eyes the standard form of Christianity and the prime symbol of Christian persecution," adding, "Deep down, it is Catholic domination that is feared."[6] For Jews, Catholicism's insistence on being the sole avenue to truth and

its history of persecuting those who denied it was deeply threatening to a population experiencing the first joys of no longer being in exile. Many Catholics, on the
other hand, saw Jews as agents of secularism, willing to forgo any religiosity in the
name of Jewish survival and security. A biting, antisemitic editorial in the Jesuit
weekly *America* rebuked what it saw as American Jewry's attempt "to secularize
the public schools and public life from top to bottom," wondering, "What will have
been accomplished if our Jewish friends win all the legal immunities they seek,
but thereby paint themselves into a corner of social and cultural alienation? The
time has come for these fellow-citizens of ours to decide among themselves what
they conceive to be the final objective of the Jewish community in the United
States—in a word, what bargain they are willing to strike as one of the minorities
in a pluralistic society."[7]

But it was not all animosity between the two groups. One vital cause brought
them together: banishing any notion of established Protestantism. By seeking to
eliminate Protestant favoritism, by putting forward arguments against the preservation of the idea of "Protestant America," Catholics and Jews found common
cause. They also unintentionally demonstrated that there was no such thing as
neutral advocacy of religion. Their argument forced them to acknowledge that in
the name of pluralism, the state had to support either all religious expressions or
none, and if it allowed all religious expressions, foreign and even "un-American"
belief systems might have to be tolerated and endorsed, which was, many felt,
unwieldy. Thus, when Catholics and Jews successfully argued on behalf of the tri-
faith image, the result was an unwitting increase in the secularity of the American
state, an event that was not at all what many of them had hoped for.

RESURGENT PROTESTANTISM

By the early 1950s, with the fight against Fascism and the rise of McCarthyism, calls
for increased religious education and inculcation were on the rise throughout America, and the public schools became a key battleground. For the schools, this was
something of a throwback. After a century of struggle that had begun during the
initial expansion of public education in the 1830s, by the late 1920s most public
schools ceased taking direction from a culturally Protestant hegemonic presence,
favoring instead rationalism and the scientific method. In the interwar years, Bibles
were not often distributed to students and prayers were rarely said in public schools.
The teaching of evolution went on trial during the 1925 Scopes case, resulting in
Christian fundamentalists largely retreating from public activism and textbook
publishers removing both God and Darwin from their product. Some atavistic laws

still existed, and in the early 1940s, thirteen states required that school be opened with Bible reading and/or prayer and thirty-seven states allowed some form of religious observance on public school grounds. But for the most part, U.S. public schools found the light through John Dewey rather than Jesus Christ.[8]

This progressive tradition came under attack in the post–World War II years. "Today," said Will Herberg in the early 1950s, "the climate of opinion is again changing. . . . There is a mounting demand that religion be given some sort of place in the program of public education. This sentiment is nation-wide." Polls bore out Herberg's assessment. In September 1953, the *Catholic Digest* reported that a whopping 98 percent of Americans said that they wanted their children to receive religious instruction. According to a Gallup poll from the early 1960s, 79 percent of Americans approved of having religious observances in school. Reciting the Twenty-third Psalm or the Lord's Prayer became relatively commonplace. Mangers began appearing on school lawns at Christmastime. Proposals advocating the installation of plaques bearing the Ten Commandments on public school campuses rose throughout the decade. For many, reasserting the United States' "Christian foundation" was the best antidote to Communism. As Joseph McCarthy famously said: "Today we are engaged in a final, all-out battle between communistic atheism and Christianity. The modern champions of communism have selected this as the time, and ladies and gentlemen, the chips are down—they are truly down."[9]

To gauge how much religion was actually being taught in U.S. public schools during the postwar period, in 1949 the National Education Association (NEA) sent a questionnaire to more than five thousand superintendents of schools in all regions of the country. The more than twenty-six hundred responses revealed that nearly half the school systems in America's large cities (more than a hundred thousand residents) had a formal program of religious education, usually taught by a religious leader from one or more faith communities. Smaller cities had fewer programs, although one can surmise from circumstantial evidence that these schools provided a more implicit form of religious education. Of the more than seven hundred school systems with formal programs in religious instruction, 15 percent held classes on school grounds during regular school hours, in violation of federal law, while around 5 percent allowed public school buildings to be used after school. Meanwhile, nearly five hundred school districts had created some sort of release-time arrangement, whereby students were free to leave school during school hours to obtain religious training. Four percent of school systems occasionally released pupils for an entire day to obtain religious training outside school. The final 10 percent of districts that admitted to having a formal plan of religious education could not be classified under any of these categories, but they were clear that there was a program in place. In addition, the numbers presented by the NEA survey are likely low because the survey occurred within a year of the Supreme Court's momentous *McCollum* decision. More than three hundred superintendents reported that they had dropped formal religious programs from their schools in the twelve months between *McCollum* and the survey.[10]

Many Americans, meanwhile, felt that this large amount of religious instruction and inculcation needed to be increased in order to provide a staunch opposition to Communism as well as to provide a moral grounding for their children. But, as Supreme Court justice William O. Douglas asked in the *Zorach* decision of 1952, if "we are a religious people whose institutions presuppose a Supreme Being," how could that idea be institutionalized in Tri-Faith America? How could programs be put in place without sanctioning any particular faith? A letter from the general assembly of the National Council of Churches put it this way: "In some constitutional way, provision should be made for the inculcation of the principles of religion, whether within or outside the precincts of the school, but always within the regular schedule of a pupil's working day." How to do this legally was the paramount question.[11]

Recalling a time when American public life was de facto Protestant and when "nonsectarian" meant mildly Protestant, Protestants most often sought a bland form of religion, such as reciting of the Lord's Prayer, which, they hoped, was ecumenical enough not to stir debate. Many times this hope was misplaced, as a Catholic, Jew, or secularist opposed it. In early 1947, for example, New York City councilman Hugh Quinn introduced a resolution to the New York City Council permitting the reading of the Lord's Prayer at general assemblies in the New York City public schools. The proposal provoked strong debate, and more than a hundred attendees showed up at the public hearing. Those who were for allowing the Lord's Prayer into public schools suggested that the action would "pave the way to create a better religious atmosphere in public schools and build up the morale of the city's youth." Those against it said the resolution would inject a dose of sectarianism into the school system, the Lord's Prayer being, in their opinion, a Christian prayer. Many clergymen opposed the resolution, as did the ACLU, the CIO, and several Jewish groups, including the powerful New York Board of Rabbis. The city council deferred the motion, futilely hoping it would go away.[12]

It didn't. In November 1951, the New York State Board of Regents, which included members from the three major faiths, recommended that each school day open with a nonsectarian twenty-two-word prayer ("Almighty God, we acknowledge our dependence upon Thee and we beg Thy blessings upon us, our parents, our teachers and our country"). Leery of the sectarian issues that would undoubtedly arise, perhaps no more than three hundred of the three thousand school districts in the state adopted the Regents' suggestion. Recognizing the resistance, the New York City school board attempted to craft a compromise in January 1953 whereby New York City schools would sing the fourth stanza of "America," the patriotic hymn, in lieu of any prayer more commonly associated with a particular creed. The compromise placated Protestants, and the Catholic weekly *America* echoed general Catholic approval. Jews, however, were less persuaded, and the New York Board of Rabbis once again objected, arguing that the fourth stanza, taken alone, constituted a Protestant prayer. (The fourth stanza reads: "Our fathers' God to thee / Author of Liberty / To Thee we sing. / Long may our land be bright / With Freedom's holy light / Protect us by thy might / Great God, our King.") Later interfaith meetings led by New York's superintendent of schools, to which Protestants, Catholics, and Jews were always invited, failed to find a solution. The controversy would eventually become the landmark case of *Engel v. Vitale* (1962).[13]

The challenges of Catholics and Jews forced Protestants to search, often in vain, for a plausible middle ground. In 1947 in the magazine *Christendom*, Protestant minister Willard Johnson wrote: "The whole problem of relationship of religion to government remains to be settled. . . . This is certainly one part of the 'American Way' which is undergoing change. The historic attitudes of all religious groups, developed at a time when church and state were either united or struggling for dominance, cannot solve the problem. New concepts must be developed for modern conditions, and they should be set forth by all creeds together."[14]

Finding new concepts was exactly the problem. Henry P. Van Dusen, president of Union Theological Seminary and a major figure in midcentury American Protestantism, argued in his 1951 book *God in Education* that American schools needed to search for a "common core" program of religious education. The three major faiths of the Western world, Van Dusen argued, were in accord on "their conceptions of God and of His relation to Truth." He proposed that American religious leaders sit down together to develop "agreed syllabi" for the teaching of religion, a fact, he said, that "should challenge American educators to fresh efforts to restore religion to its appropriate place."[15] This paralleled the interfaith work done by the NCCJ and others during World War II, but without the exigencies of war, the idea fell flat. A few prominent Protestants such as Luther A. Weigle of Yale supported the proposal, but most Catholics and Jews were skeptical.

Many other Protestants sought instead a return to the casual Protestantism of yesteryear. The frustrated *Time* magnate Henry R. Luce, son of Protestant missionaries, suggested to the Church Federation of Greater Chicago, "It is certainly time that Protestants, if they don't do anything else, should unite on a program to bring the knowledge of God to our boys and girls at school." But he offered no solution beyond this plea. At the same time, bills authorizing Bible reading were defeated after hotly contested debates in California in January 1953 and in Illinois in June 1953.[16] Other Protestants sought solace in the creation of Protestant day schools that would compete with Catholic parochial schools. These Protestant schools grew by 61 percent between 1937 and 1951, when there were about 190,000 pupils. Though tiny compared to the Catholic educational structure, they were part of a growing movement.[17]

Despite the attempt to find a "common core" or to develop parochial Protestant schools, many Protestants still felt an emotional, even proprietary interest in the public school system, hoping that "nonsectarian" could still be equated with a generalized Protestantism. Often throughout the postwar period, short religious devotionals were quietly added to the daily routine of public school children. Christmas and Easter were celebrated lavishly. The holiday carols chosen for presentation were usually religious. Bibles began to appear more regularly on public school grounds.

Despite occasional Catholic approval, the Protestant cast of this type of education was not missed by many. "Let me recall to you what the public schools I attended were like," said Howard Squadron, a Jew who grew up in the Bronx in the 1950s.

> Prayers and bible passages were recited daily. Prayer is not a generic form of expression and bible passages (and translations) were not, are not, and should not be, theologically neutral. The public school religion I encountered had in every case specific theological roots and forms. The prayers said in the public school I attended were distinctly Protestant in content.

Squadron also commented on what he saw as the cultural content of this religiosity. As he saw it:

> The use of Protestant religion was a part of a deliberate effort by the public schools to suggest to the American children of Jewish immigrants that these Protestant rituals represented true Americanism, that the rituals and rhythms of our parents' houses were alien and foreign, worse, to children who desperately wished to be accepted, even "un-American." This use of religion as a means of acculturating aliens caused many painful gaps between parent and child.

A leading historian of religion and education in the United States concluded that Squadron "captured more clearly than most the ways in which many schools operated in the United States."[18]

As members of minority faiths, Catholics and Jews were torn by the increasing religiosity demanded in Cold War America and the resurgent Protestantism that seemed to be a part of it. In general, Catholics felt religion was a vital component of a child's development, and the leading Catholic organizations wanted sanctioned religion in public schools. However, they did not want that religion to have a Protestant cast. In 1952, the Catholic bishops of America adopted a resolution warning that the nation faced a grave danger from the "irreligious decay" of its most important institutions, pointedly criticizing public schools for ignoring the importance of religion in the lives of children. They also worried about the reemphasis of Protestantism in the public schools—the very issue that prompted the formation of Catholic parochial schools in the nineteenth century. These fears led to a strong reaffirmation of Catholic parochial schools. A front-page article in the *New York Times* in 1952 claimed that Catholic schools had grown by 35 percent between 1942 and 1952, making the total enrollment four million and leading the National Catholic Welfare Conference to organize a quarter-billion-dollar expansion of the Catholic school system. Furthermore, "the increase is expected to continue," wrote the *Times*, and it was right: the Catholic parochial school system continued to grow throughout the remainder of the decade. Reflecting their rising socioeconomic status, postwar Catholics also began developing a network of private academies in which elite Catholics could enroll their children. Of course, the growth of parochial education led to increased claims of Catholic separatism.[19]

Jews also were divided about how to respond to the demands for increased religiosity in education. For the most part, they were suspicious about any religion in the public schools, although the leading Jewish organizations were split over how far Jews should go to fight it. The American Jewish Committee and the Anti-Defamation League of B'nai B'rith—two moderate Jewish civic organizations—generally sought a reconciliation of Jewish observances with Christian ones, such as parallel holidays, and were less aggressive about the addition of ecumenical prayers in the school day. In 1946, they helped Cleveland pioneer joint Hanukkah-Christmas celebrations. A similar situation was crafted at Dundee Elementary School in Omaha, Nebraska, a public school active in the intergroup relations movement. Through developments such as these, the nationalistic Jewish holiday of Hanukkah was transformed into an ecumenical celebration of religious pluralism. Hanukkah's main appeal was that it coincided with Christmas, and because it focused on children receiving gifts, it accorded with the material nature of Christmas celebrations. Hanukkah was also family-oriented, did not place barriers between Christians and Jews, and did not require special accommodations that marked Jews as culturally different from their Christian peers. Hanukkah's transformation in these years represented part of what historian Edward Shapiro has called "the Protestantization of American Judaism."[20]

But accommodation did not dominate the Jewish perspective. The American Jewish Congress (AJC), the most vocal Jewish organization at the time, was more adamantly against any incursion of religion into the public sphere. "Separation of Church and State is indispensable if we are to immunize our schools from sectarian divisiveness and strife," the AJC wrote in a forcefully worded pamphlet. "Experience has shown that whenever religion intrudes into the public school, sooner or later Jewish children will be hurt."[21]

When the Catholic and Jewish ideal of pluralism clashed, vigorous, sometimes vitriolic debate ensued. Regarding the question of how best to celebrate religious holidays in public schools, one (Catholic) diocesan newspaper stated, "We believe that the time has come for Christians in the public school system and everywhere else to declare in outright fashion that the United States by culture, tradition, and full right is a Christian country and must not be allowed to change. For that reason, Christmas in schools must be kept a distinctly Christian feast with a Christian purpose." The paper added: "Non-Christian religious groups, prompted by the presence of many of their children in public schools, are seeking to dilute or to eliminate Christ from Christmas. They are aided and abetted by the secularizing tendency in American life. If both pressures are not resisted, Christmas will lose its whole and wholly Christian meaning."[22] In the game of postwar power politics, some Catholics were evidently willing to sacrifice Jews at the altar of "Christian nationhood," even if that meant aligning themselves with the Protestants who had oppressed them for the past 150 years.

These positions were not merely intellectual principles but also positions of stakeholders. Most Jews said that successful pluralism depended on a religiously neutral state; because Jews were a small minority, this made sense. Catholics, meanwhile, were more comfortable with a form of pluralism that was respectful and even supportive of various groups' religious expressions, even if those expressions occasionally made them look like separatists. This likewise made sense, considering that they, like the Protestant majority, were Christians, and that roughly 25 percent of all U.S. citizens considered themselves Catholic, leading them to fear potential homogenization somewhat less. However, their pluralism was often narrower than that of the Jews, and, unlike even the more accommodationist Jews who favored multiple religious celebrations, many midcentury Catholics probably would not have supported celebrating Jewish holidays in schools. These differences led Catholics and Jews to oppose one another on numerous issues regarding public schools, including federal funding, release-time programs, and the observance of religious holidays.

COMING TOGETHER

On the issue of rejecting resurgent Protestantism, however, the two sides were united, and the legal precedents they created in this realm helped build a new secular defense of separation of church and state that would last for the remainder of the century and longer. Fighting resurgent Protestantism first came up in a largely unrecognized court case concerning whether it was acceptable for members of the Gideon Society to hand out Bibles to middle and high school students on public school grounds. The dispute began in 1951, when the Gideons of Passaic and Bergen counties approached the Board of Education of Rutherford, New Jersey, with an offer "to furnish, free of charge, a volume containing the book of Psalms, Proverbs and the New Testament to each of the children in the schools of Rutherford from the fifth grade up to the eighth grade, and High School." Besides Protestant proselytizing, which they did not deny, the letter also claimed that giving out the so-called Gideon Bible was "the answer to the problem of juvenile delinquency."[23]

On November 5, 1951, the Rutherford school board held a public hearing to consider the Gideons' proposal. The hearing started peacefully enough, but quickly a Catholic priest and a Jewish rabbi protested. Both men argued that this Bible was an overtly sectarian book forbidden under the laws of their respective religions. Then, as now, the Gideon Bible consists of all the New Testament, all the Book of Psalms (from the Old Testament), and all the Book of Proverbs (also from the Old Testament) in the style and manner of the 1611 King James, or Protestant, version. Despite the direct importation of several parts of the Old Testament, the Gideons excluded any reference to the Old Testament in their Bible, making it offensive to Jews, who denied the validity of much of the New Testament, and Catholics, who used a different version of the Bible, called the Douay Bible. In addition to the claim of devotional incompatibility, the rabbi and the priest also argued that the unsystematic content of the Gideon Bible could not be considered a legitimate part of the grand tradition of greater Christendom and therefore could not be accepted as an important part of the Western tradition, which might have made it applicable for educational purposes. The Gideons' only motive, they argued, was proselytizing the Protestant faith to New Jersey's schoolchildren.[24]

Despite the pleas, the Rutherford Board of Education voted with only one dissenter to allow the Gideons onto public school grounds. Nervously, the school board also crafted a complex distribution plan that was supposed to minimize any publicity the affair might generate. It stipulated that the Gideons would be allowed to distribute their Bibles only to students whose parents had signed request forms and that any announcement about distribution could not refer to the event's purpose.

Furthermore, distribution had to occur after school, when no other children would be around to witness the event and potentially feel excluded or discriminated against. By strictly limiting access, the board's clear intent was to remove the possibility that it was advocating one religion at the expense of any other.[25]

Despite the precautions, Catholic and Jewish civic and religious organizations mounted complaints. They were joined by a collection of civil rights organizations, including the ACLU and several of the civic unity groups that had emerged during World War II. In early 1952, just prior to the scheduled distribution of the Gideon Bibles, a Catholic parent named Ralph Lecoque and a Jewish parent named Bernard Tudor filed a joint injunction against the Rutherford Board of Education, hoping to get the school board to stop the affair until the matter could be sorted out by the courts. After the initial filing, the nearly immediate presence of the American Jewish Committee and several Catholic diocesan authorities made it somewhat obvious that Lecoque and Tudor were mere figureheads for the national religious organizations that had a stake in the case—an accusation made more than once by the defendants' attorneys, who at one point called the plaintiff a "dummy" being used by "the real moving party." To the defendants, this was a case of two aggressive religious upstarts challenging Protestant cultural authority.[26]

The fact that neither plaintiff showed up during the initial rounds of the trial buttressed the defendants' claim of absenteeism, but that claim turned out to be moot because the arguments were substantive. As reported in court records, the plaintiffs' central claim was that the Gideon Bible was "a sectarian work of peculiar religious value and significance to the Protestant faith," and the complainants claimed that its distribution violated "the teachings, tenets and principles" of their religions. Therefore, its presence, with direct sanctioning from the state in the form of the school board, constituted not only a breach in the wall of separation between church and state but also an offense to religious minorities. It was, in essence, sanctioning established religion.[27]

In early 1953, the case went to court. The Gideons signed on as co-defendants with the Rutherford Board of Education, and by that time Ralph Lecoque's son had transferred to a parochial school. Lecoque's departure affirmed the plaintiffs' argument that reinforcing Protestantism was necessarily divisive, but it was also a blow to the plaintiffs, who had sought to frame the case as two sides of America's religious triangle fighting for dignity and respect. Efforts to replace Lecoque with another Catholic parent (Mrs. Walter Natyniak) were rejected as coming too late. The case, therefore, became simply *Tudor v. Board of Education of Rutherford and the Gideons International*.[28]

In March 1953, New Jersey trial judge J. Wallis Leyden heard testimony. Suggesting the depth of companionship that Catholics and Jews felt regarding the case, the American Jewish Congress and the diocesan authority of the Roman

Catholic Church joined forces on behalf of Bernard Tudor. They retained Leo Pfeffer as prosecutor. Pfeffer had a long-standing connection to the American Jewish Congress, but he was also a polemical author and attorney with a reputation for defending a high wall of separation between church and state. Indeed, he sometimes came off as a rabid defender of an implacable wall of separation. His presence heightened the case's publicity and meant it was sure to become an important testing ground for the extent to which advocated Protestantism could be brought anywhere near America's public schools.[29]

Pfeffer's witnesses included a host of religious experts who described the exact points of conflict that Catholics and Jews had with the Gideon Bible. For Jews, the argument was simple. "[The New Testament] presupposes the concept of Jesus of Nazareth as a divinity, a concept which we do not accept," testified Rabbi Joachim Prinz. Other rabbis echoed this appraisal. Although the Catholic plaintiff had been removed from the case, the prosecutors nevertheless quoted the canon law of the Roman Catholic Church, which holds that "editions of the original text of the sacred scriptures published by non-Catholics are forbidden *ipso jure*." According to canon law, reading an alternative form of the Bible is proscribed under the pain of sin.[30]

But all this was irrelevant if Pfeffer could not paint the Board of Education's decision as an "effort to uphold Protestant Christianity through the public school system," which would therefore make it a First Amendment case. If the distribution of Bibles was done carefully enough so as not to antagonize a Catholic or a Jew, what did it matter if the minorities found the Gideon Bible offensive? Completely ignoring the numerous stipulations the board had drafted regarding distribution of the Bibles, Pfeffer said the board's decision to allow the Gideons onto campus was in "direct contradiction" to the "democratic education"—where schools were safe for differences among children—that was being lionized in the aftermath of World War II.[31] Pfeffer conveniently skipped over the fact that many Americans considered proclaiming faith in God an ideologically sound component of good Americanism, asserting instead that the board's actions had created an "unconstitutional preference . . . to the Protestant denomination," which was an obvious "infringement of the religious liberty of Catholic and Jewish public school children."[32] Giving state sanction to the Gideons was thus a dangerous throwback to the early nineteenth-century days of Protestant hegemony, said Pfeffer, and much had changed since then. To illustrate the historical point, he referred to a nineteenth-century case where more than a hundred Catholic children were expelled from Boston public schools for refusing to read the King James Bible. Citing another historical example, Pfeffer told the story of a priest whose challenge to a legislative mandate requiring Bible reading led the "infuriated Protestant community" to tar and feather the priest and run him out of town. Pfeffer paralleled the Rutherford Board of Education's decision regarding the Gideons to the "anti-Catholic nativism and 'know-nothingness' which disgraced American history in the nineteenth century."[33]

Pfeffer concluded his argument by bringing forward several child psychologists who painted a vivid picture of the millions of "minority" children who might suffer adverse psychological effects because the Gideons had come to their campus to proselytize, sanctioned, as they were, by the school (and, therefore, by the state). These "minority" children would be identified as different and would encounter pressures to conform to the majority. Speaking specifically of Jewish children, the prominent New York University psychologist Isador Chein said, "When the New Testament is given to [children] by sources which they consider to be respectable, and . . . from whom they are expected to learn, I think that there can be little question but that a great many Jewish children will be thrown into a state of conflict, perplexity, confusion, and to some extent guilty feeling." Another expert suggested that the school board decision would give the impression "that the school thought this was preferential in terms of what is the divine word, and that backing of the State would inevitably be interpreted as being behind it." What was a child to do when the two chief authorities in his or her life—parent and teacher—conflicted, all because the Rutherford school board had allowed the Gideons to distribute Bibles on public school grounds?[34]

It is worth noting Pfeffer's use of the term "minority" here, obviously referring to Catholic and Jewish schoolchildren and not any group distinguishable by race. His ultimate claim was that Catholics and Jews were doing their part to accommodate to the ideological demands of mainstream society. They were not demanding separate schools or unique divisions within the schools; they simply wanted the state to remain religiously neutral so they could participate as equal players. Shouldn't mainstream society do its part to accommodate their access to the mainstream?

The defense team thought these arguments were inflated, but it still couldn't mount much of a defense. The school district's lawyers perpetually cited the case of *Doremus v. Hawthorne*, a 1952 New Jersey case in which the state supreme court upheld the reading of the Lord's Prayer in public schools. The defense argued that *Doremus* demonstrated one court's willingness to allow the New Testament onto campus. Pfeffer quickly dispatched the claim on two grounds: first, that the New Testament consisted of much more than simply the Lord's Prayer; and second, that *Doremus* did not deal directly with religious diversity, the most important issue in the *Tudor* case. "That was a suit brought by some atheists, some individual trouble makers, and so on," Pfeffer said. In the Gideon case, sectarianism was "the basic issue," and, he implied, when good religious Americans disagreed, diversity had to be honored. Atheists might not be considered good Americans, but Catholics and Jews certainly were.[35]

The second argument put forward by the defense was that the New Testament was not sectarian but a universal book of the Western world, paramount in the creation of American democracy. Claiming that their responsibility was to the parent, not to any religious denomination, the (Protestant) school superintendent, Dr. Guy L. Hilleboe, contended that "when we have an opportunity to give those parents that kind of literature which is basic in the whole development of our democracy, from its beginnings—even before that; from the founding, from Plymouth Rock to the present time . . . I feel that there is nothing contrary, either morally or legally, in the provision of such materials." And "if any group presents to the schools material which will aid the child to better understand, not only himself, but those around him . . . our obligation is to the parent."[36]

Pfeffer countered that *Das Kapital* was also part of the Western tradition. Would Hilleboe distribute it too? Hilleboe stumbled in his answer. Pfeffer continued in this vein, asking that, since Hilleboe had lent "the facilities of the public school to The Gideon International," would he "not do the same for the Communist International?" Hilleboe meekly said no. This allowed Pfeffer to make the point that the school did in fact have discretion as to which groups would be allowed on campus, and in the case of the Gideons, it had adjudicated in their favor. Allowing just Protestants access could not, according to Pfeffer, be approved. Catholics and Jews, as minorities on the front line of the diversity debate, deserved protection. At risk, he added for a dose of lawyerly potency, were America's children.[37]

By the end of formal argument, Judge Leyden was clearly sympathetic to Pfeffer's argument. Nevertheless, on March 14, 1953, Leyden ruled that the action of the Rutherford school board might be "bad policy," but it was constitutional. "I can see no illegal or unconstitutional interference by what is proposed by the Board of Education, with the religious liberty or freedom of the plaintiff or his child, nor can I see any particular preference granted to the Protestant faith."[38] The board was right to allow the Gideons onto school property, said Leyden, because Catholics and Jews and any other religious minority had a right to a presence there as well. If America really was "a religious people whose institutions presuppose[d] a Supreme Being," keeping God off school grounds did not make much sense.

In the context of the wide-open debates about church and state in the 1940s and 1950s, one cannot help wondering if Leyden wanted his decision appealed. At that point, there was considerable flexibility in the Supreme Court's decisions when it came to the amount and manner of religious education in public schools, but allowing the Gideons onto public school grounds was something quite provocative.

And Leyden had to have known Catholics and Jews would fight what they saw as a sectarian attempt to insert Protestantism into public education. So was Leyden's decision deliberately provocative? Considering, however, that few judges like to have their decisions overturned, it is more likely Leyden's decision was one of conscience. He simply did not see establishment in the Gideons' action.

Predictably, the American Jewish Congress, local diocesan authorities, and Bernard Tudor immediately appealed Leyden's decision. As they moved forward, they structured their argument in the press as an infringement of the constitutional principle of nonestablishment. But, as everyone knew, establishment or not, the struggle in *Tudor* was really to make a strike against the de facto Protestantism in American life. The Gideons agreed to continue the injunction until the matter was finally settled. By this time, the case had become something of a testing ground for the Gideons, who were interested in having it play out in the courts so they could know their exact boundaries.[39]

Play out it did. On its own initiative, on October 2, 1953, the New Jersey Supreme Court withdrew the case from the Appellate Division of the Superior Court and placed it on its own calendar, to be argued just three days later. There was no time for the attorneys to do anything but recapitulate the original arguments, meaning that the arguments heard by Leyden were the same ones weighed by the New Jersey Supreme Court. Amici curiae from the Synagogue Council of America and the (Jewish) National Community Relations Advisory Council were rushed in, and the New Jersey Supreme Court came down with its decision in early December.[40]

The New Jersey Supreme Court was considerably more sympathetic to Pfeffer's arguments than Leyden had been. Ruling unanimously, the court claimed the Board of Education had in fact shown preference to one religion over another. It was hard-pressed to demonstrate that handing out Gideon Bibles constituted the establishment of a religion, but it nevertheless saw favoritism at work, and by inviting the Gideons onto school grounds, "the board of education has placed its stamp of approval upon" Protestant proselytes. The court quoted one of the professional witnesses in the case, Dr. William Heard Kilpatrick, who said that non-Protestant students were "not quite as free as the statement on that slip says; in other words, that he will be something of an outcast and a pariah if he does not go along with this procedure." This underscores the emerging importance of protecting the rights of minorities in the postwar period. Chief Justice Arthur T. Vanderbilt, who wrote the court's opinion, powerfully concluded: "Such favoritism cannot be tolerated and must be disapproved as a clear violation of the Bill of Rights." Vanderbilt declared that any attempt to employ "the public school system as a medium of distribution" of Gideon Bibles was ignoring the pluralism that had come to inhabit the meaning of separation of church and state in the early 1950s.[41]

Vanderbilt recognized that the key question was how best to honor pluralism. "The full force of the violation," he wrote, "is revealed when we perceive what might happen if a single school board were besieged by three separate applications for the distribution of Bibles—one from Protestants as here, another from Catholics for the distribution of the Douay Bible, and a third from Jews for the same privilege for their Bible." The question implied that public opinion would have been negative toward Jewish or Catholic proselytes. Vanderbilt's point was that schools should not become battlegrounds for ideological groups, and allowing the distribution of Bibles, even by the majority, opened the door to controversy. Favoritism, as he said, could not be tolerated.[42]

The decision was a strong one, well argued and broad in scope. In 1954, the Gideons appealed the decision to the United States Supreme Court, but the Court chose not to hear the case, which upheld the state supreme court decision but limited its scope to just New Jersey.

A SECULAR DEFENSE OF SEPARATION

The Gideon case underscored the fact that the midcentury disputes over religion in the public sphere had deep sectarian roots. Every time the state sought some sort of middle ground concerning religion, sectarian disputes bubbled to the surface. As *Life* put it in 1955, the "wall of separation" was in reality "an uneasy four-way truce among Catholics, Protestants, Jews and secularists." Will Herberg commented on this in his tellingly titled 1952 essay "The Sectarian Conflict over Church and State." The wall of separation was not entirely about keeping politics and religion apart for the sanctity of both (as the rhetoric of the debate had been) or about maintaining Protestant hegemony (as the reality had been since the early nineteenth century); rather, it was about honoring pluralism in Tri-Faith America.[43]

This represented a dramatic and largely unrecognized shift in the rhetoric and justification of separation. Despite the fact that the First Amendment often comes up in debates about church and state, the principle of separation has very little constitutional foundation. Arguments suggesting that the principle of separation was developed to prevent the intrusion of the state into church matters simply mask an uglier history. The doctrine of separation first entered public debate in 1800 as a way for Jeffersonian Republicans to criticize and intimidate Federalist Congregationalist clergymen (Jefferson's famous coining of the phrase "wall of separation between Church and State" came in 1802). In the middle of the nineteenth century, nativists and, more broadly, American Protestants adopted the principle of separation as a way to keep newly arrived Irish Catholics from obtaining the same social and political rights that Americans with a longer North American pedigree possessed. Protestants argued that a unified and powerful Catholic bloc might attempt to overturn republican government in favor of one controlled by the pope. To prevent Catholics from capturing free government, Protestants felt they had to deny Catholics equal civil and political rights, employing the language of separation. This allowed de facto Protestantism to rise to a place of privilege in the public sphere.[44]

The anti-Catholic tenor of separation discourse lasted until the 1950s, when the pluralist-centered argument for separation took precedence (although the anti-Catholic strain continued to exist at least until after John F. Kennedy's election to the presidency in 1960). Then the secular defense of separation arose, emerging primarily as an overt defense of tri-faith religious pluralism. There were early signs of this defense in the 1947 *Everson* decision, when Supreme Court justice and former Baptist Sunday school teacher Hugo Black famously said:

> The "establishment of religion" clause of the First Amendment means at least this: neither a state nor the Federal Government can set up a church. Neither can pass laws which aid one religion, aid all religions, or prefer one religion over another. Neither can force nor influence a person to go to or to remain away from church against his will or force him to profess a belief or disbelief in any religion. No person can be punished for entertaining or professing religious beliefs or disbeliefs, for church attendance or non-attendance. No tax in any amount, large or small, can be levied to support any religious activities or institutions, whatever they may be called, or whatever form they may adopt to teach or practice religion. Neither a state nor the Federal Government can, openly or secretly, participate in the affairs of any religious organizations or groups, and vice versa. In the words of Jefferson, the clause against establishment of religion by law was intended to erect "a wall of separation between church and State."

Despite this arresting declaration, in the *Everson* case Black found in favor of allowing public funds to go to parochial schools. Paralleling Vanderbilt's decision in *Tudor*, it is interesting to wonder what the school district would have done if it had been inundated with requests from several different religious schools to pay to bus their students as well. Postwar Catholics and Jews were asking serious questions about how the newly imagined tri-faith nation should act.

By the early 1950s, the consequences of a tri-faith nation were becoming increasingly evident. The principle of separation was needed to protect religious minorities. In all future cases concerning education, Leo Pfeffer would seek out

Catholic and Protestant litigants to support the claims of a Jew or an agnostic advocating on behalf of a high wall of separation. He made sure a Catholic lawyer was retained in *Engel v. Vitale*.[45] He struggled to do the same in *Schempp*.[46] His point was that the principle of separation was best understood as a guarantor of the rights of minority faiths, not just as Jewish advocacy for a secular state.

The case against the Gideons in 1953 served as a high point of Catholic and Jewish unity, one that Jewish defense organizations liked to emphasize. "One particularly reassuring aspect of the case," wrote the American Jewish Congress shortly after the *Tudor* decision, "was the cooperation of the local diocesan authorities of the Roman Catholic Church throughout the litigation." Despite the different means by which Catholics and Jews struggled to make pluralism, they came together to fight any reassertion of Protestant hegemony. The American Jewish Congress added: "We believe that this decision will stand as a landmark in the history of religious liberty in this country." It reprinted the decision in its entirety as a pamphlet.[47]

Throughout American history there had been a few other cases in which Catholics and Jews had joined together as plaintiffs, but most occurred decades before the advent of Tri-Faith America, and most of the time they lost. In 1908, for example, the Texas supreme court rejected the claim of Catholics and Jews that a public school was establishing Protestantism by compelling its students to read the King James Bible and recite the Lord's Prayer. "Christianity is so interwoven with the web and woof of the state government," said the court, "that to sustain the contention that the Constitution prohibits reading the Bible, offering prayers, or singing songs of a religious character in any public building of the government would produce a condition bordering upon moral anarchy."[48] The *Tudor* case marked the first time that the argument for minority rights won. That this all took place at the height of the Cold War, when support for religious education was most popular, suggests the power and importance of the argument—and the power of the pluralism inherent in the tri-faith idea.[49]

The unity displayed in *Tudor* faded quickly. Soon after, Catholics, tapping into another long-held Catholic tradition, began to fear secularism in the public sphere as much as they feared resurgent Protestantism. By the mid-1950s, the Catholic Church became perhaps the staunchest advocate of school prayer, Bible reading in schools, and public funds for parochial schools, and it led many of the protests against the 1962 *Engel* and 1963 *Schempp* decisions, which together formalized the "second disestablishment." Catholics also sought increased public observance of religious rituals such as the display of crèches. The 1962 *Engel* decision outlawing school prayer, said Cardinal Spellman, "strikes at the heart of the Godly tradition in which America's children have for so long been raised." About the 1963 *Schempp* decision outlawing Bible reading in public schools, Spellman said, "No one who believes in God can approve such a decision."[50]

Ironically, the Catholic turn away from state neutrality was a product of the Church's own successes. The legacy of *Tudor* was the development of a new defense for a high wall of separation, seeing it as a positive tool in helping develop the idea that state favoritism cannot be tolerated in a pluralistic nation. Some Catholics recognized this. Bishop Fulton Sheen was somewhat conflicted over what the Catholic position should be regarding public displays of religion after the early 1960s court decisions. When asked, he said he favored the introduction of a short prayer, "In God We Trust," into the school day, but, in a soft-pedaled tone unusual for him, he added, "I think that this prayer is sufficient and the answer to the problem of pluralism. 'In God We Trust' is already on the seal of the United States, it is already in our tradition and it is a perfect prayer." He concluded: "I am presenting my answer on the basis of the pluralistic views of the United States and the tradition of the United States and I do not believe that we should ask too much. . . . I am only asking for recognition."[51]

Asking for "recognition" was quite different from asking for a stern declaration of the nation's Christian foundation. And all the major church-state cases following *Tudor*, especially the ones decided in the early 1960s, would base their decision on the argument that it should protect minority faiths from the power of the majority, even when there was considerable social and political pressure to do otherwise. If one legacy of Tri-Faith America was the widespread awareness that group communalism was not going away anytime soon, another was the heightened wall of separation between church and state, and the secular defense for the wall itself.

6

Choosing Our Identities: College Fraternities, Choice,

and Group Rights

IN 1946, the Phi Mu Delta fraternity at the University of New Hampshire removed
a Jewish pledge from its list of inductees at the request of its national parent organization. Besides the cruelty involved in revoking an invitation because of someone's religion, the revocation flew in the face of Phi Mu Delta's founding principles
of "democracy, service, and brotherhood." Instead of fighting back against its
parent organization, the local chapter simply asked the Jewish pledge to move out.
A witness to the events said, "It was awful. . . . The kid's parents came to help him
move to the dormitory. I remember how terrible it was. His mother was crying.
But what was worse was his father," a Massachusetts judge. "That man didn't say a
word to anyone."[1]

A few months later, in January 1947, another major national fraternity rejected
its Middlebury College chapter's attempt to initiate a Jewish student who had
worked with the French Resistance during World War II. A pledge brother of the
rejected recruit, himself a former U.S. Navy pilot, declared that the avowed purposes of the war were being frustrated by his own fraternity. The Middlebury
chapter withdrew from the national organization and organized a new, more
inclusive fraternity, earning a good bit of respect from the remainder of the student body.[2]

Similar acts of discrimination occurred in fraternities and other social clubs
throughout postwar America—Jews denied access, quotas placed on Catholics,
other groups summarily rejected. But the rhetoric and image of Tri-Faith America

meant this kind of open discrimination would be challenged, especially when it occurred in America's colleges and universities, which were proclaimed to be training grounds for democratic citizenship. And challenged it was. In a dramatic transformation, by the early 1960s almost all of the major national fraternities had removed official barriers for racial and religious groups, and the victory was the result of Catholic and Jewish students combining with university administrators and outside civic defense agencies to demand an end to overt discrimination.

But eliminating discrimination turned out to be more complicated than simply passing resolutions and putting up a fight, and in unexpected ways. By the middle 1950s, just as overt discrimination was beginning to wane, some Catholics and Jews were choosing to separate from mainstream social groups, claiming they had a right, as minorities, to reject the anti-discrimination tenor of the times in the name of group self-preservation. Several leading Jewish fraternities, for instance, developed "a new *rationale* in which they are finding new values in Jewish separatism and are attempting to introduce distinctive Jewish content into their social fraternities." They wanted to maintain their Jewish identity.[3] For their part, in 1959, the large Catholic "superfraternity," Phi Kappa Theta, fought for survival at the University of Minnesota, which had just proclaimed a "deadline for democracy" that would deny university recognition to any group possessing a discriminatory charter. The Phi Kaps did not want to open their fraternity to non-Catholics, and they were willing to go toe-to-toe with a major university to secure that right.[4]

The postwar battle in fraternities, then, was not simply about ending discrimination against minority groups, but also about whether or not Catholics and Jews had the right to discriminate on behalf of maintaining a minority presence in American social life. What postwar Catholics and Jews fought for was the right to determine when and where their identities as minorities should matter, and for the special rights of minority groups to maintain aspects of discrimination in the name of group preservation. If discrimination against minorities such as Catholics and Jews was bad, was it equally problematic for Catholic and Jewish organizations to discriminate against Protestants?

Historians of midcentury America have often pointed to the national lionization of individual rights in the face of the communalism that sits at the ideological heart of Communism. And there is certainly much truth to the presence of liberal individualism in American social thought during these years, especially considering that within the rhetoric of Judeo-Christianity, in God's eyes an individual deserved certain rights and protections. But this ideology confronted severe limits as Catholics and Jews struggled for access to mainstream organizations but did not want to have to desegregate their own institutions.[5]

FIGHTING DISCRIMINATION

Collegiate fraternities have always been instruments of social division. They date back to 1776, when a group of students chartered Phi Beta Kappa at the College of William and Mary, in Williamsburg, Virginia (the founders chose Greek letters because Latin was already taken by the era's competitive literary societies and because Phi Beta Kappa's principal founder, John Heath, was the college's best Greek scholar). They experienced their greatest growth during the late nineteenth and early twentieth centuries, as college enrollments began a steady increase. This growth, however, coincided with a time when higher education was still a bastion of white Protestant men but was changing to accommodate upwardly mobile Catholics, Jews, and, in far fewer numbers, African Americans.

To protect themselves from unwanted outsiders, many of the new fraternities defined in their charters the kinds of men who could and could not belong, and race and religion were predictable boundaries. Probably the most offensive language appeared in the charter of the Phi Delta Theta fraternity, approved in 1912, which required that "only white persons of full Aryan blood, not less than sixteen years of age, should be eligible." Other fraternity charters limited membership to "Christian Caucasians." Some banned "the black, Malay, Mongolian or Semitic races." Sometimes "servants of the Pope" were excluded. An article in the *American Mercury* of 1931 discussed how several national fraternities "view with ill-concealed alarm the willingness of their Northern chapters to admit Roman Catholics to membership."[6] Despite some incursions, as late as the 1930s most social fraternities were considered a preserve for the ethnic, racial, and religious elite, meaning white Anglo-Saxon Protestants.[7]

As the journalist James Rorty noted in a discussion of collegiate fraternities in the 1950s, "segregation breeds segregation," and concurrent with the growth of these Anglo-Protestant social clubs was the rise of Jewish, Catholic, and African American fraternities. By the end of World War II, there were eleven prominent fraternities for Jewish men, two for Catholics, and two for African Americans.[8] As a member of a Jewish fraternity said, "If we are not permitted to join other fraternities, we must form a fraternity of our own. Nobody really *likes* to live in a ghetto. But sometimes you have to."[9]

Many professors and university administrators were alarmed at the rapid expansion of fraternities during the first decades of the twentieth century. Their frustrations were eased a bit during the Great Depression, which fiscally and numerically weakened university Greek organizations, and then again during World War II, when the number of students attending college was curtailed. Many universities simply closed their Greek systems during the war.[10]

Several of the critics thought the image of a tolerant America cultivated during World War II would, once and for all, kill off university Greek systems. Buell G. Gallagher, a Congregationalist minister and a professor of Christian ethics at the Pacific School of Religion, in Berkeley, California, gave a widely circulated speech in 1946 that said, "It is tragic to see . . . organizations flourishing which capitalize on racial and religious prejudices. Such centers of prejudice have no place in a democratic age."[11] A 1946 *New York Times* survey of twenty colleges found that every single one of the colleges it examined, from the University of the South and the University of Kentucky to the University of Rhode Island and the University of Indiana, was planning reforms that would bring the Greek societies "closer into the life of the institution."[12]

As early as 1943, however, other observers were predicting a great expansion of Greek life following the war. They saw millions of military men gaining ambition and direction and the federal government paving the way for GIs wishing to go to college.[13] These predictions were correct. From 1946 to 1956, the number of national fraternity chapters on campuses around the country jumped from 2,600 to 3,500, with undergraduate memberships up 60 percent. By 1948, fraternity memberships, like university enrollments, were at all-time highs, in many cases doubling prewar levels. Fraternities were wealthier too, buying the mortgages of their buildings and even building new, luxurious houses. After suffering two decades of decline, Greek social societies were entering into what is now seen as a golden age.[14]

But this new crop of fraternity men seemed different from previous generations. By 1947, one estimate suggested that nearly 50 percent of all fraternity members were ex-servicemen. Other estimates were higher.[15] These men "were older, more sophisticated, conscious that they were late getting launched in their careers, in acquiring a wife and getting a home."[16] As a postwar fraternity man put it, we "had had our fill of stratified idiocy" in the military and would not stand for hazing rituals in an elective recreational setting.[17] In one instance at the University of Washington, a dozen pledges, all overseas war veterans, walked away from their chapter during the initiation rituals, with one holding, "No 18-year-old kids are going to warm our bottoms."[18]

Besides challenging the traditional role of the pledge, returning soldiers had been thoroughly imbued in the wartime rhetoric of American tolerance. As one Colby College student said, "Many of us have served in the armed forces in the past three or four years and we came to know men of all types, races, creeds, and colors. We learned to judge men for personality and character, and I think we should continue to do so."[19] In polls, this postwar generation of students overwhelmingly supported eliminating discriminatory clauses in university organizations such as Greek societies.

Support of this kind continued to mount throughout the 1950s, at one point topping 80 percent of the undergraduates. The pollster, Elmo Roper, said most students declared it "silly and prejudiced to judge people on preconceived notions about their race or religion," adding, "Many of them might argue that it is not only undemocratic to draw the color or religion line, but also that an individual's personality becomes warped and slanted when he holds such views."[20]

Together, these tolerance-imbued students, faculty, and administrators took aim at the restrictive charters of the major fraternities. At Amherst College, for instance, the administration decreed shortly after the war that "any man good enough to be admitted to Amherst College should be good enough to be admitted to one of its component social groups," thereby outlawing any group whose "charter had any limitations on membership based on race or religion." Amherst's fraternities were given until 1951 to remove discriminatory clauses from their charters. Alfred S. Romer, the head of a corporation that owned the house of one fraternity, said the Amherst trustees had "of course, anti-Semitic bars particularly in mind."[21] Similar challenges emerged within five years of the war at major universities in Arizona, California, Rhode Island, Illinois, Colorado, Connecticut, Massachusetts, Minnesota, New York, New Jersey, Washington, Michigan, Pennsylvania, Florida, Maine, Ohio, and Wisconsin.[22] By 1957, the National Interfraternity Council (NIC), the umbrella organization overseeing the vast majority of the major national fraternities, had a list of seventy-two colleges across the nation where "agitation is taking place."[23] Notably missing from this catalogue were schools from the South, but the South was alone in resisting the trend. "This is not a whim or a localized attack," said one NIC report. "It has occurred on too many fronts."[24] The push to democratize the social and cultural life of collegiate America was broad and unsystematic, but there were widespread demands that America at least try to live up to its wartime rhetoric.

Institutional racism meant there were small numbers of African Americans in the nation's colleges during the first half of the twentieth century and therefore few incidents of discrimination against them in fraternities. There were still occasional challenges, as in 1948 when Thomas Gibbs's invitation to the Phi Kappa Psi fraternity at Amherst sparked significant debate in the national press. The national Phi Kappa Psi organization expelled its Amherst chapter for committing, ironically enough, "unfraternal conduct" by initiating Gibbs.[25] For the most part, though, there were too few African Americans gaining entrance to predominantly white social fraternities to spark much debate.

In contrast, Jews were numerically overrepresented in America's universities, especially at high-status schools in the Northeast, Midwest, and California. Unlike Catholics, who were heretofore predominantly working-class and numerous enough to develop a handful of their own institutions of higher learning, American Jews lionized the secular education system of the United States. Before World War I, Jews constituted roughly 40 percent of Columbia University's enrollment, 20 percent of Harvard's, and perhaps as high as 80 percent to 90 percent in some New York City schools such as Hunter College and the City College of New York. Immediately after World War I, the elite colleges of the Northeast began instituting quotas to limit Jewish admission. They were incredibly effective. In just two years, the percentage of Jews at Columbia dropped from 40 percent to 22 percent. Rumors spread that other elite colleges had limited the percentage of Jews they admitted to the percentage of Jews in the United States as a whole, which was about 3 percent. Despite these admissions quotas, Jews remained demographically overrepresented in American colleges, but the antisemitic tone had been institutionalized.[26]

Discrimination did not go away after students enrolled either, and nowhere was it more prevalent than in the fraternity system. Several fraternity charters explicitly barred Jews, but even if there was no explicit discriminatory clause, most of the major non-Jewish fraternities would not have thought to invite a Jew to join, simply because it likely had never done so before.

To rectify the perceived injustice, American Jewish defense organizations became the driving force advocating the end of restrictive charters of fraternities. They convened councils, monitored discrimination, and drafted reports. And after one very public debate over discrimination in a fraternity at Williams College in 1953, the American Jewish Committee commissioned a study detailing discrimination within the entire system of American collegiate fraternities. The report, entitled "White Men of Full Aryan Blood," called the fraternity system a "breeding ground of bigotry" that was stuck in an era mired in "racist philosophy." The authors urged several organizations to join together to combat the problem and challenge this "unfraternal conduct."[27]

Answering the call, in 1954 B'nai B'rith (itself founded in 1843 as a counterpart to the flourishing Christian men's fraternal organizations of the era), the American Jewish Committee, and a selection of other civil liberties organizations formed the National Committee on Fraternities in Education (NCFE). The NCFE's mission was to eradicate what it called "Aryanism," or the "acceptance and rejection of persons for membership on grounds of race, religion, and national origin." The use of the word "Aryan" was of course potent after the Holocaust, and the organization became a clearinghouse for tallying and investigating instances of discrimination within the fraternity system, mainly actions against Jews but also against Catholics and African Americans. Instances of discrimination against these two groups were limited, however, because "Roman Catholics have tended

to segregate themselves and to be barred in some measure from Protestant fraternities or subjected to quotas," while African Americans constituted "less than 1
percent [of the population] at most fraternity colleges."[28] The group cited no cases
of discrimination against members of national origin groups such as Germans or
Italians, suggesting their decline in national prominence.

After its initial founding, the NCFE was funded almost entirely by the American
Jewish Committee.[29] Nevertheless, the American Jewish Committee used its
leverage to create a blue-ribbon panel of professors, clergymen (Protestant, Catholic, and Jewish), and civic leaders to serve on its board.[30] In 1955, NCFE's
chairman, Brooklyn College sociologist Alfred McClung Lee, a Unitarian and a
longtime advocate of goodwill, published a book, *Fraternities Without Brotherhood*,
that attempted to expose a "basic threat to democracy in the United States," the
American fraternity system.

To the NCFE, the ideal democracy was one where a person could and would
ignore any "criteria of money, social class, religion, or race," all of which are
"attributes that are inherited rather than achieved." Once these superficial criteria were demoted, "men can see one another as individuals" and act free of group
discrimination.[31] At the same time, Lee believed that universities were basic
training grounds for the leaders of democratic society and, as such, should be
regulated to ensure they served the broad interests of the public. He concluded:
"The existence of an organization that permeates a major portion of a student's
experiences with an Aryan philosophy is hardly consistent with the total educational philosophy of the American college." It was, therefore, the "civic responsibility of the college fraternity" to help make "a better civilization," one free of
discrimination based on descent.[32] Throughout the 1950s and 1960s, the NCFE
lobbied university administrators to force the removal of discriminatory clauses,
tallied and publicized instances of abuse, and supported students who challenged
the restrictive clauses.

The National Interfraternity Council (NIC) emerged as the NCFE's primary
opposition. As early as the 1940s, the NIC had been arguing that within a democratic society, no one should be able to tell anyone else with whom they could or
could not associate. As David Embury, president of the NIC in 1947 and a longtime NIC board member, put it: "I would sing the praises of discrimination. I love
the discriminating tongue, the discriminating eye, the discriminating ear, and,
above all, the discriminating mind. . . . The person for whom I can find no love and
no respect is the indiscriminate person. . . . To be indiscriminate is to be common,
to be vulgar. . . . I think that every bird-lover must admire both the red-breasted
robin and the golden oriole. . . . No one, however, expects to find both of them in
the same nest. Nature, in its wisdom, has not so ordained."[33]

Embury, a high-church Protestant with solid blue-blood credentials, contended that university administrators had no place dictating what private social organizations could do. "If I form my fraternity of bow-legged men, let us say, at Amherst, and, because it succeeds there, groups of bow-legged men from Dartmouth, from Williams, from Bowdoin, and elsewhere petition and receive charters established from chapters of the bow-legged fraternity in their schools also, all are bound by this membership restriction which forms *one of the common ties, one of the distinguishing characteristics of this particular group*." He added:

> I, for one, will fight to the last ounce of my strength to defend the right—the democratic right—of any man or group of men to form a fraternity or other association with any membership restriction or qualification that they, in their absolute discretion, may see fit to impose:—a fraternity of blacks for blacks, of whites for whites, of Jews for Jews, of Gentiles for Gentiles, of Catholics for Catholics, of Protestants for Protestants. Of course, it is also the undisputed privilege of any group to form an organization with none of these restrictions if that be their pleasure. But it is one thing to say that a group *may* omit such restrictions—that is democracy. It is quite a different thing to say that a group *must* omit them—that is regimentation.[34]

Embury's argument was simple: choosing one's friends was a social right, not a civil right, and because college fraternities were voluntary social organizations, they were not subject to regulation.

Embury was on solid, if challengeable, constitutional grounds. The "peaceable assembly" clause of the First Amendment to the U.S. Constitution could be interpreted to mean that any group could assemble under whatever auspices it chose. Indeed, his argument underscored a long-acknowledged tension within classical liberal philosophy between tolerance and autonomy; unlike Lee and the NCFE, which prioritized the tolerance aspect of liberalism, Embury prioritized autonomy. And "autonomy" became the central argument of the NIC for the next two decades. In 1949, it urged fraternities and sororities to "review their membership policies in the light of changing social conditions" but suggested that clauses only "be eliminated by those fraternities who deemed it advisable." In 1953, it adopted a similar resolution attesting to "the right of each fraternity to establish its own criteria for membership." And in 1957, despite all the challenges rapidly emerging, it reaffirmed this position without a dissenting vote.[35]

In addition to this defense of autonomy, many in the NIC saw the forced elimination of discriminatory clauses as merely the first step in the enforcement of diversity. As the president of Phi Kappa Psi, W. Lyle Jones, said in 1957, "Elimination of 'clauses' is only the beginning. Next in line is a system of quotas, whereby you prove your purity and adherence to a new social order—all in the name of freedom!"[36] Although this argument against what has come to be called affirmative action rarely came up in public discussions, it was apparent that the NIC's ultimate fear was that administrators were going to force organizations to have a certain number of Jews, Catholics, or African Americans.

Despite the rhetoric of "democracy" coming from both sides of the argument, at the grassroots the issue was just plain divisive. In 1952, the Delta Chi fraternity sought the opinion of its alumni about what to do about the whites-only clause in its charter, and it attempted, in good faith, to broach the subject of changing its restrictive clause. Warren W. Etcheson, the administrative secretary, compiled more than twenty-seven hundred responses, with a little more than half in favor of removing the restrictive clause. Still, a little less than half were not in favor of such a change.[37] Etcheson threw his hands up in frustration: "It is virtually impossible to present a representative sample of the replies. They range all the way from the downright vulgar and vituperative outbursts to glowing phraseology of ideals and brotherhood. The whole thing has displayed considerable ignorance concerning our membership qualifications. One person wrote that if we admit Negroes, the next thing we know we will be admitting Jews. Many were 'shocked' to learn that we had a 'white' clause. Several wanted to know why Negroes don't organize their own groups, apparently unaware that there are several national fraternities for Negroes, some larger than Delta Chi. But it's a 'damned if you do' and 'damned if you don't' proposition. Great numbers on both sides demand that they be permitted to resign if their view is not upheld." Baffled by the storm, and persuaded by articulate factions on both sides, Etcheson wrote, "The only replies I have no real sympathy with are those that suggest we remove the restriction yet practice it. I will support and defend any action taken except that so-called 'middle-ground.'"[38]

THE DECLINE OF DISCRIMINATORY CLAUSES

Despite the grassroots divisiveness, throughout the 1950s NIC board members sensed a shift in public opinion against overt discrimination. They were losing the rhetorical battle. Fearful of what might result, the group became increasingly defensive. Viewing Jews as the driving force behind the insurgency and sensing that American Jews would be hampered by Red-baiting, the NIC hired the Pinkerton Detective Agency "to obtain a spot check on various individuals recently listed as members of the 'National Committee on Fraternities in Education.'"[39] The Pinkerton reports pointed out that some of the NIC's perceived adversaries were involved with, or had their bills paid by, the American Jewish Committee, which indicated (in their minds) possible association with Communists. One such potential Communist was a man named Dr. Robert Risk, an NCFE board member and a dentist from Indianapolis, Indiana, who was deemed to have "a somewhat unsavory reputation and has been suspected by some as being a Red. Recently he was mixed up with a doctor in Indianapolis who was barred from practice for unapproved methods of surgery."[40] A twenty-one-year-old Jewish woman named Marilyn Tessler was the subject of continued surveillance ("7am Using a rented auto, left Boston. Tailed subject . . ."). She was targeted for organizing an essay contest on the question "Should social fraternities and sororities be abolished?" The Pinkerton report repeatedly pointed out her Jewish faith, acknowledging that her neighborhood was "ninety-five percent Semitic" and that her father-in-law "is a Rabbi and is employed at a Jewish poultry slaughter house."[41]

The surveillance did not turn up much evidence of Communist subversion, nor did it slow the tide of public opinion, which was clearly beginning to turn in favor of the anti-discrimination reformers. In 1948, for instance, a collection of twenty-four small local fraternities that had been founded to promote interfaith and interracial relations consolidated to form Beta Sigma Tau, the first national fraternity with such an expansive mission. In 1954, a group called Students for Democratic Action began Operation Brotherhood, a nationwide effort "to rid the university campus of discrimination," with fraternities being a specific target.[42] The NIC sponsored a group called the Edgewater Conference to fight the organization, but, the NIC noted, the Edgewater Conference was "rapidly becoming known as the Ku Klux Klan of the fraternity world."[43]

University administrators also went on the offensive, with some eliminating from their campuses any social group that had a discriminatory clause in its constitution. Some universities went further, targeting fraternities even if they removed their discriminatory clauses. When the State University of New York (SUNY) adopted a resolution in 1953 banishing any social organization that barred students "on account of race, religion, creed, national origin or other artificial criteria" (but leaving loopholes for academic or religious organizations), the NIC fought back. It viewed the case as a key "show-down" between administrators and social fraternities.[44] It mobilized resources and tried to frame the case as one between a democracy of choice and authoritarian dictates premised on forced tolerance. It argued that SUNY's resolution denied fraternity members' basic civil rights, encroached on their freedom of assembly, denied them equal protection of the law, and adversely affected existing contracts. In the end, a special three-judge federal district court upheld SUNY's right to ban national fraternities from all twenty-two of its campuses, arguing, "A state may adopt such measures . . . as it deems necessary to its duty of supervision and control of its educational institu-tions."[45] The U.S. Supreme Court denied an NIC appeal, and universities gained considerable control over the organizations that operated under their auspices.

Following the SUNY case, there was a flurry of action by universities to restrict racial or religious discrimination in fraternity charters. Most often, universities set deadlines by which they would withdraw university approval from groups prac-ticing discrimination (supporters called these "deadlines for democracy").[46] A study by the Illinois Committee on Human Rights in Higher Education found that by 1964, slightly more than half of the 252 universities they polled had taken a formal position outlawing discriminatory clauses in university-sponsored organi-zations. More than 70 percent of New England schools had taken action against discriminatory groups, contrasting with 3 percent of schools in the South. Schools in the rest of the nation—in the West, the Midwest, and the Middle Atlantic—all hovered around 50 percent.[47]

Following this flurry of university action, many national fraternities quickly rid their charters of discriminatory passages regardless of what the NIC advocated. In the wake of the New York state ruling, Phi Delta Theta removed the phrase "full Aryan blood" from its bylaws, replacing it with the slightly less transparent "social attributes that will make them acceptable to all other chapters of the fraternity." Other fraternities followed suit. From 1945 to 1948, the number of national frater-nities with restrictive clauses in their charters had fallen from more than sixty to thirty-seven. By 1962, just two still had them.[48]

As their legal defenses crumbled, NIC members grew less careful about how they defended "autonomy." One prominent NIC member, L. G. Balfour, revealed to another, "Confidentially, the trouble now [for the Sigma Chis] at Chicago is due not only to the fact that there are a great many Jews in the chapter, but that they gave a formal dance recently and entertained quite a few colored girls. I think we will remove our chapter shortly."[49] He also commented about one anti-discriminatory fraternity that "there was one Christian in the lot and the balance were collored [sic] or Jews."[50] Another prominent NIC member described a fraternity at Ohio State as "an unsavory mess . . . with white girls dating colored boys and vice versa, and engaged in social practices that certainly would not be tolerated by any good fraternity."[51] In reaction to the California legislature's 1959 decision to set its own "deadline for democracy" for all state schools, the NIC fought the resolution on the grounds that it would be a "forerunner of an attempt to require fraternities to prove by actual practice that they do not restrict membership on the basis of race, color or creed."[52]

Although it would be easy to chastise the national fraternities for their position, their argument about autonomy was legitimate. From the NIC perspective, it was good Americanism to fight encroachments by the government, especially when the government sought to restrict individual freedoms. And if it was true that it did not want to force its members to alter their charters, it was also true it had harbored within its auspices several Jewish and Catholic fraternities throughout the twentieth century. Indeed, by 1946, two Jews had even served as NIC chairman, and the NIC official monthly, *Fraternity Month*, printed glowing articles about the success of these minority fraternities.[53] They were not all bigots; they just did not want to be told what to do.

RACE AS A SPECTER, RELIGION AS A REALITY

That religion, not race, was the animating force for much of the debate is suggested not only by the fact that the NCFE was founded and funded by Jewish organizations but also because religion featured prominently in the NIC's open debates. In 1948, the NIC considered voting on a resolution declaring its belief that a fraternity "has the right to select its own members . . . [and] the fraternity may, if it chooses adopt restrictive rules for its own membership."[54] Before the proposal reached a vote, however, Alvin T. Sapinsley, a member of Zeta Beta Tau (ZBT), the largest Jewish fraternity in the nation, rose with a suggestion: "Rather than to rush into a decision here today, hastily . . . and have the newspapers print a result and either magnify it or distort it," the NIC should table the resolution and send it back to the various national chapters for consideration. Sapinsley received an ovation for this invitation to punt on the issue, perhaps simply for offering a quiet way of disarming a potentially troubling situation.[55]

Discussion was less constrained at the concurrent meeting of undergraduates under the command of David Embury. There, debate grew so heated that the NIC chose to divide race from religion as a topic of discussion. Concerning race, discussion was relatively lively but also clear-cut. The most dramatic moment came when Embury suggested that "all who felt that it was desirable to admit Negroes and whites in the same fraternities should also give their position on intermarriage." Embury's statement met with what the *New York Times* called "violent protest" from many of the student participants. Nevertheless, the session put to vote the question "Should the fraternities that have discriminatory clauses in the constitution in regard to color eliminate such clauses?" The nonbinding vote was 25–12 in favor of keeping the discriminatory clauses, with eighteen representatives abstaining.[56]

Regarding religious groups, discussion was equally heated, but delegates questioned whether it was "un-American" to discriminate on the basis of religion, a question of national identity that had not come up during the discussion on race.

"Any type of religious discrimination . . . limits the acquisition of an open mind, a liberal viewpoint or a democratic outlook," argued Alan G. Johnson, a Pi Kappa Alpha from Syracuse University, while John Dickmeyer, a Kappa Sigma from the University of Massachusetts, added, "People are further advanced today than they were fifteen years ago. The only way we can live sensibly as Americans is through inter-faith organizations." Despite these arguments, many students opposed the interfaith resolution, arguing that racial integration was mostly theoretical, something that was unlikely to influence most American fraternities, while religious integration was a realistic possibility at universities across the nation. One delegate proclaimed, "In a democracy we are assumed to have the right to choose our own friends. . . . If you do not care to have a Catholic or a Jew as your friend, that is your privilege."[57] In the end, students held firm in the idea that local chapters should defer to the dictates of the national organizations. The overwhelming vote against removing the discriminatory clauses, one that demonstrates the contentiousness of the prospect of including Jews and Catholics in elite social organizations, was 44 to 19.[58]

Religion also emerged as the principal obstacle within particular fraternities. Some, such as Sigma Alpha Epsilon, developed "a tacit understanding and sort of a gentleman's agreement that no colored boys or non-Christians would be initiated."[59] Others, such as Kappa Delta Rho, added "religious emphasis" to their ritual, to which, they knew, Jews could not subscribe. The American Jewish Committee called this "a rather threadbare cloak of purely discriminatory practices."[60] Still others, such as Alpha Tau Omega (ATO), chose to strengthen the discriminatory clause in 1954, remarkably adding "Christian" to its historic limit of "white men only."

The ATO act was both a direct attack on Jewish inclusion and a show of resistance to popular opinion. Harry E. Pople Jr., an ATO from the Massachusetts Institute of Technology, pointed out what would have been obvious: "It seems to me that since the major contention in the colleges is the discriminatory clause in the Constitution, that our best bet is to leave it somewhat disguised so that we will not cause some of the Brothers to get into trouble on their campuses. Seems to me it might be well to disguise it somehow."[61] But John N. Yates from the University of Colorado protested: "On this point I think it is time for most of us to stand up and be counted. I think this [Christian] clause that we are putting into our Constitution is a basic one which our Fraternity was founded upon and not one to be hidden or shoved under the table. I very much think it ought to be adopted and passed so that we can show to other fraternities in the nation just where we do stand on this so-called rash discriminatory clause. I think as members of the Christian faith we should stand up and say, 'Yes, we are members of the Christian faith and we want Christians as our Brothers.'"[62] Debate ended after Kenneth F. Murrah of Georgia stated: "I believe that if we can't stand on a campus in the north or in the south and say that we are a Christian fraternity, then let's get off that campus because we don't need a chapter in a university whose administration is anti-fraternity. And I believe to be against that clause is to be against the Alpha Tau Omega Fraternity."[63] Without further debate, the motion to block Jews passed.

The Christian-only sentiment was not fleeting either. In a remarkable vote in 1957, ATO polled its members about what it should do about the religious and racial restrictions in the charter. Of the 118 chapters around the nation, 113 replied. Ninety-one voted to retain the Christian part of the membership clause, while just 72 voted to keep the "white" clause.[64] In 1960, a similar questionnaire revealed similar results: of the 112 chapters returning the poll, 66 wanted to retain the "Christian" clause, and only 40 voted to retain the "white" part of it.[65] In 1964, ATO began the process of eliminating both membership restrictions, and in 1966 it became one of the last national fraternities to do so.

By the late 1950s, the anti-discrimination forces were clearly carrying the day. Almost all the charters of national fraternities had dropped their discriminatory language. The state had intervened several times to ensure the end of overt discrimination. Technically, Catholics, Jews, and other minorities were welcome to join any fraternity they might choose. When the NIC reiterated its autonomy argument in 1957, one member of the American Jewish Committee called it "the dying gasp of its fight on behalf of the college fraternity system," adding that "overt restriction is practically ended" and "practically dead."[66]

In 1965, one university dean, Clyde S. Johnson, who was also the research editor of the NIC, noted, "No hard facts are available with respect to the inclusion of minority group members within campus fraternity systems," but his impression was that "concern about admitting Roman Catholics to chapters almost entirely Protestant has all but disappeared generally. . . . All of the fraternities catering to Jewish men now have representatives of other faiths. . . . The number of Negroes found in campus systems which once included whites only is still very small, compared to the percent in the national population, but this is also true of their proportional representation in higher education generally." Johnson concluded: "Fraternity memberships have become more representative of the national pluralism than was true a decade or two decades ago."[67]

The reality was more complex. By the late 1950s Catholics and Jews were regularly welcome in all fraternities on campuses that had no historically Catholic or Jewish fraternities. But where Catholic or Jewish fraternities existed, integration proceeded far more slowly. "At campuses where Jewish fraternities exist there is very little cross-rushing and Jewish students seldom become members of Christian fraternities," read an American Jewish Committee report from 1956.[68] After an extensive study of segregation in the fraternity system in the early 1950s, Brooklyn College social scientist Simon Marcson concluded, "The overwhelming majority of the quarter of a million college fraternity and sorority members literally live for three or four years in an environment erected upon principles of segregation."[69] Various "gentlemen's agreements" limited membership to those who were "socially acceptable."[70] Data from particular institutions corroborate this conclusion. At Dartmouth, where there was no Jewish fraternity, "virtually all" fraternities had accepted a Jewish member between 1954 and 1960.[71] At the University of Missouri, a researcher found that "considerable anti-Semitism exists and is manifest in exclusion policies."[72] At Brown University, some fraternity chapters developed quotas for Catholic and Jewish membership, with one such fraternity setting a 25 percent limit for Catholic men. This change was so recent at Brown, however, that the social scientist who studied the problem concluded, "In practice, few Jewish students belong to any fraternities except the one which is exclusively Jewish."[73] At Williams College, a 1957 report concluded that "Roman Catholics have a full and equal opportunity for membership in fraternities," while "most fraternities have Jewish members but prefer to limit the number who belong at any one time."[74] The American Jewish Committee concluded in 1962 that "in actual practice, all of the fraternities that have changed their restrictive clauses have accepted Jewish members but on a significantly varying scale."[75]

"RELIGIOUS CONTENT" AND MINORITY RIGHTS

A second force for autonomy emerged to oppose the American Jewish Committee and the NCFE, from a more surprising source: Catholic and Jewish fraternities themselves. An American Jewish Committee report of 1956 read: "For the most part the Jewish fraternity leaders are deeply concerned about the maintenance of their organizations as distinctly Jewish and so have been among the last to drop their own bars against non Jews."[76] The largest Catholic fraternity, meanwhile, "maintains its right to exclude non-Catholics, despite anti-bias regulations at many campuses."[77] Catholics and Jews were beginning to understand the merits of autonomy, merits that seemed particularly important for a minority group seeking preservation in a pluralistic society.

There were several reasons for this resistance. For one thing, these religiously defined organizations did not want to compete for the most desirable Catholic or Jewish men against larger, more established fraternities. Worried they would not survive in the face of competition, they resisted calls for integration. Another reason for their reticence, especially for Jews, was their fear that parents would not support, financially or otherwise, the historically Catholic or Jewish fraternities if they began to integrate outsiders into their membership and abandoned their socioreligious mission. It was an open question whether parents "are prepared to accept exposure of their children to a situation of social association, with possible consequences of inter-marriage."[78] A third reason was the basic notion that within a pluralistic nation, minorities were an enriching presence worthy of protection. And fourth, no group likes to be completely subsumed within the majority.

Maurice Jacobs, one of the two Jewish past presidents of the NIC, summed up the problems that might arise if Jewish fraternities were displaced from their exclusive mission. If they were forced to consider non-Jewish men, they would "not be able to attract the same high type non-Jews that they attract among their own," forcing them to become "third and fourth rate." Plus, Jewish causes might get buried by national causes in an integrated fraternity. "Where will our community get its future leadership if not from this college-trained group?" Jacobs wondered. Jacobs pointed out the "fear of most Jewish parents," namely, intermarriage. "When people are thrown together at a tender age," he asked, "what happens?"[79] The integration of Jewish fraternities might begin a process that would jeopardize all of American Judaism. "It has taken us over 60 years to build what we have," Jacobs concluded. "Let's not destroy it so quickly, merely because of a theory of the sociologists, who have been wrong before, and will be wrong again." Tellingly, Jacobs, a publisher by trade, was the first to print a Hebrew prayer book in America and a founder of the American Jewish Historical Society, signifying his deep interest in preserving Judaism in America.[80]

Jewish fraternity men were in a terrible bind, having to balance their own desires for autonomy with the Jewish defense organizations' desire for openness. In 1958, Fred H. Turner, an NIC board member and editor of its *Bulletin*, wrote to a colleague: "It seems to me that we continue to get public support and participation in NIC from the Jewish groups, but at the same time there is a constant behind the scenes sniping activity which is certainly doing no good."[81] His NIC colleague fired back: "Confidentially, you should know, however, that we now have positive proof that the NIC Jewish fraternities are acting in unison, following the advice and actually the instructions of the American Jewish Committee. We know this group has gone so far as to threaten one Jewish fraternity with dire penalties should they fail to revise their charter, which now restricts their membership to Jews."[82] What those penalties were or could be, he declined to say. But he was right in his prediction: by 1960 all the historically Jewish fraternities had removed their discriminatory clauses.

This did not mean Jewishness left the historically Jewish fraternities. Rather than basing their demands for autonomy on fear of what might happen, many fraternity men embraced the idea that Jews should want to identify as Jews and that Jewish fraternities had a responsibility to make that choice appealing. They promoted an affirmative sense of their Jewish heritage, adding what came to be called "Jewish content" to their ritual. Finding "new values in Jewish separatism," these fraternities began emphasizing their particular religiosity. In the late 1950s, Alpha Epsilon Pi (AEPi) was the most active in crafting some of these new measures, including an argument that Jewish fraternities had a right to be "equal but separate."[83] The phrase was of course a play on the "separate but equal" premise that had, until 1954, justified legal racial segregation in the United States. But AEPi defended its use of the principle as "a new stress on the essential validity of cultural diversity."[84] In order to maintain diversity, minorities needed protection. As the president of one large AEPi chapter said in 1956:

> We can no longer base the cause for our existence on the fact that many fraternities will not accept Jewish boys—for most fraternities will accept them today. We must and are developing a positive program whereby our Jewish youth will be kept aware of its heritage and responsibility to the Jewish community, as well as to the community at large. The methods by which this is to be implemented into our individual chapters are now being studied and devised in many of our Jewish fraternities by committees composed of both lay and rabbinical members. The program decided upon within each fraternity may have a slightly different approach, but I am certain the end result will and purpose will be the same—*the retention of our Jewish college youth in our Jewish way of life.*[85]

The notion that Jews might have something to gain if they maintained their Jewish identities was defended in numerous places. In the *National Jewish Post and Opinion*, Rabbi Philip Bookstaber wrote, "I refuse to give up the potential good, with all its evils, that a group of Jewish boys, organized into a Jewish fraternity, can accomplish, as against the hysteria now prevalent under the terms of no discrimination and no bias."[86] At a 1955 meeting with the American Jewish Committee, dozens of Jewish fraternity leaders implored the organization to cease its push for fraternity integration. "Please don't destroy what some of us have worked on for over forty years—equal rights for the Jewish groups on campus. Equal rights within the National Interfraternity Conference where we always have at least one man on the Executive Committee. . . . We are against, practically unanimously, . . . what the AJC is doing in this field."[87] Others pointed out that if the integrationist argument was taken to its logical conclusion, it "would mean that no organization such as the [American Jewish] Committee itself, organized for a Jewish purpose, should exist." Another added: "If your intention is to encourage the complete assimilation and disappearance of Jewish students from the American college scene . . . then your present program . . . is definitely achieving that purpose."[88] Summing up this autonomous perspective, Alvin Sapinsley, the former president of ZBT, said, "[Jews] have a right to determine for themselves the extent of their Jewishness."[89]

At the University of Michigan, meanwhile, one Jewish student wrote about "the Jewish problem" at the university, by which he meant the persistent "Jewish clannishness and almost complete disregard and contempt for the gentile community." Suggesting that "Jews are certainly the most conspicuous minority" on campus, he described a section of buildings known around campus as "The Gazza [sic] Strip" because of the preponderance of Jews occupying them. He described the Jewish fraternities as "the most blatantly discriminatory groups on campus" and noted that they publicly pressured Jewish freshman not to rush non-Jewish houses. Overtly declaring their separatism, they avoided pan-fraternity events.

But what most baffled the student was that this separatism was a matter of choice. After describing the university's "complete random" roommate placement process for freshmen, he described how upperclassmen and even freshmen after one semester were able to choose where they lived. The result? "Jewish ghettos— areas where more than 80 percent are apparently Jewish . . . And this is inspite [sic] of . . . active discouragement by the University." He worried that this would result in increased antisemitism. A personal study of his revealed that non-Jews said they had become more hostile to Jews since coming to campus. Jews were, the Gentiles reported, "too clannish" and "openly anti-gentile."[90] Upon hearing about the case, Lawrence Bloomgarden of the American Jewish Committee expressed his frustration at "the self-segregative policies of Jewish fraternities and sororities," and he complained that "on most other campuses . . . similar situations prevail."[91]

Not everyone complained. One rabbi, the Hillel Foundation's director at Washington University, said, "Everybody knew that a Jewish Greek house was Jewish. Jewish parents in many cases expected their sons or daughters to 'take a bid' to this or that house, and were not reluctant to be taxed by the extra costs, on the assumption that the Jewish fraternity made possible intradating amongst the Jews, thus guarding against the risk of mixed marriages."[92] Jewish parents, meanwhile, often rejected their children's attempts to integrate, claiming their children were not about to jeopardize their Jewish heritage in the name of a sociological ideal.

The idea that Jews should preserve discriminatory qualities contributed to the tremendous growth experienced by Jewish fraternities during the late 1950s and early 1960s. ZBT, the largest and oldest Jewish fraternity, grew from thirty chapters to more than eighty after the war. These numbers might simply reflect the growth of fraternities in general and continued discrimination within the Greek system, or they might suggest the hope of Jewish youth to retain their particular institutions. What they do not reflect is the integration of historically Jewish fraternities: by 1958, perhaps only as few as forty non-Jews had joined the three largest Jewish fraternities, which had a total undergraduate membership of about ten thousand.[93] Discrimination or not, Jewish fraternities were still filled with Jews.

Catholics followed a similar trend. In 1959 the two leading Catholic fraternities, Phi Kappa and Theta Kappa Phi, merged to become one "superfraternity," Phi Kappa Theta. The goal was to consolidate Catholic Greek life, limit competition between the two organizations, and fight to maintain Catholic identity in a united way. Through the 1950s, the two fraternities had been intense rivals, but during the early 1960s, freshly united, Phi Kappa Theta was often fighting alone to preserve its discriminatory charter, which limited membership to just Catholic men. Unlike Jewish fraternity members, Catholics were unencumbered by communal demands to integrate, and thus they held on to their restrictive charter longer than any other social fraternity in the United States. "I wonder which college is going to lock horns with them?" pondered one former NIC president in 1961.[94] During the early 1960s, Phi Kappa Theta added twenty-five chapters across the nation. It finally dropped discriminatory restrictions from its charter in 1969, with the new membership clause admitting any young man "regardless of religious persuasion, as long as he could understand and agree to accept the Fraternity's religious heritage," according to one of the fraternity's historians.[95]

Catholics too were arguing for the importance of choice and for minority rights. "Family living is too intimate to allow for known cleavages which can destroy harmony and unity," said Reverend James A. McInerney, a Dominican priest and the scholarship director of Phi Kappa Theta. "Fraternities worthy of the name are a cooperative sharing of intimate daily life. Private individuals and private organizations alone should determine their lawful purpose and their lawful needs. Strength is in diversity, not in the dreary sameness of mediocrity. Much of the so-called integration tends in this direction, but I fear maliciously, and not from any high ideals."[96]

Commonweal was more torn. Biased exclusion was clearly problematic, and collegiate social fraternities should "abandon an obviously bankrupt policy." However, the "choosing of one's friends and associates is a social right which cannot be confused with civil rights." And at the end of the day, this argument was "correct if not compelling."[97]

"EQUAL BUT SEPARATE"

These kinds of demands emerged in numerous social arenas throughout the late 1950s and early 1960s. Demands that discriminatory clauses be removed from charters of powerful, majority-run organizations appeared everywhere. The New York Athletic Club was attacked in 1957 for its restrictions against Jews and African Americans. The California Tip Toppers (whose members had to be at least six feet four inches) came under fire for restricting Jews. Major men's and women's social clubs were also exposed for racial or religious biases.[98] The Anti-Defamation League passed a resolution denouncing resorts and hotels that practiced religious discrimination after hearing the results of a study showing that more than 22 percent of nearly three thousand hotels studied "clearly discriminate against Jews."[99] During the 1950s and early 1960s, most of these overt restrictions had fallen by the wayside, helped by federal laws such as the Civil Rights Act of 1964, which allowed the federal government to cut off all federal funds to colleges if they allowed fraternities to continue discriminating.[100]

Minority organizations, however, faced no such demands. In most of these debates, and especially the debate about collegiate social fraternities, nobody explicitly made the point that there was a difference between a powerful group's demand for autonomy and that coming from a group possessing less power. But it was clear that a hegemonic group's discriminatory claims could all too easily be interpreted as an attempt to deny minority groups access to places of power. The results could be seen not only as undemocratic but also as malevolent. The demands for maintaining discriminatory clauses emerging from groups possessing less power, on the other hand, might also be undemocratic, but they emerged out of an affirmative desire to maintain group unity in an America that was just beginning to recognize and accept its diversity. One discriminatory act is meant to restrict, the other to perpetuate. There is a distinction between the two forms of discrimination, even if this distinction means that the rhetoric of anti-discriminatory, "tolerant" democracy, based on the concept of individual rights and the brotherhood of man under the Fatherhood of God, might lose coherence.[101]

While rationales for minority group rights have emerged in force since the 1990s, during the 1950s and 1960s Catholic and Jewish fraternity members were making this distinction in practice, demanding that the United States alter its stringent grounding in individual rights in order to accommodate and more fully recognize some of the dominant minority groups in what now had to be seen as a pluralist society. The benefits and costs associated with making this distinction continued to resonate many decades later. In 2005, the playwright Steve Karp produced an autobiographical play called *Fraternity*, which described the anxiety Karp felt as an undergraduate at Tufts University in 1961 when he was invited to become a member of Delta Tau Delta, a popular non-Jewish fraternity with a long history of racial and religious discrimination. Delta's president had sought to challenge the fraternity's discriminatory heritage, and he invited Karp and one other Jew to be test cases. Despite having some reservations, Karp joined the fraternity, making it easier for other Jews to integrate Tufts's Greek system. He worried, however, that joining a non-Jewish fraternity might mean he was shedding his Jewish identity simply to earn social acceptance. He rationalized that he might be seen as a trailblazer, opening doors for others to follow. "I didn't know how I would come out as a Jew," Karp said of the experience. He, like many of his peers, was conflicted.[102]

But he was glad to have the choice. Gone were the days when Catholics and Jews were told which houses they could join and which they could not. Replacing them were the more confusing days when one could choose to identify by one's religion or not. That this choice created mixed feelings in so many young men was a sign that this victory came at a cost. That it pushed some Catholics and Jews to make demands on behalf of minority groups in a liberal individualist society is an unaccounted part of midcentury American liberalism.

7

Keeping Religion Private (and Off the U.S. Census)

SINCE ITS FOUNDING in 1790, the U.S. Bureau of the Census has never asked a formal question about religion on the decennial census. During the eighteenth, nineteenth, and twentieth centuries, it had become axiomatic in government circles that such questions, requested in official form, would infringe on rights protected by the free exercise and establishment of religion clauses of the First Amendment to the United States Constitution.[1] But that does not mean government officials thought religion was unimportant. In the 1880s, the decade of the first great migrations from southern and eastern Europe, the bureau began asking questions about the religious preferences of the American public. But it did so only hesitantly, through non-census-year population surveys, which do not legally mandate an answer and which are based on questions addressed to church and synagogue officials, not the general public. These Censuses of Religious Bodies (CRBs) were tabulated most recently in 1916, 1926, and 1936. Not many people complained about the CRBs, but the questions were not posed to citizens directly, and the results were always thought to be inaccurate considering they came from the leaders of the various congregations.

Immediately after World War II and the Holocaust, Congress decided against reporting on religion in a 1946 survey, even after the data were two-thirds tabulated. Fearful of analogies with the "Final Solution," Congress simply refused to fund the remainder of the survey.[2] But with the postwar rise in importance of religious identities, other organizations filled the statistical void. During World War II, George Gallup, the father of American polling, began breaking down most of his data by the "three faiths of democracy." Gallup's handful of polls on religion before the war most often used the categories "Protestant" and "Catholic" in its tabulations. Jews were added into regular consideration only during the buildup to war, and by the 1950s, Gallup was determining not only how many Americans belonged to what faith but also how many Jews voted for Adlai Stevenson, how many Protestants liked Ike, and how appealing Joseph McCarthy was to American Catholics.[3] He began asking about interfaith marriages in the early 1950s too, although, revealingly, the phrase "interfaith marriage" was never used; in postwar America it was evidently clear that "intermarriage" or "mixed marriage" signified religion, not race.[4] In 1955, the phrase "or synagogue" was added to Gallup's common question "Did you, yourself, happen to attend church during the past month?" Once there, the phrase never left.[5]

Another prominent American pollster, George Roper, also began asking about religious identities in the 1950s, as did numerous field polls in the major newspapers and national magazines. Churches themselves began polling as well, doing tabulations and cross-tabulations, trying to figure out how the development of suburbia was influencing American religious life, where parishioners were coming from and going to, and why people were flocking to church on Sundays. They were all struck, universally if sometimes cynically, by the tremendous growth of churches throughout the 1950s and by the tri-faith characterization of that growth.[6] But if the breadth of these data gatherers was impressive, there was a clear lack of consistency. The *Yearbook of American Churches*, the *Catholic Directory*, and the *American Jewish Yearbook*, three authorities on each of the respective faiths, all had different ways of tabulating members. Furthermore, they weren't exactly impartial about the results.

The most authoritative quantitative survey available was clearly the United States Census, and, beginning in the mid-1950s, the Bureau of the Census engaged in a very public debate about whether the federal government should put a question about religion on the census of 1960. The possibility of the federal government venturing so deep into unknown terrain sparked a nationwide debate on the merits and demerits of tabulating people by their religion. The discussion escalated within government circles, and the dispute went all the way to President Eisenhower before it was resolved.[7]

In the end, the debate testified to the rise of religiosity in postwar America, and to the tri-faith character of that social manifestation. But it also helps document the rise of yet another principle in American public life: the right to religious privacy. The right has no constitutional foundation, and the principle of "religious privacy" did not emerge until the middle of the twentieth century. During the 1950s, leaders of American Jewish organizations championed the new principle as a sort of super-separation of church and state, which would guarantee that their rights would never be compromised by having the government ask about and locate people by their religion. Thus, they formulated and articulated the new principle while they fought against the inclusion of a question of religion on the U.S. Census. Catholics overwhelmingly rejected the idea of religious privacy, seeing religion as profoundly social as well as transcendent. Protestants fell somewhere in between. But because of Jews' willingness to put up a fight in the census debate, and because of the problems inherent in working through American religious pluralism, the federal government simply backed down, allowing the principle of religious privacy to flourish, as it has ever since.

"ONE OF THE MAJOR UNDERLYING SOCIAL FACTORS IN AMERICAN LIFE"

The postwar debate about adding a question on religion in the United States Census was unusually contentious. Unlike the off-year Census of Religious Bodies, the decennial census mandates a response by law, although people often leave a few questions unanswered and those who do almost always go unpunished. Only one person had been prosecuted for refusing to answer a Census Bureau official's question—a Rhode Island farmer who "willfully and maliciously" refused to reveal the size of his wife's farm in the 1890 census. But, if it wished, the bureau could be more active in prosecuting such cases.

For the 1950 census, the bureau quickly and quietly rejected a proposal to include a question about religion. Its acting director, Philip Hauser, sought to avoid controversy; recalling the congressional opposition to the 1946 survey, he led a coalition of bureau officials against its inclusion in 1950. "It is our conclusion," read Hauser's official statement, "that in view of the controversial nature of the question, the intense opposition to it in certain quarters, and the doubtful reliability of the information collected, it therefore seems unwise to jeopardize the success of the whole decennial census in order to obtain the admittedly useful information on religious affiliation."[8]

In 1953, under a new administration and with "religious groupings represent[ing] one of the major underlying social factors in American life," as one prominent census official put it, the bureau's leaders grew less wary. Now headed by the Eisenhower appointee Robert W. Burgess, a professed Baptist, and operationally run by the widely respected demographer Conrad Taeuber, the Census Bureau began to consider a wider range of questions.[9]

The possibility of adding a question on religion interested both men, but Taeuber was especially interested. The son of a clergyman, a University of Minnesota

Ph.D., and a twenty-year civil servant, Taeuber had a national reputation for his able analyses of population trends in the United States. He and his wife, Irene B. Taeuber, had written the standard work on American demographics, *The Changing Population of the United States* (1958). Throughout his career, he had been aware of the deficient nature of American religious statistics, but he had begun to think seriously about the problem after a 1952 luncheon held by Rupert Vance, a distinguished sociologist at the University of North Carolina, which featured a talk on developing more reliable statistics on religious preferences. By the time he joined the Census Bureau, he strongly advocated including religion in the U.S census.[10]

He found a receptive ear in his boss, Robert W. Burgess, who had been a respected statistician and economist at Western Electric Company. Burgess left no record as to why he was interested in the question on religion, but he was an adamant believer in the social utility of statistics. Without them, he said, "we would be faced with an intolerable uncertainty regarding any long-range efforts to maintain public and private services to society." He took it upon himself to educate the public not to fear statistics at a time when gathering statistics and crunching numbers were on the rise because of demographers' widespread adoption of computers.[11]

In 1956, when secretary of commerce Sinclair Weeks decided against promoting the 1956 CRB (amid a cost-cutting effort that eliminated nearly half the Census Bureau's first-priority survey questions), Burgess and Taeuber immediately began to argue for including a question on religion in the 1960 decennial census. As he was prone to do, Burgess strove to spark public dialogue. He felt that once the question was in the open, it could not be evaded, so he issued a brief statement in fall 1956 saying that the question was "under consideration" by the bureau.[12]

The ACLU reacted to Burgess's press release immediately. As one of the nation's principal advocates of individual privacy, the ACLU said it would not support any question dealing with an individual's belief on the grounds that doing so would infringe on individual liberty. But the group softened its opposition by adding the caveat that it would not oppose a question on religion if the bureau allowed respondents to refrain from answering. Burgess knew that making a question on the decennial census optional would require congressional action, and he considered seeking it. Both Burgess and Taeuber felt that ACLU support would undermine the First Amendment qualms people might have and would make it easier to gain approval. Therefore, the bureau's initial public stance was to seek approval for the question while weighing attempts to make it optional.[13]

Catholics immediately became among the strongest advocates of the question. In September 1956 the Jesuit weekly *America* fired off a misinformed editorial condemning Burgess and the Census Bureau for rejecting out of hand any possible question on religion. *America* was clearly in favor of such a question, and it (wrongly) saw Burgess's reaction to the ACLU as implying some waffling in the face of civil liberties groups. Objection to including a question on religion, *America* argued, "might have validity in connection with applications for employment. But it does not seem applicable when the questions objected to are for census purposes and are to be answered anonymously." The Catholic Church had long favored a census question on religion, despite concerns about the connections people might draw between Catholics and income levels reported by the Census Bureau. *America*'s support was new only in its stridency, not in its argument.[14]

At the invitation of the magazine, Burgess responded to *America*'s mostly incorrect allegations. He showed that both he and the bureau were open to a question on religion—if only they could find more supporters. He concluded his letter by saying, "We would welcome your views on the need for such data as part of the 1960 census program, including the uses which would be made. Our objective must be that of providing the most useful body of statistics possible within the framework of the legislation and the budget the Congress provides." Burgess then edited his remarks and issued them as another official press release, hoping to spark more debate.[15]

Sensing the need for some official defense of why a question was being considered, in December 1956 Burgess elaborated his position in yet another widely distributed press release. Religious data, he wrote, would be helpful to churches as well as business interests, school planners, criminologists, and sociologists, a "considerable number" of whom had requested such a question. The results could supply marketers with better target information, city planners with better data for planning public schools, and sociologists with valuable data on a vital division in American society. The bureau did not believe that the "long-established principle" of separation of church and state was "in any way jeopardized" given the confidentiality of the responses and their use for statistical purposes only. Thus the question did not invade privacy any more than other questions on the census, such as the one about the highest grade of school completed.[16] Here Burgess might have drawn an easy parallel between the question of religion and the question of racial identification or "mother tongue," each of which had appeared on the census in various forms throughout the nineteenth and twentieth centuries. For unknown reasons, he never made the connection, though likely neither Catholics nor Jews would have appreciated the direct comparison to racial minorities. Nevertheless, Burgess pledged that any question dealing with religion would probably have a clause that allowed respondents to avoid answering it.[17]

With Burgess crafting an ideological defense, Taeuber began testing the question in the field. Relying on an administrator who was expert in the Canadian census (which included a question on religion), Taeuber inserted the question in one of the bureau's routine Current Population Surveys. After much study, Taeuber phrased the question, "What is your religion? Baptist, Lutheran, etc." That formula minimized potential areas of conflict (by not openly asking, for example, "Are you a Jew?") and helped prevent the formation of a residual category of "Protestant" for those unwilling to admit to religious apathy but not serious about religion. Despite the phrasing, the bureau demonstrated the persistence of the tri-faith formulation in its tabulations, which read "Protestant," "Catholic," "Jew," "other," and "no religion," with the Protestant category only occasionally broken down by denomination. The phrasing was later criticized by several social scientists, notably the sociologist William Petersen, who argued that the question should have read: "Have you a religion?" Then, if the answer was affirmative, there should have been a follow-up question: "What is it?" The divergence between Petersen's questions and the bureau's conveys vastly different understandings of religion. Petersen's question—"Have you a religion?"—implies that religion is a choice and not a fixed part of someone's identity, whereas Taeuber's phrasing— "What is your religion?"—suggests that religion is universal and fixed. The fact that Petersen aired his criticism at all indicates that the meaning of religion—as an individual choice or as an identity given at birth—was an open question in midcentury America, but Petersen was certainly in the minority.[18]

The first trial occurred in Milwaukee in November 1956. Of the 431 households tested, the bureau bragged that "less than one-half of one percent" refused to answer the question on religion. "Although responses to the inquiry on religion were wholly voluntary, virtually all persons gave the information without hesitation," read the official report. The data were not terribly surprising, nor was the question evidently disturbing to anyone questioned. Bureau officials felt confident they were ready to conduct a large-scale study.[19]

That study came five months later, when Taeuber included the question in a broader, nationwide survey of 35,000 households. Like the smaller survey, the large survey went off without a hitch, leading Taeuber to think a nationwide tally might occur in 1960 if the question could finally win approval.

OPPOSITION

By the time the data from the large survey were released, a nationwide debate had started over whether the decennial census should include a question on religion, and the results of Taeuber's survey would be shrouded in controversy. Trouble began in November 1956, when the National Catholic Welfare Conference buttressed Catholics' usual support for the question by giving its official approval to inclusion of the question. Rather than simply show support, however, the NCWC made the question its top political priority of 1956 and 1957. According to NCWC documents, "the [NCWC's] Public Affairs Committee's sole project in October 1956 was to figure out strategies by which a question on religion could be added to the Census," a project it deemed so important it was "to be effected by every proper lobbying technique available." Perhaps more important from a public perspective, the NCWC declared that the Catholic presses should be enlisted in this "crusade for a 'religious question'" and that the national secular press should be made aware of the question's deep sociological importance. The NCWC worried that getting a question on religion in the census "won't be easy because one religious group (The Jews) will oppose" the question "on the principle of separation of Church and State."[20]

It was a forceful memo, and, as American Catholicism's most important political voice, the NCWC possessed tremendous political and cultural strength among American bishops, several politicians, and ordinary Catholics. Shortly after the memo's release, Thomas B. Kenedy, Catholic representative to the Association of Statisticians of American Religious Bodies, editor of *The Official Catholic Directory*, and an intellectual with ties to the NCWC, led an interdenominational group to confer with Burgess about how to handle the publicity that was sure to result from the debate. Kenedy's lobbying seemed to work on Burgess, and Kenedy left the meeting with "reliable assurances that a question will be placed on the 1960 census."[21]

Kenedy emerged as a leading public supporter of including the question, and through his words we can discern the Catholic argument for the question's inclusion. His overt argument was that the data would be useful to charitable groups, hospitals, and schools, allowing them to better deploy their resources. Secular social planners and charitable organizations would find the information useful too. As cities hollowed out and America suburbanized, such statistics would be beneficial to groups trying to keep tabs on their flocks. This civic and sociological argument was strong enough to win the support of the American Sociological Association, the Association of Statisticians of American Religious Bodies, the Census 1960 Advisory Committee, the Population Association of America, and other secular demographic agencies.[22]

Kenedy and the NCWC may have had an ulterior motive, believing that the census data would provide demonstrable proof of the numerical power of Catholics in the United States. Previously, the debate about whether Protestants or Catholics had numerical superiority had been hampered by the fact that the Catholic Church counted in its ranks everyone born Catholic, while Protestant churches waited until their members were thirteen years old before including them. An official tally by the Bureau of the Census would alleviate confusion and perhaps clarify the extent of Catholic power in the United States. For a minority group whose place in American life was suspect because its members were supposedly unable to adhere to democratic principles, a third party's demonstration of their large and continuous presence would help solidify their standing and legitimize their group identity. Furthermore, a demonstration of the large number of American Catholics would be sure to impress politicians, who frequently debated issues important to midcentury Catholics, including federal funding of public schools, the legality of school prayer, and whether the United States should send a permanent diplomat to the Vatican. For those and possibly other reasons, following the NCWC's call, the National Council of Catholic Men, the Catholic Press Association, the *Catholic Digest*, the *Catholic Review*, and the *National Catholic Register*, the national Catholic weekly, all came out in support of the measure.[23]

As the NCWC had predicted, by early 1957 Jews came out in opposition to the question. Jewish groups were quick to notice the proposition because the executive secretary of the Jewish Statistical Bureau, Dr. H. S. Linfield, was deeply protective of his professional turf and did not want to be made extraneous by tabulations done by the Census Bureau. When the Census Bureau announced its intention to explore the question, Linfield took note.[24]

Other Jewish statisticians, including Marshall Sklare, were similarly aware of the question and encouraged their organizations to weigh the matter carefully. It did not take them long to settle on a position, and in spring 1957 the major Jewish organizations discussed strategies to fight inclusion of the question. They too were unequivocal about who their opposition was. "One thing is clear," said a memo from a member of the American Jewish Committee. "The moving force behind the proposal . . . has, for a number of years, been Catholic." The American Jewish Congress took the lead role in the fight and ultimately took the debate to the mainstream American press.[25]

The Jewish groups at first argued that the question would violate the principle of separation of church and state and would yield dubious information that would only provide fodder for bigots. At the American Jewish Congress's urging, in the summer of 1957 numerous rabbis and community members wrote the Census Bureau denouncing the potential inclusion of the question on those grounds. The American Jewish Congress also effectively lobbied the ACLU to change its position, suggesting that its previous stance (to support the question if answering it was made optional) was not legally coherent considering the mandatory nature of the decennial census. The ACLU somewhat sheepishly turned against the question, even if it was made optional. This merited coverage in the *New York Times*. Most effective, however, was the decision of the American Jewish Congress's president,

Israel Goldstein, to send a letter to newspapers across the country invoking James Madison's opposition to the "census of religions" and pointing out the inherent invasion of individual privacy the question would bring. (Leo Pfeffer actually wrote most of the letter, which Goldstein, as the AJC's president, signed.) Tens, if not hundreds, of newspapers ran this explanation: "Under Federal law, persons questioned by census takers are subject to conviction and imprisonment as criminals should they refuse to answer the census taker." By forcing people to divulge their religion, the letter said, the Bureau of the Census would infringe on the free exercise of religion.[26]

This constitutional objection was the key legal component of the American Jewish Congress's argument. It was a dubious argument, though, because the bureau only rarely convicted, much less imprisoned, anyone for refusing to answer a question, nor had it decided conclusively against making the question optional, nor did it see itself as placing undue pressure on individuals who did not have a religion or who were of a minority faith. Citing all these reasons, Burgess replied to Goldstein's arguments: "I do not believe . . . that the asking of a simple question on religious affiliation or preference constitutes interference with freedom of religion." He pointed out that many polling groups asked questions about religion and nobody complained. And, he argued, the problem would be minimized because the answers would remain confidential. Nonetheless, the constitutional objection became the pillar of the American Jewish Congress's official thinking.[27]

A second, more defensive reason involved fears of what the data would reveal about American Jewry. Rabbi S. H. Markowitz of Philadelphia expressed fears that "for the first time in our three century experience on this continent, an official government publication will contain information on Jewish income and occupation. . . . Do you want the following questions answered by no less an authority than the U.S. government? 1. What is the average Jewish income? 2. How many Jewish bankers are there in the U.S.? . . . 3. Where do Jews live?" Sociologist Marshall Sklare was concerned about "the problem of cross-tabulations," admitting that "the most sensitive [cross-tabulation] from our point of view would be running religion against income." A memo from the American Jewish Committee pointed out, "The possibilities for mischief of cross-tabulating religion and income are obvious." The wealth of American Jews, they worried, would revive gentiles' fears that Jews were planning to hoard American wealth in an effort to undermine Christian society just as society was beginning to lose its long-standing suspicions about Jews.[28]

A third, related motive for the Jewish community's staunch opposition was memories of Jewish persecution, both in the United States and especially in Germany and central Europe, which had led many Jewish leaders to fear revealing their precise location to authorities. Just fifteen years earlier, Franklin D. Roosevelt had claimed that "if there was a demagogue around here . . . to take up anti-Semitism, there could be more blood running in the streets of New York City than in Berlin." The depths of American antisemitism in the 1930s and early 1940s would hardly be forgotten by Jewish leaders of the 1950s. Dorothy Good, the earliest scholarly commentator on the Census Bureau's consideration of a question on religion, wrote in 1959 of Jewish fears that the gathering of religious information "might become the entering wedge for the kind of secret governmental files . . . that were detested features of the Nazi and Fascist regimes." Many Jews reported a purely "emotional reaction" against the question, one that led them to "search" for "reasons or rationalization" for their feelings. Those rationalizations "ran the gamut from: it wasn't good for the Jews to be numbered . . . [to] this was a movement involving church and state." All of these reasons led to a generalized feeling that one's religion should remain private.[29]

With hindsight, one can see a discrepancy between this rhetoric of fear and the decline of outward antisemitism in America in the late 1950s. Nevertheless, censuses have played a significant role in the long history of human rights abuses. Most famously, the Nazis had spent considerable energy developing statistical measures of Germany's population, which proved vital in their pernicious relocation efforts. Germans were early adopters of the Hollerith (IBM) counting machines, and Nazi statisticians had encouraged the development of increasingly sophisticated counting and sorting machines, many of which would eventually be used throughout the industrialized world. Other censuses facilitated abuse too, including those that identified Japanese Americans, Native Americans, and minorities in the Soviet Union. In light of this long history, American Jews had substantial reason for concern.[30]

Some Jewish organizations were sympathetic to the question's inclusion, particularly members of the National Jewish Welfare Board (NJWB), an umbrella organization that ministered to local Jewish community groups across the nation. The census data would have facilitated such groups' tasks of planting Jewish community centers and providing job assistance for Jews. Moreover, Jews had gained such social acceptance since World War II that some could not fathom the thought that the data would be used perniciously. "It is my feeling," said Sanford Solender, the director of the Jewish Center Division of the NJWB, "that in a democratic nation, in which difference is respected and the right of persons to enjoy such religious choices and affiliations as they desire is honored, it is entirely justified that information about such affiliation be deemed a normal part of the objective social data to be secured about the population through the regular Census." Affirming his confidence that the Census Bureau would keep the information confidential, Solender bluntly asserted that he did "not agree with the American Jewish

Congress' position . . . and [I] hope that their position will not unduly influence those who are determining the Census policy."[31]

Solender's opinion was never made public, mainly because of fears that American Jews would look weak if they divided on such a critical matter. When Solender made his pitch about supporting the question to Samuel D. Gershovitz, an executive of the NJWB, Gershovitz said, "I don't think we should come out [for the question] unless officially requested to do so by the U.S. Census Bureau—and then after consultation with our leadership . . . particularly in view of Am. Jewish Congress's opposition, as well as [that of] other civic defense agencies." He soon admitted, "The civic-defense agencies seem quite anxious on the subject—making it quite difficult for such an organization as ours to take a different position." Meanwhile, nearly all other major Jewish groups—the Anti-Defamation League of B'nai B'rith, the Union of American Hebrew Congregations, the American Jewish Committee, the Jewish National Community Relations Advisory Council, and the National Council for Statistics of Jews—came out publicly against the proposed question.[32]

Protestants were split on the matter. As the *Christian Century* said in 1957, because religion had become "hardly more than a matter of sociological identification in America," many Protestants were hard put to understand all the fuss about just "another automatized item punched on an ibm card."[33] Most liberal Protestants were lukewarm supporters of the question, although they were rarely in the forefront of the debate. Their typical argument was similar to that of the social scientists: they shared the humanistic belief that all knowledge is inherently good and that the question might reveal data useful for civic planners. As Burgess argued, "Providing objective information is one of the major means by which we can deal with the tendencies toward discrimination and group conflict." Following this argument, the United Christian Missionary Society, the Board of Home Missions of the Congregational and Christian Churches, the Board of National Missions of the Presbyterian Church, USA, and other liberal Protestant church groups came out in support of the measure. In this camp also resided Paul Blanshard, the famous critic of Catholicism, who, in the *New York Times*, voiced support for the census question because, he said, "church affiliation is an important social datum in American life. It has great social significance . . . [and] exact knowledge about church statistics" would be eminently valuable. His open support for the question aligned him with the Catholic Church and organizations associated with it, remarkable given the antipathy between him and American Catholicism throughout the 1940s and 1950s.[34]

Other religious groups tended to oppose inclusion of the question, usually warning of the potential inaccuracy of the data to be collected. Groups such as the Christian Scientists and Mormons were doctrinally opposed to outside tabulations of their members. Joining them in opposition were the General Conference of Seventh-Day

Adventists and some Baptist groups. With the exception of the Catholics, nearly every religious group that had experience of violent persecution in the United States came out against putting a question on religion in the 1960 census.[35]

The American Jewish Congress lobbied mainline Protestant groups to oppose the measure, with moderate success. The argument it made was not about the importance of separation of church and state but about religious privacy. In an October 30, 1957, article in the *Christian Century* entitled "Is It the Government's Business?" Leo Pfeffer argued that the question was "an unwarranted invasion" of the right of privacy. "Life would hardly be worth living," he wrote, "if man could not keep quiet when he wanted to . . . [F]orced speech no less than forced labor is slavery." The journal neither endorsed nor rejected Pfeffer's opinion, but the editors offered tacit support, suggesting that the only viable basis of opposition was "the mores of American life, which permit all religious matters to remain entirely private." These mores, however, were something new, or, if not new, then previously unarticulated.[36]

By late summer 1957, Jewish groups had clearly taken up the opposition, and Catholics had assumed the role of the proposal's most fervent supporters. Both lobbied the Protestant mainstream and urged their own flocks to make the public aware of their positions. The Catholic journal *Commonweal*, produced by laypeople, somewhat surprisingly came out against the question, proclaiming, in the face of heavy institutional Catholic opposition, that the "rights of conscience are sacrosanct, and this fact is of such paramount importance that it outweighs all the arguments in favor." Perhaps an understanding of religion as a private matter made more sense to Catholics outside clerical ranks than to those within it. *Commonweal* earned a sharp rebuke from the Reverend Joseph B. Schuyler, a Jesuit professor of sociology at Fordham University, who argued that the question was worthy of inclusion "since religious adherence is as much a factor in national socio-economic life as occupation, income, and national origin." The editors of *Commonweal* rebutted: "Even on purely pragmatic grounds, enough people are opposed to the question's inclusion to make us doubt that its results could possibly justify the religious dissension it is capable of arousing." *Commonweal*'s seeming inability to persuade its co-religionists proved how solid American Catholicism's institutional voice was in the 1950s.[37]

A "STAB IN THE BACK" TO CATHOLICS

Over the next few months, a vigorous battle sprawled across editorial pages throughout the country. The Bureau of the Census's regional offices were under orders to forward clippings about the debate to national headquarters, and more than one hundred such articles were collected in the summer of 1957. No consensus ever formed, and the positions of the NCWC and the American Jewish Congress only became more entrenched. A statewide survey performed by the *Minneapolis Tribune* revealed that one in three Minnesotans thought the inclusion of the question was a "good idea," while 22 percent thought it was a "poor idea."[38] Some bureau officials were skeptical about the wisdom of including the question because of the ACLU's change of position. If the question on religion was made optional, others worried about what would prevent other questions, such as the historically despised one on income, from becoming optional as well. A Justice Department opinion on this question would have helped, but the Justice Department rarely offered preliminary legal opinions, and to ask department officials to do so would be a delicate political maneuver that Burgess apparently was unwilling to perform.

In mid-October 1957, the American Jewish Congress became convinced that Census Bureau officials would not include the question if "they feel there is strong public opinion against the inclusion of such questions." In a final push to sway the Census Bureau, the American Jewish Congress directed its members to write the bureau, senators and representatives, clergymen, and local newspapers to express their opposition. The memo, in conjunction with the efforts of the American Jewish Committee and the Jewish Community Relations Council, was effective: American Jews bombarded their representatives in Washington. The question on religion seemed to be disrupting the progress of the decennial census.[39]

The tactic worked. By late November 1957, Burgess came to a conclusion: the matter was too touchy and the Jewish opposition was too persistent, so he would stop pushing for a question about religion in the 1960 census. Burgess had begun to sense that the debate had generated such a fierce dynamism that it might turn people against the entire 1960 census, and he was unwilling to take that risk. Taeuber hoped Burgess would delay a decision long enough for the results of the nationwide survey to become known. Taeuber thought the results would help generate support for the question by demonstrating the usefulness of the data. But Burgess did not wait. At his next staff meeting, Burgess announced his decision. He sought and received consensus from his staff.[40]

Taeuber and Burgess, both unhappy about the decision, went on the road to make the announcement in person to groups that had requested the question's inclusion. At a November 21 meeting of the Association of Statisticians of American Religious Bodies in Takoma Park, Maryland, Taeuber's obvious regret stifled most protest, save one Catholic voice who charged that the decision had been a "stab in the back." In explaining the reasoning behind the decision, Taeuber rejected the constitutional argument and claimed instead that the Jewish dissension had worked. Thomas Kenedy's notes from the meeting paraphrase Taeuber as saying, "In the minds of a considerable number of persons doubts exist as to the propriety of asking such a question. Therefore, to use the power of the Census would not be in the best public interest." The Census Bureau's final press release on the matter also pointed to the Jewish opposition without naming it. The release read in part: "At this time a considerable number of persons would be reluctant to answer such a question in the Census where a reply is mandatory. Under the circumstances it was not believed that the value of the statistics based on this question would be great enough to justify overriding such an attitude."[41]

Catholics were obviously upset. Cardinal Spellman wrote to the secretary of commerce, Sinclair Weeks, saying, "I wish to say that I do not agree with Mr. Burgess' conclusions, and if it is not too late, I would appreciate it very much if you will permit Archbishop O'Hara of Philadelphia to explain our views on the matter." But it was too late. The moment had passed.[42]

Demographers and sociologists were also upset. Several wrote the bureau to protest discarding the question, and even Business Week took the bureau to task. In 1959, sociologist Donald J. Bogue fumed that religion was not going to appear on the 1960 census even though "most sociologists consider religious affiliation a factor of paramount importance in explaining many aspects of human behavior." He compared religion to "educational attainment, occupation, and income" as "an axis around which much of a person's life is oriented," and he lamented that there would be no statistics because of "policy considerations." Even the American Jewish Year Book expressed frustration, claiming that "such an inquiry, although questioned under other grounds by the major Jewish community organizations, would have offered an excellent opportunity for the development of basic decennial estimates of Jewish population and other demographic details. Attention could then be placed on keeping these figures up-to-date between census years," rather than having to come up with the numbers de novo.[43]

Not everyone was dismayed. The American Jewish Congress's in-house article on the decision trumpeted its win with the title "A Victory for Religious Liberty." It unabashedly noted: "It is sobering to reflect that this invasion of a most sacred American freedom could have gone virtually unheeded had the American Jewish Congress not alerted the public to its true meaning." Israel Goldstein called the decision a "far-reaching victory for traditional American freedoms." The minutes of the American Jewish Congress's next executive committee meeting suggested that "Congress members should emphasize this victory in their membership campaign as an outstanding example of the important contributions which the Congress is steadily making in order to preserve religious liberty."[44]

Yet the debate did not conclude there. There was still another delicate matter to attend to, and here the newly developed principle of religious privacy triumphed yet again. Almost as soon as the decision not to include a question on religion in the 1960 census was announced, data from the gigantic March 1957 survey were finally tabulated and analyzed. Would the results prove that the American Jewish Congress had been correct in contending that the data would be useless for social planners and would instead provide fodder for America's antisemites? Or would the NCWC be proven correct in its assertion that the data would be useful to social planners and demonstrate the considerable Catholic power in the United States?

Knowing the results would be reviewed critically, Taeuber decided the bureau would publish two bulletins, one a short synopsis consisting of simple breakdowns by age, region, and rates of intermarriage, the other a more detailed study that cross-tabulated religion by income, occupation, residential patterns, and other potentially touchy social indicators. By making the first report a benign spread-sheet of uncorrelated data and putting almost all the correlative data in the second volume, Taeuber hoped to soften any offense the results might give.[45]

The first report, issued on February 2, 1958, emphasized the key finding that a great majority of Americans were willing to answer a question about religion. Taeuber had spread the sample over 330 areas that included 638 counties and some 40,000 dwelling units. Completed information was acquired from approximately 35,000 households. The data were then extrapolated through inferential statistical methods to create nationwide numbers.

The results were generally banal and expected. Two of every three people who were at least fourteen years old regarded themselves as Protestant, one of every four as Roman Catholic. A little more than 3 percent of the population claimed to be Jewish. A full 96 percent of Americans polled reported a religion. Less than 3 percent reported no religion (about 75 percent of those in the "no religion" category were men), and 1 percent made no report.[46]

Suggesting the importance of the three primary religious divisions in the postwar period, the survey found very little intermarriage across the divisional lines. "Among all married couples in which one partner was reported as Protestant, Roman Catholic, or Jewish, in ninety-four percent of the cases the other partner was reported in the same major group," it read. A random sample would have reported a match in only 54 percent of the marriages. The data, however, were marred by the bureau's failure to take account of those who had changed faiths to accommodate a spouse, making the bureau's data on intermarriage rather crude.[47]

The first report also noted the substantial presence of Catholics in the Northeast, still the cultural capital of the United States. In that region, Catholics constituted slightly more than 45 percent of the population. Protestants made up a little more than 42 percent. Jews were statistically overrepresented in the region too, constituting 8.5 percent of the population.[48]

Reactions to the first round of data were generally favorable. The bureau's chief statistician was asked to present parts of the information to the American Sociological Association. Notes of congratulations poured in. Demographers, sociologists, and culture watchers were eager for the second report. With the correlative data, demographers felt, the United States would be well on its way to obtaining a greater understanding of the religious sociology of its nation.

To their great frustration, though, the second report would never see the light of day. In late May 1958, nearly four months after the release of the first report and just as the second report was about to go to press, renewed opposition suddenly emerged. First, some Jews began to question the reliability of the bureau's data. Because Jews constituted only slightly more than 3 percent of the population, the statistical variability involved in sampling might easily produce errors, they argued. They also pointed out that the report had incorporated important Protestant denominations into the "Other Protestant" category, thus insulating groups such as the Episcopalians and the Mormons from the results of cross-tabulations. Those two groups, as the Jewish statistician H. S. Linfield pointed out, were similar in size to the Jewish group. Why should they be left out of the cross-tabulations? "In this procedure," Linfield said, "we see a complete denial of the principle of equal treatment of all religious groups in government records, and a threat to the liberties of all religious groups."[49]

This argument almost certainly masked other areas of disenchantment—the bureau, after all, prided itself on the soundness of its data, and in general it had good reason to do so. In a letter to the bureau, a rabbi from Pennsylvania spelled out the Jews' concerns more clearly. The first volume was "bad enough," he said, but the second volume, which will give statistics on "how many Jewish barbers, their average income, places where Jews live . . . etc., etc.," will be "much worse." "I am sure you realize how such information could be used by various propaganda agencies and by groups of anti-semites who have been producing scurrilous enough material without having the actual statistical figures to pervert and misuse," he said. This letter was a representative example of Jewish opinions expressed to the bureau.[50]

The timing of this second wave of opposition coincided almost exactly with the proposed release of the second volume. Although Jewish groups had been against the release of the data since at least January, in April they realized that it wasn't their constitutional argument that had persuaded Burgess to remove the question on religion from consideration but their vocal dissent. Adapting and broadening this tactic, several Jewish leaders called a meeting on May 5, 1958, bringing together like-minded Jewish and non-Jewish groups to forge a letter-writing campaign protesting the data's release, all while citing the new principle of religious privacy. Christian Scientists responded, as did some Baptists, the ACLU, and the

Religious Liberty Association, a nondenominational group that promoted the free practice of religion while fighting any incursion from the state. This tactic got the attention of several members of Congress, including Representative Abraham J. Multer of New York (an active Jew) and Senator Wallace F. Bennett of Utah (a prominent Mormon).[51]

Delayed by rewriting, a final draft of the census bureau's second volume was sent to the Commerce Department's Office of Public Information in late April. As it was being reviewed there, the assistant secretary of commerce, Frederick H. Mueller, heard about the renewed rancor and requested all the correspondence concerning the reports. Because the Bureau of the Census is part of the Commerce Department, all decisions about releasing further material required Mueller's approval.[52]

Then the report languished. Two months later, an anxious Burgess finally received a letter from Mueller. After consultation with the secretary of commerce himself, Mueller decided "it would not be feasible to publish any more statistics of this nature." The report, he declared, would never be released. A stunned Burgess recognized that this represented the first time a completed Census Bureau report would be withheld from the public because of political concerns, and he contended that his bosses had given in to "demagogic pressure." He considered taking the matter to President Eisenhower himself. He was a friend of the president's pastor, Dr. Edward L. R. Elson, who had preached on the importance of the data, and Burgess thought he could win the president's ear through Elson. Mueller told Burgess that the president was well aware of the matter through Senator Bennett, the Mormon alerted when the Jewish groups sought "like-minded others" to help their cause. According to Mueller, the decision not to release the report was made in consultation not only with the secretary of commerce but also with the White House.[53]

Burgess was flummoxed by the White House's action. To those who inquired about the "missing" data, he wrote, "While we may not agree with some of the interpretations, nevertheless it appeared wise not to override the strongly held views of a considerable number of people." When Jewish groups applauded the decision to ban the second report, Burgess reminded them that Israel included a question on religion in its census.[54]

The American Sociological Association passed a resolution protesting "this suppression of reliable statistical information." The chairman of its Social Statistics Committee judged it a "dangerous principle" for the government to acquiesce to pressure groups. "We would like to believe that the American public is not afraid of facts and that all groups in the population will in the long run be benefited by more accurate information," he wrote. The suppression of the data was starkly visible when the bureau's chief statistician repeatedly had to answer "no comment" to questions he received after giving a necessarily abbreviated paper on the data at the American Sociological Association national convention. The acclaimed sociologist William Petersen, of the University of California at Berkeley, wrote:

> The principal argument for including a question on religion in the census, in short, is the humanist one that knowledge is good, and more complete and accurate knowledge is better. Religion is not only a personal experience and a sacred theology; it is also a social institution. As such, it should not be protected from empirical research and analysis by a high wall of magical taboos. I know of no other instance in its long and honorable record when data actually assembled by the Census Bureau were suppressed. This morally disturbing, possibly even illegal, act would be inconceivable with respect to statistics on any other subject.[55]

But the subject was religion. What would have emerged had the report been released? Nobody can say for certain because the report has since disappeared, perhaps destroyed after the debate. The National Archives, the Library of Congress, the archives of the Bureau of the Census, and the Department of Commerce libraries all have removed or destroyed any information about the "missing" data. Fortunately, in 1967 Congress passed the Freedom of Information Act, and at least one scholar, the Brown University sociologist Sidney Goldstein, obtained the tabulations (not the completed report) from the federal government. Ignoring much of the controversy, Goldstein published an article on the data in 1969 in the *American Journal of Sociology*.[56]

The data reveal few surprises to scholars knowledgeable about the sociology of midcentury religion. Jews on average obtained more schooling and had higher incomes than Protestants or Catholics. Catholics brought up the rear in both those categories. More than three-fourths of Jewish men were white-collar workers, while about a third of Catholic and Protestant men were. Perhaps the most surprising statistics were that Catholics were consistently below the national average in marriage rates in every age group and that on average they had fewer children than Protestants. This contradicts the widely held notion that Catholics married at a younger age and had larger families than members of other religious groups. It is, however, difficult to draw conclusions about any particular group from the data because the report reveals a snapshot of the population at a single time and not a collection of information that shows change over time. As Andrew M. Greeley, Marshall Sklare, and others were soon to show, the dynamics of American Catholicism and American Judaism were undergoing dramatic changes in postwar America, and without correlative data on either chronological end of the 1957 tabulations, the census data do not provide much information about the transitions those groups were experiencing.[57]

JEWISH POWER AND RELIGIOUS PRIVACY

Twice, then, postwar Jews powerfully influenced the debate about the U.S. Census, each time using a different tactic, each time relying on the right to religious privacy. In the first case, they created mass pressure that made large swaths of the population resist the census as a whole; in the second, they targeted influential lawmakers from other minority faiths in order to gain influence at the highest levels.[58] Catholics failed in the census debate because they would have had to prove that the question would not be divisive—something American Jews would not allow them to do. To the Jewish defense agencies, religion was an entirely private matter, operating strictly within the realm of the individual or the group. This stress on individual privacy is somewhat typical for a minority group concerned about its status in a particular culture. But there is something almost tragicomic about the response of American Jews to the census debate and their declaration that freedom of religion meant freedom from being asked what their religion was. They were concerned about any proposal that might enable someone to make a broad objective statement about Jews in America. Nonetheless, the issue sheds light on Jews' public struggles to create a more pluralistic mainstream. The assertion of Leo Pfeffer and others that true religious pluralism required a nonreligious or at least nondenominational public sphere may have appeared hysterical at times, but it was part of a genuine effort to formulate what pluralism might look like in the American nation.

Catholics, meanwhile, viewed religion as not only a spiritual matter but also a public, communal, and even political phenomenon. That view led them to embrace the politicization of the census debate. They had stakes in the demonstration of their numerical power and of their loyal, long-standing presence as a significant minority group in the United States, which would, they hoped, curtail the impression they were inherently attracted to authoritarianism. During the census debate, the Jesuit sociologist Joseph B. Schuyler wondered, "Have you ever stopped to consider what a religious affiliation census . . . could contribute to the potential self-knowledge of every parish and diocese? . . . I would suggest that this is not a matter of separation of Church and State . . . but of completely democratic community preference." If certain communities sought to retain their unique identities, why should they not be allowed to do so? And why should they not be allowed to do so with the best information possible? Schuyler was suggesting the inevitability of the persistence of minority groups, and he thought knowledge about them might help America accept its inevitable pluralism.[59]

To sociologists and demographers, meanwhile, religion was a social phenomenon comparable to ethnicity, race, or class. That idea was reflected in their desire to have, for the first time in American history, pertinent and reliable information on American religious groupings, the same goal that drove Will Herberg to write *Protestant-Catholic-Jew*. To them, it was a basic fact that Jews tended to socialize with other Jews, Catholics with other Catholics. Why not account for it with the most powerful statistical tool of them all?[60] The fact that the Bureau of the Census disaggregated nearly all of its data into the three categories of Protestant, Catholic, and Jew suggests the cohesiveness that the bureau assumed each group to have. Judging by the census categories, Mormons were a species of Protestant, albeit a unique and identifiable one. Similarly, evangelicals were, as a social category, nonexistent.

In addition to all this, religion was supposed to be a great unifier in Cold War America. Most Protestants viewed it that way, which was why so many of them were concerned about Catholic divisiveness and Jewish claims to privacy. As the *Christian Century* had put it in 1951 when it published a long editorial entitled "Pluralism—A National Menace," with religious pluralism now threatening "the basic concepts upon which American democracy is founded," the worry was that America would "have no common will . . . [which] makes for national instability." In the end, they feared, America would be "vulnerable to communist propaganda" because religious minorities did not want to continue to acquiesce in the de facto Protestantism of American life. If discrimination was wrong, so was divisiveness, and it was uncertain how a census of religion might affect that balance.[61]

In the end, the debate about the census played out according to each group's understanding of its power interests, with Catholics seeing the census question as a possible enhancement to their standing, Jews seeing it as a threat to theirs, and mainline Protestants feeling unthreatened. The debate also highlights the parameters of Tri-Faith America. As Burgess repeatedly emphasized, the question was under consideration not because he or Taeuber wanted to assist religious groups but because of "the belief that religious groupings represent one of the major underlying social factors in American life."[62]

In Tri-Faith America, with each of the three religious groups vying to enact its vision of a pluralist nation, the argument for religious privacy had certain merits, foremost among them that pluralism would not be infringed by the government and that small religious minorities would not be subjected to perpetual denigration backed by the power of official statistics. Somewhat ironically, then, religion was to be a private matter in a nation that celebrated its religious pluralism.

8

From Creed to Color: Softening the Ground for the Civil Rights Movement

___

ON JANUARY 14, 1963, 657 clergymen representing Protestant, Catholic, and Jewish faiths gathered at the Edgewater Beach Hotel in Chicago for the first-ever National Conference on Religion and Race. Luminaries such as Paul Tillich, Abraham Heschel, Morris Adler, Sargent Shriver, and Albert Cardinal Meyer of Chicago mingled together in the hotel's hallways. The writer from *Ebony* said the conference "looked like a living Who's Who of the Religious World."[1] President John F. Kennedy opened proceedings with a written statement urging the tri-faith leaders to make concrete the ideals of the interracial conference, thereby releasing "the spirit and power of all the citizens of the United States."[2] Martin Luther King Jr., in a riveting final-day speech, labeled the conference "the most significant and historic [convention] ever held for attacking racial injustice." He concluded by saying:

> The churches and synagogues have an opportunity and a duty to lift up their voices like a trumpet and declare unto the people the immorality of segregation. We must affirm that every human life is a reflex of divinity, and every act of injustice mars and defaces the image of God in man. The undergirding philosophy of segregation is diametrically opposed to the undergirding philosophy of our Judeo-Christian heritage and all the dialectics of the logicians cannot make them lie down together.[3]

In King's words, the theological common ground that emerged in Tri-Faith America and that had positioned "Judeo-Christianity" at the center of American moral authority underscored the importance of individual equality in God's eyes, and thus mandated an end to racial segregation. He was directly tapping into tri-faith rhetoric and, he knew, was engaging an audience accustomed to vouching for the benefits of pluralism and therefore receptive to claims of equality. Other civil rights leaders at the conference and elsewhere did exactly the same thing; indeed, by providing a language and an audience, the image of Tri-Faith America helped make possible the civil rights movement of the 1960s. Somewhat ironically, though, the use of the tri-faith rhetoric by civil rights activists also marked the decline of Tri-Faith America, as other, nonreligious divisions seemed more significant than those between Protestants, Catholics, and Jews. A key year in this transition from creed to color was 1963, and a key event in 1963 was the National Conference on Religion and Race.

THE NATIONAL CONFERENCE ON RELIGION AND RACE

Mathew "Mat" Ahmann was the reason the conference happened. In the summer of 1962, Ahmann, who had helped found the National Catholic Conference for Interracial Justice in 1960, approached Rabbi Philip Hiatt of the Synagogue Council of America and Reverend J. Oscar Lee of the National Council of Churches with the idea for a tri-faith conference on interracial justice. African American civil rights was clearly emerging as a national issue, and America's three prominent religious groups had yet to come together to show unified concern. When Hiatt and Lee agreed to participate, Ahmann encouraged the National Catholic Welfare Conference to join as the third sponsor. Ahmann became secretary for planning and organization, and made sure his name was significantly less visible than those of the three major religious organizations.[4]

Ahmann hoped the presence of the three groups would make it clear the civil rights movement was not just a political or social movement but also a moral one. If the religious organizations representing the largest factions of each faith came out in support of civil rights, the demands made by civil rights leaders would certainly become broader and more powerful nationally. During his speech at the conference, Rabbi Abraham Heschel, the nation's preeminent Jewish theologian, said, "We are here because of the faith of a 33-year-old Catholic layman. I want him to come to the stage." When Ahmann came to the stage, Heschel pulled Ahmann's head down and kissed him on the head, provoking the audience to rise in applause.[5]

Ahmann timed the event to coincide with the one hundredth anniversary of the Emancipation Proclamation, and the mostly white conferees, some of whom had been fighting for civil rights for decades in organizations such as the Federal Council of Churches, the American Jewish Congress, or the National Catholic Welfare Conference, could not believe they had been so blind to the enormity of the problem. Together, they "acknowledged the collective guilt of the religious bodies in America; guilt for malpractice which contributed to the climate which produced the Civil War; guilt for the racial abuses still found in religious bodies; and even more, they acknowledged the massive fear of positive action to open our society so that every man is accepted by every other man"—at least so said the joint "Appeal to the Conscience of the American People," ratified and released on the final day of the conference.[6] An internal report written after the event claimed, "The mood of the Conference can be described with three adjectives: serious, self-critical, committed," adding, "Never before have I seen a delegate group as filled with the spirit of *mea culpa*. It took courage for such a group to so flagellate themselves before the entire world and before those whom they had so deeply wronged."[7]

This was the first time Abraham Heschel met Martin Luther King Jr., sparking a friendship that lasted until King's death. In his speech at the conference, Heschel argued that divisions, be they denominational or racial, were not within the controlling spirit of religion. "Religion and race," he began. "How can the two be uttered together? To act in the spirit of religion is to unite what lies apart, to remember that humanity as a whole is God's beloved child. To act in the spirit of race is to sunder, to slash, to dismember the flesh of living humanity. . . . Perhaps this conference should have been called Religion *or* Race. You cannot worship God and at the same time look at a man as if he were a horse." Reflecting on the events that prompted the conference, Heschel said, "It was easier for the children of Israel to cross the Red Sea than for a Negro to cross certain university campuses."[8]

Jews were not alone in the self-flagellation. The Very Reverend Monsignor John J. Egan, director of the Archdiocesan Conservation Council of Chicago and heavily involved in issues of social justice, said in his speech, "If there is one underlying theme which unites Catholics, Protestants, and Jews, it is the belief in a personal God to whom we all have the obligation to give witness; and in the essentially related belief that all men, as special creatures of God, possess a unique dignity by virtue of their creation. This notion of kinship in God is so deeply embedded in the tradition of all our faiths that it cannot be rejected without at the same time rejecting our place in the community of the Judaeo-Christian faithful." For a Catholic priest to so clearly connect his faith to others was fairly remarkable, although not unprecedented. But in Egan's eyes, the demands of the civil rights movement supplanted the importance of religious divisions. They demanded that "Judeo-Christian morality" live up to its central unifying feature: that all men were "special creatures of God" with "a unique dignity by virtue of their creation." After cataloguing the assorted historical challenges to the "Judaeo-Christian tradition" during the previous hundred years, from Marx to Spencer to authoritarianism, Egan charged: "It is the people of God who alone bear the responsibility for racial intolerance. . . . Neither the Jew nor the Christian can escape it. He can only fulfill it, or fail at it; and failing at it, he bears false witness not only to his neighbor, but to God."[9] To reject the ideals of Judeo-Christianity was to disavow God.

Catholic participation at the conference abounded. In attendance were the head of the archdiocese of Chicago, Albert Cardinal Meyer (who had just returned from the first session of the Ecumenical Council in Rome, which later would be called Vatican II), and several of American Catholicism's "most renowned prelates," who participated "on a simple delegate level, often sitting in workgroups, forums, [and] plenary sessions unnamed and with no regard to rank." This was not about Catholic status but about the moral wrong that was racial segregation. Non-Catholics saw this and hoped the issue of race might bring about a greater "thaw" in relations between Catholics and non-Catholics. "Perhaps such optimism is premature," said one Jewish observer, "but it is possible that a fresh wind is beginning to blow through the atmosphere of inter-religious relations. Certainly in the area of race relations, communities can expect increased Catholic participation."[10]

The civil rights movement thus was diminishing the importance of divisions between Protestants, Catholics, and Jews. Franklin H. Littell, a Protestant church historian at the Chicago Theological Seminary, admitted in his speech, "The fact that [the conference] represents Protestant-Catholic and Christian-Jewish cooperation is *almost* as important as the theme itself." Most of Littell's speech concerned the previous decades' movement to overcome Protestant hegemony in the name of religious pluralism, which set in motion what he saw as an almost teleological pattern of social acceptance, with African Americans next in line. During the two decades following World War II, Littell said, "the Catholic community has emerged from its minority-consciousness to a status of parity in the new multi-faith complex. So have the Jews." By 1963 the spotlight had turned to African Americans. "The old America of white, rural and Protestant dominance is dying," said Littell, a white Protestant. To those in the majoritarian position, "either they can accept the logic of a voluntaristic and pluralistic situation . . . or they can end up as embittered and negative minorities which the course of history has passed by." The United States, Littell said, was now a place of tolerance, a place where pluralism had become cemented to the national image. White Protestant monism was dead.[11]

Littell's speech received acclaim not only for its vigor but also for arguing that "the most useful and relevant contribution the churches could make to racial justice would be . . . to become truly the Church—disciplined as a community of witnesses, loving in service to the Least Brother, intercessory for the helpless and defenseless." Heretofore, American Protestantism had built defensive walls instead of bridges. Now it needed to translate what it had learned in Tri-Faith America to the African American civil rights struggle.[12]

In his rousing concluding speech, King rallied the mostly white audience to take action in this world rather than waiting for the next, spelling out what America's churches and synagogues could do "to face the challenges of this day." These included stressing the importance of the individual in the grand tradition of Judeo-Christianity, preaching from the pulpit the nonbiblical character of segregation, and pointing out that all race hate is "based on fears, suspicions, and misunderstandings, usually groundless." These were all familiar tropes in Tri-Faith America, which, many conferees were beginning to realize, was an overwhelmingly white conception. King then challenged the group:

> Men everywhere and at all times will know that our Judeo-Christian faith transformed the jangling discords of America into a beautiful symphony of brotherhood. In a real sense this conference has been a blessing. Never before have the major faiths come together to grapple with the tragic problem of race and color prejudice. The fact that such an historic conference is being held may be indicative of a greater sensitivity to racial injustice on the part of the Church and the Synagogue. For four days now, we have dwelled in this sun-lit mountain of transfiguration. We have listened to eloquent words flowing from the lips of Christian and Jewish statesmen. . . . And now the valley of injustice, with all of its ghettos, economic inequities and demoralized children of God, stands before us in grim stark, and colossal dimensions. . . . Will we march only to the music of time, or will we, risking criticism and abuse, march only to the soul-saving music of eternity? More than ever before we are today challenged by the words of yesterday, "Be not conformed to this world: but be ye transformed by the renewing of your minds."[13]

To make his point, King strategically tapped into the religious language of Tri-Faith America ("Judeo-Christian faith," "brotherhood," "come together") and the sympathy manifested by the acknowledged pluralism in the tri-faith vision ("the Church and the Synagogue," "Christian and Jewish statesmen").

Uplifted by King's words, the conferees approved "An Appeal to the Conscience of the American People." It began, "We Americans of all religious faiths have been slow to recognize that racial discrimination and segregation are an insult to God, the Giver of human dignity and human rights. Even worse, we all have participated

in perpetuating racial discrimination and segregation in civil, political, industrial, social and private life. And worse still, in our houses of worship, our religious schools, hospitals, welfare institutions, and fraternal organizations we
have often failed our own religious commitments." After asking the forgiveness
of God for these sins, the religious leaders asked the forgiveness of "our brothers,
whose rights we have ignored and whose dignity we have offended." It concluded:
"We affirm our common religious commitment to the essential dignity and
equality of all men under God. . . . We dedicate ourselves to work together to
make this commitment a vital factor in our total life." In essence, the conference
was simply including race in the concept of the brotherhood of man under the
Fatherhood of God.[14]

Repeatedly (and incorrectly) hailing the conference as "the first time that official
spokesmen of the nation's three major religious organizations have met on a social
issue," the press followed the event closely.[15] Having religious leaders of the three
major American faiths—representing, the newspapers said, more than a hundred
million Americans—speak openly about racial inequality lent gravity to the civil
rights movement, signifying that it was a moral problem engulfing the entire nation. Chicago newspapers vigorously covered the event, and several television
channels moved popular programs to air four and a half hours of the conference's
speeches.[16] The African American newspaper the *Chicago Defender* hailed the conference as "the most ambitious attempt yet to galvanize America's religious bodies
into effective action on racial problems," but cautioned, "How much action they
will stimulate remains to be seen."[17]

To promote the conference's ideals, the conferees adopted ten "pilot cities" to
focus continued efforts.[18] In each city, members of the three prominent religious
communities convened conferences, petitioned local lawmakers regarding open
housing and fair employment, attempted to integrate various religious schools,
and encouraged dialogue and integration.[19] Taking cues from the national conference, the newly formed Chicago Conference on Race and Religion, for instance,
demanded that all religiously related fraternal groups eliminate discriminatory
practices and that churches and synagogues refuse free land from home devel-
opers who discriminated. It asked participants to petition the federal government
to cease subsidizing segregated hospitals, schools, and institutions of higher education. It encouraged changes to textbooks in both religious and public schools.
Protestants, Catholics, and Jews were to travel throughout Chicago demanding
structural changes in order to alter a profound moral problem.[20]

In some ways, this was the Tolerance Trio all over again, with racial harmony
now supplanting religious amity as the principal goal. As such, the NCCJ saw an
opportunity to show that its thirty-five years of experience could benefit the newly

recognized national cause. In a memo sent to the leaders of local NCCJ branches in each of the ten pilot cities, the national NCCJ office passed along a form letter local officials could send to those motivated by the National Conference on Religion and Race. The NCCJ should, the cover letter stressed, demonstrate "what we have to offer: know-how, materials, and programs." Local leaders should stress that their experience qualified them to help promote tolerance.

There was, however, a good bit of fear in the letter too. The NCCJ seemed worried that its fight for interreligious harmony was being demoted in importance in American life. "I am distressed," said Gordon W. Lovejoy, an NCCJ official, "by the long-term implications to NCCJ programming and fund-raising if we are not *actively* involved in efforts being made by Catholic, Protestant and Jewish clergymen who are working at the greatest moral and civil challenge of our day—religion and race."[21] Even at the height of the civil rights movement, the NCCJ could not let go of the notion that racial and religious equality were equal challenges in postwar America. Nevertheless, the NCCJ offered its services to the cause, while suggesting that it had long been active in the push for civil rights.

The NCCJ's interest in adapting to changing times clearly demonstrates the decline of the perceived social importance of religious identities by the early 1960s.[22] It also showed that some of the lessons of Tri-Faith America had softened the ground for the civil rights movement by creating a language civil rights leaders could tap into and by making American pluralism an accepted part of the nation's identity. Most Americans had readily accepted their nation's Judeo-Christian underpinnings as well as the fact of their nation's pluralism; going back to "native, white, Protestant" superiority was hardly realistic. The NCCJ was right to see itself being marginalized by a different cause by 1963. But in some ways, that marginalization was a result of the fact that its mission had succeeded.

A LANGUAGE TO TAP INTO

At the National Conference on Religion and Race, the three African American civil rights leaders invited to speak each discussed, underscored, preached on, lionized, and heralded the values of brotherhood, the importance of the individual in God's eyes, and the sacrilege of unbrotherly hatred. They made civil rights a religious cause, perfectly suited to the ears of the tri-faith audience. Benjamin Mays, chairman of the conference, mentor to Martin Luther King Jr., and president of Morehouse College in Atlanta, told the conferees: "It matters much what happens to the soul of America, to our democracy, and to our Judeo-Christian faith. If these lights go out, may God have mercy on our souls. If we cannot build the brotherhood of man in the United States I despair of its ever being built anywhere in the world."[23]

These concepts had been a vital part of nearly all the rhetoric in the 1960s civil rights movement. While various movements for African American civil rights had in the past unsuccessfully utilized the language of secular equality (Communism in the 1920s and 1930s) and labor rights (A. Philip Randolph and his peers in the 1930s and 1940s), the most successful civil rights language was that borrowed from Tri-Faith America in the 1950s and 1960s.[24] Toward the end of his "Letter from Birmingham Jail," for instance, Martin Luther King Jr., wrote: "One day the South will know that when these disinherited children of God sat down at lunch counters, they were in reality standing up for what is best in the American dream and for the most sacred values in our Judaeo-Christian heritage, thereby bringing our nation back to those great wells of democracy which were dug deep by the founding fathers in their formulation of the Constitution and the Declaration of Independence."[25] In 1956, King imagined himself as Apostle Paul, writing a letter to American Christians. He lambasted Protestants for their sectarianism ("This narrow sectarianism is destroying the unity of the Body of Christ. You must come to see that God is neither a Baptist nor a Methodist; He is neither a Presbyterian nor a Episcopalian. God is bigger than all of our denominations. If you are to be true witnesses for Christ, you must come to see that America"). He criticized Roman Catholicism for its pride ("I am disturbed about any church that refuses to cooperate with other churches under the pretense that it is the only true church. I must emphasize the fact that God is not a Roman Catholic, and that the boundless sweep of his revelation cannot be limited to the Vatican. Roman Catholicism must do a great deal to mend its ways"). And he emphasized the unity demanded by a broader understanding of God ("I must say to you, as I have said to so many Christians before, that in Christ 'there is neither Jew nor Gentile, there is neither bond nor free, there is neither male nor female, for we are all one in Christ Jesus.' Moreover, I must reiterate the words that I uttered on Mars Hill: 'God that made the world and all things therein . . . hath made of one blood all nations of men for to dwell on all the face of the earth')."[26] King's approach, true to his ministerial roots, was religious. And while the religion he was preaching was Protestant, the words he used were well within the mold of American Judeo-Christianity.

Even civil rights leaders critical of mainstream religion drew from the rhetorical well of the tri-faith concept. James Lawson wrote in the original "Statement of Purpose" for the Student Non-Violent Coordinating Committee (SNCC): "The philosophical or religious ideal of nonviolence [is] the foundation of our purpose, the presupposition of our faith, and the manner of our action." This faith, he wrote, grew "from Judaic-Christian traditions" and sought "a social order of justice permeated by love."[27] John L. Lewis, SNCC's most effective leader, suggested the Judeo-Christian tradition led in another direction:

> I think that somewhere in the history of Judeo-Christian tradition is the idea that there can be no salvation without the shedding of blood and there may be some truth in that. Personally, though, I now accept the philosophy of non-violence . . . but I think that when we accept non-violence, we don't say it is the absence of violence. We say it is the present assumption—much more positive—that there might be the shedding of blood. You know what Gandhi says: If I had the personal choice to make between no movement and a violent movement, I would choose a violent movement.

A cursory knowledge of the Bible (or of Reinhold Niebuhr) affirms Lewis's point that "Judeo-Christianity" can be leveraged in both violent and nonviolent directions. Either way, Judeo-Christianity was the accepted bedrock of American morality.[28]

As early as 1957, *Time* noticed the power of Martin Luther King Jr.'s argument for civil rights, not because of its eloquence but because of its Judeo-Christian foundation. In a cover story, written shortly after King's successful Montgomery bus boycott, *Time* described King's argument: "Christian love can bring brotherhood on earth. There is an element of God in every man. No matter how low one sinks into racial bigotry, he can be redeemed." If one were to select a few of the most valued phrases in Tri-Faith America, one could hardly do better than preaching "brotherhood" or affirming that "there is an element of God in every man." According to *Time*, King "struck where an attack was least expected, and where it hurt more: at the South's Christian conscience."[29]

Southern civil rights activists, both black and white, drove this point home. At the Southeastern Regional Methodist Student Conference in Virginia, a group of thirty-seven college students and counselors wrote a letter to Virginia governor Thomas Stanley saying the U.S. Supreme Court's recent 1954 decision in *Brown v. Board of Education* was "in keeping with the spirit of democracy and Christianity and should not be side-stepped in any way." Others claimed more flatly that "segregation is un-Christian." The Southern Baptist Convention proclaimed *Brown* to be "in harmony with the constitutional guarantee of equal freedom to all citizens, and with the Christian principles of equal justice and love for all men."[30] Students arrested in Lynchburg, Virginia, for staging a 1961 sit-in defended their action by saying: "We have taken seriously the most basic principles of our Judeo-Christian heritage. . . . These, we believe, represent a Higher law than the law of governments."[31]

Southern church leaders supportive of segregation were at a loss about what to do about the usurpation of the religious high ground. If they chose to attack the religious ideals of the civil rights movement, they either argued that the ideal of worldly brotherhood was unbiblical, a fantasy dreamed up by northern sociologists, or that desegregation ultimately would lead to miscegenation, which was, in their view, unbiblical. In a widely circulated 1954 sermon called "Integration or Segregation?" the Reverend James F. Burks of Bayview Baptist Church in Norfolk, Virginia, argued that because God had created earthly divisions by language, race, sex, and more, humans should not strive to overcome them. The biblical ideal of brotherhood was meant to be spiritual, not physical, and humans who sought to create it on earth were not only fools but ungodly. "If integration of races is based upon the contention that men are all 'one in Christ,'" he said, "then the foundation is not secure. The idea of 'Universal Fatherhood of God and Brotherhood of Man' is MAN'S concoction and contradicts the Word of God." Burks added: "Those who are 'one in Christ' are such through a spiritual union and certainly not physical."[32]

Clearly one specter residing beneath the fear was interracial sex and marriage. As one parent wrote in a letter to Virginia governor Stanley after the *Brown* decision, if schools were integrated, "in less than ten years we will face the problem of intermarriage." Another said: "Having attended my beloved little county church from infancy I believe I know the fundamentals of the teachings of God's Holy Word. . . . [N]owhere can I find anything to convince me that God intended us living together as one big family in schools, churches and other public places." And another: "I believe that the integration of the races in our public schools will result in intermarriage of the negro and white races, and I am sure that the NAACP will next try to have the law repealed prohibiting intermarriage of the two races. I believe that the Lord would have made us all one color if he had intended that we be one race."[33]

But civil rights activists would not concede the high ground. They insisted that struggles for brotherhood could not be divided between the spiritual and physical worlds. They demonstrated that segregation (as opposed to slavery) was not to be found anywhere in the Bible. When Martin Luther King Jr. organized the 1965 civil rights march in Selma, Alabama, "clergy of all faiths"—ministers, priests, and rabbis—answered his call. Once the rhetoric of Tri-Faith America had been marshaled in the cause, the tri-faith character of the civil rights movement was irresistible.[34]

CREATING A BROAD WHITE ACCEPTANCE OF AMERICAN PLURALISM

In 1964, sociologist Milton Gordon remarked on the extent to which almost all Americans had embraced pluralism. In his landmark work *Assimilation in American Life*, Gordon defined pluralism as "the *right* of ethnic groups [broadly understood] to maintain some degree of cultural difference and some degree of ethnic communality, [while seeing] this cultural variation as essentially beneficial for American culture as a whole."[35] To his surprise, the main group resisting pluralism in 1964 was not former power holders in American life but African Americans. "They do not envisage the retention of a Negro subcommunity with its own institutions as a desirable long-range goal for Negroes in the United States," he wrote. He quickly noted that Malcolm X and the Black Muslims would disagree with this sentiment, as would a small contingent of African American groups interested in African culture. But mainline African Americans were hesitant about any sort of particularism. To Gordon, this was understandable considering the role segregation had played in the African American past and because "their ties to their various ancestral cultures are extremely tenuous or nonexistent."[36]

For everyone else, however, pluralism was the new national mode, and the chief advocates, noted Gordon, were Catholics, Jews, and sympathetic Protestants. "America has become," Gordon wrote, "a national entity of Protestants, Catholics, and Jews—where membership in, or identificational allegiance to, one or the other of these three great faiths is the norm, and where the legitimacy of the institutional presence and ramifications of this presence of the three denominations is routinely honored in American public opinion."[37] Gordon cited Herberg's *Protestant-Catholic-Jew* often, but he was careful not to advocate on behalf of Herberg's "triple melting pot" theory, favoring instead the more complicated notion that "American society has come to be composed of a number of 'pots,' or subsocieties, three of which are the religious containers marked Protestant, Catholic, and Jew, which are in the process of melting down the white nationality background communities contained within them; others are racial groups which are not allowed to melt structurally; and still others are substantial remnants of the national background communities manned by those members who are either of the first generation, or who, while native born, choose to remain within the ethnic enclosure." He labeled the process one of a "multiple melting pot," bringing about "the 'pluralism' which characterized the contemporary American scene." Pluralism was the new way in which the nation understood itself.[38]

Sociologists such as Gordon had noted the new mood for at least a decade. In 1956, Horace Kallen, one the nation's leading observers of American pluralism, wrote that since World War II "Americanism seeking a cultural monism was challenged and is slowly and unevenly being displaced by Americanization, supporting, cultivating a cultural pluralism." To Kallen, the very image of America had changed since the battle with totalitarianism, and the new image was one of a tolerant and pluralist nation.[39] Along similar lines, in 1954 Nathan Glazer affirmed the widespread acceptance of the pluralistic nature of American life, suggesting that since World War II group identities had transformed from being "national cultures" to becoming part of a pluralistic American ideology.[40] In all their work in the 1950s, sociologists such as Gordon Allport, George E. Simpson, J. Milton Yinger, George R. Stewart, Stewart G. Cole, and Mildred Wiese Cole made similar claims, pointing out the growing number of Americans willing to embrace the idea that the nation was a pluralistic place.[41] When the civil rights movement arose in the 1960s, many Americans had already rejected the monistic understanding of the country.

No group was more adamant about its role in getting American society to recognize its inherent pluralism than the National Conference of Christians and Jews. As early as 1955, the NCCJ was congratulating itself for having helped make the dominant image of the nation less centered on its white Protestant heritage, asserting, "The [NCCJ's] strong moral cleansing action, deriving chiefly from religious motivation and frank discussion of the once hush-hush problems of prejudice, has been an important factor in removing some of the worst areas of discrimination from life in the United States."[42] The NCCJ pointed out that 1952 was the nation's "first year without a lynching," suggesting there had been a "vast social revolution that has brought more progress in interracial relations in America in the last two decades than during the entire previous period since emancipation."[43] While the "NCCJ does not claim to have brought the new day in human relations single-handedly . . . by hewing to its longe-range [sic] program directed through the trunk line organizations of human endeavor, it has been a great and far-reaching force in shaping a public opinion favorable to civil rights action, fair employment legislation and the ending of segregation in the armed forces and the public schools."[44]

The leaders of the NCCJ were keenly aware that they had not challenged racial disparities enough in the past, but they nevertheless still thought they had changed American culture in such a way that racial progress was possible. One NCCJ official unsubtly quoted newspaper columnist Roscoe Drummond, who had said, "The headlines . . . say that the Supreme Court is ending segregation in the public schools. It is nearer the truth—and even more significant—to say that the pattern of events, particularly during the last two decades, have rendered segregation no longer acceptable to the nation and that, in effect, the court is now confirming the precedents."[45] The NCCJ underscored its own work during World War II as a harbinger of change, saying, "Unquestionably, NCCJ put a picture in the minds of many responsible leaders in the armed forces that contributed to the breaking down of racial barriers and the eventual integration of all services. Wherever possible, in all wartime trio appearances, the integration of audiences was encouraged. All of its efforts among servicemen helped advance the idea for which Dwight D. Eisenhower, as both soldier and President, has stood: in the armed forces, there is no more necessity for segregating peoples of different color than there is for segregating people of different faiths."[46]

The NCCJ clearly inflated its historic commitment to civil rights, but it saw its goodwill work as having been transformative in getting the nation to change its perception of itself. In 1955, its Religious Commission stated: "We once again reaffirm our common moral concern for racial injustice. . . . Wherever human dignity is outraged, it becomes imperative for Catholics, Protestants and Jews to raise their united voices in protest and to join with new resolution in education tasks that will help to eradicate the prejudice and fear out of which racial injustice is born."[47] A self-evaluation in 1958 claimed the NCCJ "has from the beginning included those of diverse national and racial origins."[48]

Among religious leaders, the NCCJ was not alone in recognizing the importance of African American civil rights by the late 1950s, although these recognitions led to various degrees of action. Nevertheless, religious leaders were some of the most visible white supporters of the movement, even if they were criticized (and self-critical) for not doing enough or for acting too late. When the Little Rock Nine approached Little Rock Central High School in the famous 1957 confrontation with Orval Faubus, four ministers, two black and two white, escorted them. Catholics marched in numerous civil rights rallies, often dressed in religious attire, and in 1958 the American Catholic bishops released a pastoral letter called "Discrimination and the Christian Conscience," which denounced segregation, called race a moral and religious problem, and argued that racial uplift was inevitable once the bonds of inequality were removed.[49] Following the pastoral letter, Catholic theologians and many bishops rejected race as a meaningful concept in a universal church. Even the Pope began rewarding bishops such as Joseph Rummel and Joseph Ritter, who had worked hard to integrate their dioceses. Jews had long supported civil rights as part of their broad campaign against prejudice.[50] By the early 1960s, it was clear that some of the staunchest white supporters of racial civil rights had emerged from the religions within America's religious triangle. When President Johnson was drumming up support for the Civil Rights Act of 1964, he invited 150 Protestant, Catholic, and Jewish leaders to the White House, saying, "It is your job—as men of God—to awaken the conscience of our beloved land, the United States of America. . . . Inspire and challenge us to put our principles into action."[51] When in 1965 Protestants, Catholics, and Jews marched together in Selma, Alabama, all the priests, nuns, ministers, and rabbis who participated dressed in their religious garb to underscore it as a moral affair.

There also emerged by the late 1950s searching examinations in all three faiths of the place of race in religion, finding that segregation was not and could not be biblically sanctioned. In *Segregation and the Bible* (1958), Everett Tilson wrote that the

Bible yields "something more and superlatively better than a particular solution to a particular problem," without, of course, providing "a set of blueprints for its actualization."[52] Protestantism's most famous preacher, Billy Graham, was similarly anti-racist. After some early waffling, he announced in 1954 that his revivals would not have segregated seating. Segregation, he said, could not be biblically sanctioned and thus would not be tolerated. Punctuating the point, in July 1957, Graham invited Martin Luther King Jr. onstage in one of his New York City crusades. That year he also published an article in *Ebony* titled "No Color Line in Heaven."[53] Meanwhile, in March 1957, *Social Progress*, the monthly publication of the Presbyterian Church U.S.A., wrote, "Racial segregation is a problem of such size and urgency that it dwarfs all other social issues in American life today."[54] T. B. Matson, in his *Segregation and Desegregation: A Christian Approach* (1959), wrote, "There is no place right now where it seems more difficult for the child of God to measure up to the high demands of the Christian religion than in the area of race relations."[55]

Of course not everyone agreed this was the best way for "men of God" to act. Catholic archbishop Thomas J. Toolen, head of the Mobile-Birmingham diocese, did "not believe that priests are equipped to lead groups in disobedience to the laws of this state."[56] The *Ave Maria*, a respected Notre Dame–based weekly, said social action by religious leaders went beyond their call of duty: "when a clergyman's collar or a nun's habit appears in a public protest, they are implicating the Church— whether they want to or not—whether the Church should be implicated or not." The newspaper called for a meeting to determine "what means of witness and protest are appropriate and what means are not."[57] The debate over how much social action religious leaders should engage in continued throughout the 1960s and led, ultimately, to the transformation of American religious sociology, which went from division among Protestants, Catholics, and Jews to division between people of faith who advocated active social justice campaigns and those who did not.[58]

THE WORK THAT RACE HAD DONE IN TRI-FAITH AMERICA

Pointing out the ways in which the tri-faith ideal helped allow the civil rights movement to blossom does not exonerate tri-faith activists from being shortsighted on the question of race. The worried letter sent by the NCCJ in response to the activities of the National Conference on Religion and Race exposed a vital fact about Tri-Faith America: from its inception in the 1920s to its maturation in the 1950s, it was a profoundly white identity. Nearly all the key faith organizations—the National Catholic Welfare Conference, the National Council of Churches, the Synagogue Council of America—were slow to incorporate African Americans into leadership roles or to examine the role the organizations played in perpetuating racial divisions. Meanwhile, the groups that helped codify the tri-faith idea, such as the NCCJ, had at crucial moments in their history chosen to limit their mission to religious goodwill.

More pointedly, the Catholics and Jews moving to the suburbs were well aware their new neighborhoods were racially exclusive. They knew when they were debating what should be reflected in American education that African Americans were more or less excluded from the conversation because of their numbers or because of segregation. In Herberg's *Protestant-Catholic-Jew*, black people were reduced to a footnote on page 25. When sociologists attempted to account for the socioreligious groups in American life, they managed to concoct a group called "Negro Protestants," but this group was not a significant part of the "religious factor" that was then influencing American life; it was just a sociological presence taking up space in postwar Detroit.

Black Americans were keenly aware of the shortcomings of this national vision. Modjeska Simkins, the secretary of the NAACP in South Carolina, was harshly critical of mainstream religion, both black and white. She denounced "the made-in-America brand of 'Christianity'" that "smell[s] to high heaven. Living here in the 'Bible Belt,' we surpass the rest of the Nation in 'stomping' the church floors and desecrating our highways with Bible verse signs. Inscribing these verses on the tables of our hearts and living them daily are white horses of another color. . . . Brothers in Christ were of course without color, but that was not how Americans of faith acted."[59] Martin Luther King Jr.'s "Letter from Birmingham Jail" evinced similar criticism on the whiteness inherent in the concept of Tri-Faith America. "In deep disappointment I have wept over the laxity of the church," he wrote. "But be assured that my tears have been tears of love. There can be no deep disappointment where there is not deep love. Yes, I love the church. . . . Yes, I see the church as the body of Christ. But, oh! How we have blemished and scarred that body through social neglect and through fear of being nonconformists." Benjamin Mays, the chair of the National Conference on Religion and Race, said, "In questions of ethics and morals, we believe that religion should lead and not follow. It may be that if religion had taken the leadership, emancipation might have come without a Civil War and without the hatred that the War engendered. It may be that if the Church and Synagogue had led the way in desegregating their congregations, the May 17, 1954 decision of the United States Supreme Court might have been unnecessary. The so-called secular society would have followed the leadership of the Church and the Synagogue."[60] Indeed, several African American church leaders refused to attend the National Conference on Religion and Race because of the slowness of religious organizations to come to the civil rights cause.[61]

It was a sad irony that those most adamantly preaching brotherhood were so blind—sometimes willfully so—to America's racial divide. At the same time, acceptance of the pluralistic vision inherent to the tri-faith concept would have been severely hampered, perhaps fatally so, if that vision had been too inclusive of racial minorities before the 1960s. Polls demonstrated that racial equality declined in importance between World War II and 1960 for most Americans. Most white Americans pretended to be blind to this fact and did not want their economic gains threatened by racial discord. "We just can't afford to be democratic," said one white postwar suburbanite in 1959, reflecting on the equity he thought he might have to sacrifice in the name of equality.[62] If groups such as the National Conference of Christians and Jews had steadfastly demanded that racial equality be an important part of their postwar mission, they would have been turned down for grants, denied access to Ad Council revenue, and generally marginalized. Therefore, the NCCJ backed off until, as the worried letter from 1963 shows, the middle stages of the civil rights movement had transformed the sociological calculus.

Despite this sometimes willful blindness, it was clear to all that because racial disparities were so obvious in the United States, African Americans almost always made the best litigants in challenging discrimination, the best exemplars of brotherhood denied. In housing and schools it was cases centered on African Americans that regularly broke down legal barriers. Catholics and Jews then frequently used those decisions to catapult themselves into many facets of American life. They justified their entrance into the suburbs, for example, by citing *Shelley v. Kraemer*, the 1948 case about a black family in St. Louis. In some ways, Catholics and Jews took advantage of these black litigants to earn mainstream access.

Furthermore, throughout the 1940s and 1950s the major goodwill organizations could not ignore segregation and be true to their cause. Thus, they often used vague language of tolerance in many of their campaigns. To petition on their behalf, they chose as their spokesmen widely respected, popular African Americans such as Jackie Robinson rather than controversial figures such as Paul Robeson. They quietly engaged in activities supporting racial tolerance, doing so without much fanfare. After cataloguing injustices against religious groups, a 1954 NCCJ annual report said: "Prejudices and discriminations among God's creatures of different color must be outgrown. They are sinful; they play into the hands of Communism; and they slow down the united action of the free world's development." The NCCJ did not ignore race, nor was it unaware of the deep problems created by racial segregation. But the call in this report came, as with many similar calls, at the bottom of the report. It was followed by no substantive demands for action.[63]

Thus the relationship between Tri-Faith America and the nation's racial disparities is deeply illogical. The very foundation of Tri-Faith America—the brotherhood of man under the Fatherhood of God—left no room for segregation. And the organizations promoting the tri-faith ideal had solid, if uneven, records fighting racial discrimination. Yet many of these organizations chose not to insist on racial equality as part of their mission, as part of their call for "brotherhood." Worse, they took advantage of the fact that the pluralism they advocated could not have emerged had they been truer to their principles.

FROM CREED TO COLOR

In his famous speech at the 1963 March on Washington for Jobs and Freedom, Martin Luther King Jr. concluded: "When we allow freedom to ring, when we let it ring from every village and every hamlet, from every state and every city, we will be able to speed up that day when all of God's children, black men and white men, Jews and Gentiles, Protestants and Catholics, will be able to join hands and sing in the words of the old Negro spiritual: Free at last! Free at last! Thank God Almighty, we are free at last!" King deliberately made mention of the groups that had come to-gether in the past to insist on a pluralist definition of the United States. Indeed, under the symbolic shadow of Abraham Lincoln, King was on stage with Mathew Ahmann, the young Catholic who had organized the National Conference on Religion and Race. The Reverend Patrick J. O'Boyle, the Roman Catholic archbishop of Washington, D.C., gave the invocation. The Reverend Eugene Carson Blake spoke to the vast crowd on behalf of white Protestants. Rabbi Joachim Prinz, head of the American Jewish Congress, was one of the ten organizers of the event. Along with everything else it was, the 1963 March on Washington was a tri-faith affair. Perhaps it was unsurprising that King used the word "brotherhood" three times in his fifteen-hundred-word speech.

But by the middle of 1963 it was clear the rise of public concern about race had removed religion from its perch animating much of America's social discourse. The civil rights movement had single-handedly changed most Americans' under-standing of their country, forcing a recognition from white people that black people were a vital part of the nation, always had been, and needed to be recog-nized as such. In that year, *Time* both proclaimed the end of the postwar religious revival and named Martin Luther King Jr. its Man of the Year, making him the first African American to win this recognition.[64] Sidney Poitier also became the first African American man to win an Oscar for a starring role, for his performance in *Lilies of the Field*. *Time* did not much care for the film, but it noted, "The selection

The seminal moment of the civil rights movement—the 1963 March on Washington for Jobs and Freedom—was, among other things, a tri-faith affair. The widespread acceptance of the notion that America was a tri-faith nation gave civil rights leaders such as Martin Luther King Jr. a language to tap into and an audience already accustomed to avowing American pluralism. Here, the planners of the march meet with President Kennedy. They included (left to right) Secretary of Labor Willard Wirtz, Matthew Ahmann, Martin Luther King Jr., John Lewis, Rabbi Joachim Prinz, Rev. Eugene Carson Blake, A. Philip Randolph, President Kennedy, Vice President Johnson, Walter Ruether, Whitney Young, and Floyd McKissick. Cecil Stoughton/White House, John F. Kennedy Presidential Library and Museum.

of Sidney Poitier at least coincided with the sentiment of the times."[65] Polling data from 1963 also show racial issues becoming, by far, "the most important problem confronting the nation." Despite occasional blips in the pollsters' data, as for instance during the 1954 *Brown v. Board* case, race had hardly ever appeared as one of the country's most pressing problems. It remained relatively low on the list until 1963, when it suddenly topped Americans' concerns. It remained there for a decade. *Black Like Me* (1961), John Howard Griffin's first-person account of a white man who took tanning pills and toured the Deep South as a black man, sold more than five million copies and was transformed into a film in 1964. The book was almost as popular as the one it was modeled on, Laura Z. Hobson's 1947 bestseller, *Gentleman's Agreement*, which told the story of a Christian pretending to be Jewish. But different times required different obfuscations. The civil rights movement had transformed what were viewed as the nation's most prominent divisions, from creed to color.

Conclusion: The Return of Protestant America?

IN 1962, WHEN tri-faith rhetoric was at its height and pluralism was beginning to be equated with civic secularism, Billy James Hargis, a fiery Protestant minister long known for his over-the-top anti-Communist tirades, was in Colorado Springs with his son when he learned that the U.S. Supreme Court had outlawed prayer in public schools. It was the first of the two decisions that formalized the second disestablishment of religion in America. Hargis and his son saw the headline on a newspaper lying around an ice cream parlor. "All the way home," Bill junior recalled, "my dad talked about how this was really the beginning of the end for America, that the country had turned its back on God, and that any country that did that couldn't stand. . . . It made a profound impression on me and really put the fear of the Lord in me. I felt like this was a tragic event and, looking back on it, I still do."[1]

The minister, long marginalized from the Protestant mainstream for his vicious Red-baiting and for publicly deriding the concept of the "brotherhood of man under the Fatherhood of God," drove his son back to their hotel. "I dissolved into tears," Bill junior said, "and my mother came and found me and she took me to my father's office there in the hotel, and he opened up the Bible with me, and that's the day I accepted Christ as my personal savior and became a Christian." Bill senior had a different response. He organized a protest movement, one that so stridently protested the Court's decisions that in 1964 the IRS revoked his organization's tax-exempt status.[2] The success of Tri-Faith America and the arrangements made in the name of honoring religious pluralism had begun to provoke a backlash. Conservative Protestants wanted to take back what they saw as "their country."

Hargis was not alone among conservative Christians in seeing danger in tri-faith ideals. A pastor in Lynchburg, Virginia, named Jerry Falwell first got the idea to build a Christian school in 1963, after the Supreme Court handed down the second of its two decisions, this one removing enforced Bible reading from the classroom. Falwell said he became afraid "the Christian world view was not only going to be pushed back but eliminated, and that another might replace it," and so he created several private Christian academies. "There were those who thought we were probably starting Lynchburg Christian Academy to have a white-flight school—that kind of thing—but from day one I made it clear that Lynchburg Christian Academy . . . would be for any and all who loved Christ and who wanted to study under born-again teachers in a Christian environment with academic excellence," Falwell said. With a mission of opposing secularism (or "secular humanism," as conservative Christians derisively called it), the school was opened in 1967 and spawned a nearby university called Liberty University in 1971. Liberty became (and is) the largest evangelical university in the world, instrumental in educating conservatives associated with the religious right, including members of the media, lawyers, and politicians. Building on its success, in 1979 Falwell co-founded an organization called the Moral Majority, helping provide an avenue for the religious right to enter American politics.[3]

This protest movement began even before the Supreme Court decisions of 1962–63, albeit slowly. In 1955, several evangelical Christians around Billy Graham founded *Christianity Today* as a dissenting voice to the mainline *Christian Century*. The *Christian Century* was deemed to have become too theologically soft, too absorbed in ecumenism and the ideals of Tri-Faith America rather than doctrinal evangelical Christianity. Billy Graham and the evangelicals around him designed *Christianity Today* to provide an alternative voice.

Also in 1955, the mainline National Council of Churches expelled its Lay Committee, which was, to the ministerial leaders of the National Council, growing overly conservative and harshly critical of the National Council's social agenda. The chair of the Lay Committee, J. Howard Pew, the conservative financial angel of the group, recovered from the expulsion by forming alliances between political conservatives and religious fundamentalists. It was his money that supported the institutions of what came to be called the religious right, and it was mainline Protestantism's support of tri-faith ideas that spurred him into his oppositional role.[4]

Despite this emerging revolt, by the middle 1960s many of the sticking points between Protestants, Catholics, and Jews seemed to have been settled—in the courts, in classrooms, in schools, throughout the community. A Catholic had served as president of the United States. Antisemitism was at historical lows. No one seemed to be clamoring for a return of "Protestant America." Politicians and cultural critics used the concept of Judeo-Christianity regularly, both for its implied unity and for its display of moral authority.

By the 1970s, though, conservative Protestants were openly claiming that affirming pluralism had led to secularism and that secular ideals had dislodged those brought forward by Jesus of Nazareth. Their country, they argued, which stretched back to the Puritans, through the fiery sermons of the First and Second Great Awakenings, and through the rise and fall of turn-of-the-twentieth-century fundamentalism, had been taken from them by those willing to dabble in secularism in order to safeguard pluralism, and they were ready to fight back. "One of the features of the seventies was nostalgia," said the evangelical social critic Os Guinness, speaking of the early activities of the religious right. "And, of course, if you go back to the nineteenth century, you start harking back to 'Christian America.' Now, who were the natural heirs of Christian America? The evangelicals thought they were." Evangelical leader Pat Robertson announced on his television program, *The 700 Club*, that "in the next five years we have an unprecedented opportunity for America to fulfill the dream of the early settlers who came right here to Virginia in 1607, that his land would be used to glorify God."[5] It was no accident that the 1980 Washington for Jesus rally was held on April 29, the anniversary of the date on which the first British settlers landed in Jamestown.[6]

Activists of the religious right all focused on perceived slights by an overly lenient mainstream, which was, these conservatives thought, departing from pure Christian principles in the name of pluralism. All the arenas of contestation in Tri-Faith America once again became political. Many grassroots evangelicals, for instance, first became politicized in local debates over textbooks, some of which they deemed overly permissive and morally liberal. In West Virginia, Texas, and California, conservative activists, acting in the name of Protestant Christianity, rallied to fight what they saw as the country's departure from Christian ethics. Meanwhile, Christian schools like Falwell's proliferated throughout the 1970s, with evangelical parents opting out of the secularized public option.[7] Indeed, it was a battle over the tax status of Christian schools that served as the true impetus for the formation of the religious right. It was not abortion or gay rights but the threatened tax status of the nationwide web of Christian schools that served as a catalyst for the unification of religious political conservatives.[8]

Despite these purely Protestant underpinnings, evangelical activists also knew the power of the language of "Judeo-Christianity." This led them to try, mostly successfully, to co-opt the name. In the textbook debates of the 1970s, for example, one of the pamphlets issued by evangelical leaders objected to any material that contained suggestions of moral relativity. "To the vast majority of Americans," said the pamphlet, "the terms 'values' and 'morals' mean one thing, and one thing only; and that is the Christian-Judeo morals, values and standards as given to us by God through His Word written in the Ten Commandments and the Bible."[9] When *Christianity Today* editorialized against abortion, it argued that abortion was a repudiation of the Hippocratic oath and Judeo-Christian ethics.[10] Ronald Reagan wooed conservative Christians by endorsing tuition tax credits, complaining that the Supreme Court had "expelled God from the classroom," and observing that everyone in favor of abortion had already been born. He summed up his complaints by talking about the enormous challenges facing "traditional Judeo-Christian values" in 1970s America.[11] Because of the term's historical flexibility, those opposing the religious right had a difficult time making the case that these conservatives were distorting the true meaning of the phrase.

The religious right benefited from the term's vagueness in another way too. Since the late 1970s, there has been a remarkable transition in the country's religious sociology. Rather than the divisions being mostly between the "three faiths of democracy," as had been the case from the 1910s to the 1960s, by the 1970s conservative Protestants, Catholics, and Jews all began to feel they had more in common with one another than with their co-religionists who happened to be liberal. No matter what their faith, Protestant, Catholic, or Jewish political liberals, who were also often theologically liberal, found more in common with one another than with strict literalists or the more conservative among their own faith. Meanwhile, those within the religious right, adopting the idea of "co-belligerency," felt there might be nothing wrong with befriending a Catholic or Jew who would march with them in anti-abortion rallies or "pro-family" parades. Indeed, the premillennial dispensationalism that served as one centerpiece of evangelical theology required the return of world Jewry to Israel. Politically conservative Jews, who were usually fierce defenders of Israel, took the outstretched hand. There were some slip-ups, of course, as when Bailey Smith, president of the Southern Baptist Convention, observed publicly in 1979, "It is interesting at great political rallies how you have a Protestant to pray, a Catholic to pray, and then you have a Jew to pray. With all due respect to those dear people, my friends, God Almighty does not hear the prayer of a Jew."[12] While this statement was intended to be a clear attack on the acknowledged pluralism of Tri-Faith America, it directly countered the idea of co-belligerency, which was, and would continue to be, on the ascendant during the latter half of the twentieth century. Indeed, leaders of the religious right had to apologize on behalf of Smith, fearing his comments might threaten their political ambitions.

No longer were antipathies between Protestants, Catholics, and Jews animating social change; rather, the force behind change was the aversion between liberals of all faiths and conservatives of all faiths. This has led in unpredictable directions that would have shocked Americans of the 1950s. In the first decade of the twenty-first century, it was conservative Protestants seeking government aid for private religious schools. These latter-day Protestants stood diametrically opposed to their midcentury brethren, who tried to limit Catholic access to precisely these kinds of services. At roughly the same time, a group of Hasidic Jews in the suburb of Kiryas Joel, outside New York City, institutionalized religious housing segregation in order to preserve communal norms. These Jews would have seen the arguments of their American Jewish forefathers from the suburbs of the 1940s and 1950s as badly shortsighted, although they would have appreciated the efforts of activists fighting to instill "Jewish content" within the fraternity system. Meanwhile, in 2008, Protestant fraternities began suing universities for discrimination, because the fraternities wanted to limit their membership to Protestants. Unlike the Protestants of the 1940s and 1950s, who wanted to keep Catholics and Jews out for social reasons, the 2008 lawsuit was intended to enhance the faith of members against prominent secularism. "We want to be a light on this campus," said Daniel Weaver, a chapter president of the Lambda Sigma Phi fraternity, using the minority-rights argument put forward by postwar Catholics and Jews to fight for the preservation of evangelical Protestantism.[13]

A final factor changing America's religious sociology, one that has yet to supplant the liberal-conservative divide, has been an increase in the number of faiths practiced in the United States. Changes in immigration law since 1965 have allowed a variety of new immigrant populations to come to the United States, especially from Asia, Africa, and Latin America, carrying their own religious traditions, including Hinduism, Buddhism, Islam, and more.[14] The nation's increasing religious diversity has made it difficult to refer to the United States as a "Judeo-Christian nation." In April 2009, for example, President Barack Obama stressed at a press conference in Turkey that the United States did not consider itself "a Christian nation or a Jewish nation or a Muslim nation. We consider ourselves a nation of citizens who are bound by ideals and a set of values." Gone are the days when everyone wanted to proclaim America's "Judeo-Christian tradition"; now it is mostly conservatives who eagerly make the claim. For his proclamation in Turkey, Obama was roundly chastised by those who insisted, as did Republican activist Frank Donatelli, that "the better answer would have been to say that we are a nation that considers itself a product of the Judeo-Christian tradition because that happens to be accurate." Despite the fact that the "Judeo-Christian tradition" was an invention of the middle of the twentieth century, its rhetorical power persists.

If it was unsurprising that the successes of Tri-Faith America would provoke a backlash, it was perhaps more surprising that, as the tri-faith ideal grew successful, many Catholics and Jews felt less compelled to retain their religious identities. Success and acceptance had bred indifference.

The successes were obvious. Andrew Greeley's sociological studies of Catholic advances during these years showed that American Catholics had used the postwar years to achieve economic, educational, and social parity with white Protestants. By the 1960s, Catholics were more likely to go to college than white Protestants. Their earnings were on average slightly higher, and they were just as likely, if not more likely, to choose a white-collar career. They were as likely to live in the suburbs as Protestants, and they were (slowly) dropping their support of the Democratic Party, although they still remained, in general, slightly left of center within the American political spectrum, at least until the culture wars of the 1980s and 1990s.[15] These transitions affected individual Catholics' identities. In 1963, half of American Catholics still had Catholics as their three best friends, especially if they had gone to Catholic schools. But only a quarter of American Catholics had all Catholic neighbors, and less than half felt it was important to have Catholic friends. In their attitudes toward Jews and African Americans, 1960s Catholics were basically indistinguishable from Protestants, and most Catholics (70 percent) disagreed with the statement "Most Protestants are inclined to discriminate against Catholics," a distant cry from what this percentage would have been the previous decade.[16]

Jews were succeeding as well. Marking a significant symbolic transition, by the early 1960s Jews were fully accepted as faculty members on university campuses, allowed to teach courses on previously restricted subjects such as Western civilization and Western literature.[17] The number of Jewish senators and representatives was on a slow increase that would not stop until the 1990s. Some Jews were even moving their way up corporate ladders that had been denied to them earlier in the century, including at Bank of America, Chrysler, and DuPont, although big business remained the one arena infested by subtle anti-Jewish discrimination.[18]

Jews had other reasons to feel less alienated too. The two impulses that historically set Jews apart in the United States—antisemitism and Zionism—had become less visible in American life by the middle 1960s. The decline of antisemitism was spectacular and quick. In 1948, one in five Americans reported not wanting a Jew as a neighbor, but by 1959 only 2 percent of Americans said they had similar concerns. Another poll taken in 1959, a year before John F. Kennedy's election, revealed that slightly more Americans were willing to vote for a Jew for President than for a Roman Catholic. By 1962, 75 percent of Americans said they would object to an antisemitic candidate solely because he or she was antisemitic.[19] Meanwhile, the success of Israel had given the Zionist commitment less urgency. Israel's fate would occasionally stimulate American Jewry to redeclare its allegiance to the faith (especially after Israel's wars in 1967 and 1973), but Zionism was no longer a central notion of American Jewry.[20]

The thought of Jews and Catholics losing much of their uniqueness sparked vigorous, sometimes contentious conversations within the respective communities about what it meant to be Jewish or Catholic. For Jews, reconsiderations of Jewish identity are legion, but in the 1960s there was a new tenor to the debate. When in 1961 *Commentary* held a forum titled "Jewishness and the Younger Intellectuals," the panelists expressed varying views on how Jewishness had affected their lives, but all agreed that by the early 1960s it no longer dominated their self-image. Twenty-eight-year-old Philip Roth pointed out, "Small matters aside—food preferences, a certain syntax, certain jokes—it is difficult for me to distinguish a Jewish style of life in our country that is significantly separate and distinct from the American style of life. . . . What a Jew wants and how he goes after it, does not on the whole appear to differ radically from what his Gentile neighbor wants and how he goes after it."[21] Similarly, historian Samuel Shapiro suggested, "The postwar prosperity and the consequent decline of anti-Semitism have . . . tended to make us as smooth and bland as any other group of successful middle-class Americans. Except for the *yarmelkes* and the (usually concealed) Torah, the synagogue in my suburb would be hard to distinguish from some local churches." Left unsaid, of course, was that his family was allowed to live in a religiously mixed suburb largely unmolested, a profoundly new occurrence.[22]

In the same series, Andrew Hacker, then a young professor of government at Cornell, reflected on the problems inherent to this easy kind of access. He told a story from his college years, a dozen years prior, when he had attended a "small New England college which had thirteen fraternities, none of them Jewish." He noted, "In the pre-war years this did not matter: the admissions policy of the college was candidly anti-Semitic and there were never enough Jews on the campus to set up a fraternity chapter of their own." Since the end of the war, however, not only had the college "been admitting a high proportion of Jews, but in addition the fraternities have been exhibiting an unusual tolerance," with "each house tak[ing] in several Jews each year." The result, he said, was "that these students are soon bound in the brotherhood to their Gentile classmates. The Jewish boys half-consciously understand that they are expected to dress, talk, act like the Gentiles who have embraced them—though this is never suggested in so many words." There were other accommodations as well. Hacker said that he and other young Jews consciously kept their grades close to the house average and "they tend to date Gentile girls."[23] To him, all this added up to them losing their Jewishness. "Quite clearly this problem is going to become accentuated in the whirl of suburban life, in corporate employment, in academic preferment." Feeling frustrated that acceptance was potentially leading to absorption, Hacker concluded: "The toleration we have so long asked for is now beginning to have consequences that we may not have the strength to resist. . . . [T]he Gentile world has been too hospitable to impress my Jewishness upon me" and "circumstances do not drive me to find an identity in Jewish culture and the Jewish tradition. . . . But yet: I have a deep pride in this culture and tradition," and he hoped Jews would "continue to retain a Jewish self-consciousness despite the temptations to become a thoroughly assimilated American."[24] But the question remained: how did one do that?

In a thoroughly depressed-sounding piece from June 1961, sociologist Daniel Bell went through the options, dismissing them one by one.[25] Orthodoxy was "too constricted." Ritual was "too shallow." Should Jews celebrate a common experience and, if so, which one? Bell rejected the life of the shtetl for its "narrowness of mind, its cruelty, especially to school children . . . and its invidious stratification." He dismissed the immigrant experience of the Lower East Side or "Jew Town" in Chicago for "frequent coarseness, the pushing, the many other gross features of that life." He also found fault with associations based on Jewish civic organizations, which risked "accommodation" rather than self-fulfillment. And Israel, he said, was "no answer" because it was a "false *galut*," just another form of exile from the world.[26]

What was left? Bell looked inward. "For me," he said, "to be a Jew is to be part of a community woven by memory." He struggled, however, to locate a collective bank of memories, and he concluded his essay with a famous rabbinical quotation: "It is not thy duty to complete the work, but neither art thou free to desist from it." He took comfort in knowing that "one realizes that one does not stand alone, that the past is still present, and that there are responsibilities of participation even when the community of which one is a part is a community woven by the thinning strands of memory."[27]

Bell's point was summed up in Marshall Sklare's 1964 study of recent literature on Jewish intermarriage, which showed that that Jews were intermarrying at higher rates than expected.[28] Sklare concluded that until the early 1960s, American Jews had been quiet about social absorption, assuming that intermarriage was only an occasional aberration and that Jewish solidarity would keep the community together. Several studies on intermarriage between 1962 and 1964 became, in Sklare's mind, "one of the first signs that this community may at last be preparing to recognize that a problem does exist." He wrote:

> Having finally established themselves in such a [free] society, Jews are now coming to realize that their survival is still threatened—not by Gentile hostility but by Jewish indifference. This is what finally makes intermarriage so

bitter a dilemma to confront. On the one hand, it signifies the fulfillment of the Jews' demand for acceptance as an individual—a demand he has been making since the Emancipation; on the other hand, it signifies a weakening of Jewish commitment. In short, it casts into doubt American Jewry's dual ideal of full participation in the society and the preservation of Jewish identity.[29]

Many postwar Jews sided with Daniel Bell in emphasizing a shared historical experience. But with the life of the shtetl and the ethnic allegiances of the Old World too far removed, support for Israel and remembrance of the Holocaust became central pillars of American Judaism. Postwar Jews retained memories of and constructed memorials to those lost to Hitler's atrocities, and the Eichmann trial introduced the word "Holocaust" to Americans as representative of the mass murder of Jews by the Nazis. Hannah Arendt's book on the trial, although vigorously debated within Jewish circles, brought Jewish suffering to the center of debate.[30] While memories of the Holocaust had existed in American Jewry ever since World War II, their prominence only increased in the late 1960s, when the Six-Day War provoked feelings that Israel was under threat and that American Jews needed to pledge their support to their co-religionists, lest another Holocaust occur.[31] In the aftermath of the Israeli wars, the Holocaust moved to the center of American Jewish identity.[32]

Catholics faced a similar identity crisis in the early and middle 1960s. Most Catholics had been somewhat confident, even combative, about their place in America throughout the 1950s, secure in the notion that their image as solid anti-Communists suited the times. This confidence began to falter during the early 1960s, however, and a surprising note of defensiveness and even fear emerged in 1963 when Daniel Callahan, an associate editor at *Commonweal*, wrote an article called "The New Pluralism." John F. Kennedy's election and the Supreme Court's decision in *Engel* suggested that Catholic differences were becoming muted in American society. He asked if "Catholicism [is] compatible with the new pluralism, set now within a context in which, step by step, religion is losing its traditional privileges." A secular, pluralist vision of America put forward by "a large Jewish-secular minority (supported by many Protestants)" had changed American culture since World War II, making secularism the "context" of religious debate and limiting interfaith squabbles. The problem for Catholics was that Catholic identity had long been nourished by antipathy toward Protestants (and vice versa), but as secularism was emerging as the only plausible civic solution to pluralism, Callahan worried that the Catholic vision was becoming less important to the life of the nation. He hoped Catholicism had "sufficient inner resources to survive and flourish" despite the change in culture. But he was aware that as Catholics earned greater levels of achievement and as the United States became increasingly accepting of Catholicism, Catholic identity in America would have to transform itself from a besieged immigrant faith to something more attractive.[33]

Others were less certain about the "inner resources" of American Catholicism. Two months after Callahan wrote his article, Catholic political theorist Francis Canavan rebuked him in the pages of *America*. Canavan's concern was that this "new pluralism" was premised on secularity and was therefore bound to corrupt American Catholicism. Secularism was not pluralism, he said. Instead of removing religion from the public square, the state should honor "a genuine pluralism . . . that permits and encourages private, including religious, institutions of welfare to serve the public as effectively as state institutions do." As one positive example, Canavan pointed to the GI Bill, which gave veterans money to spend on any sort of education they chose, religious education included. What had to be defeated, said Canavan, was not pluralism but secularism.[34]

A few months later, Notre Dame historian Philip Gleason pointed out that each author had defined pluralism differently and therefore "one man literally does not know what the other is talking about."[35] Callahan's "new pluralism" was one of acceptance, Canavan's one of rejection. In the debate, however, there was ample concern about the survival of Catholic identity in pluralist (and secularized) America.

These Catholic uncertainties increased throughout the 1960s. At first the cause seemed to be Vatican II, the papal conclave held between 1962 and 1965 that substantially liberalized the faith by altering long-standing traditions and endorsing the idea of religious pluralism. In a church where to be Catholic meant, in the words of one observer, "mass on Sunday, fish on Friday and no 'pills' any day,'" the conclave provoked probing questions about what it meant to be Catholic if these things were no longer required. In 1967, Donald J. Thorman, a researcher whose work focused on the Catholic laity, suggested: "The problem is that many lay people simply no longer know how to answer the question: What does it mean to be a Catholic Christian." With all the various cultural and ritualistic "stuff" now transformed, Thorman felt, "the characteristic note of today's American Catholic is confusion, indecision; we are treading water, waiting, wondering what is going to happen next." Thorman concluded: "Things used to be so simple and neat," but Vatican II "opened new visions of Christianity that make all the old definitions . . . seem pallid." He titled his article "Today's Laymen: The Uncertain Catholic."[36]

In yet another vital intervention, Philip Gleason saw the crisis another way. Demoting the importance of Vatican II, Gleason wrote: "The identity crisis itself took place earlier than, and independent of, Vatican II." Gleason thought American Catholicism had gone through a "crisis of Americanization" between World War II and the late 1960s, when American Catholics had lost their ethnic and class distinctiveness. They shared a number of experiences with other Americans, including World War II, the expansion of higher education, and the automobile and mass media cultures, which brought "all segments of the population together" and furnished "a common fund of experience." More to the point, they "tended to make younger Catholics more like other Americans." Like it or not, American Catholics were assimilating.

To keep Catholic identity relevant, Gleason argued that Catholic institutions had to adapt, but he thought it would be nearly impossible to do so. American Catholics were "orienting themselves to new reference groups and taking their values from new sources." Attempts to reinvigorate the ethnic component of American Catholicism—what later would be called the "ethnic revival" of the 1970s—were too hollow. In the end, a melancholy Gleason reminded readers, "While the Church must be engaged in the world, it cannot be completely assimilated to the world. Catholicism has come disastrously close to becoming a culture religion in other times and places; for it to become a culture religion now—even in the name of relevance—would be a religious catastrophe and would contribute nothing to the solution of the problems of society."[37]

In the end, Catholic identity in America came to be nourished by aligning with one of the sides within the nation's new religious sociology. Catholic priests and some laity put culture war issues, including opposition to abortion rights and homosexuality, at the forefront of their Catholic identity. Other Catholics, mostly laity and nuns, have taken up the fight against poverty, both within the United States and throughout the world. They argue among themselves as to what the Church's priorities ought to be, and as they do, conservative Catholics seem to have more in common with conservative Protestants and Jews, while liberal Catholics quite easily align with liberal Protestants and Jews. Ironically, both sides claim to be acting in the name of Judeo-Christian morality.

Despite the identity crises provoked by success, and despite the creation of a formidable opposition in the form of the religious right, the success of the tri-faith idea shaped American life during the second half of the twentieth century and has continued to do so well into the twenty-first. It formulated principles of group communalism, group rights, and religious privacy, all of which remain cherished today. It helped usher in the second disestablishment of religion in the United States, which still stands as a law of the land. And acceptance of the tri-faith idea also softened the ground for the civil rights movement, which set the terms for all future debates about American diversity. Despite all this, perhaps the greatest demonstration of its success was the visceral reaction it provoked, a reaction that has been as formative in shaping American public life since the 1980s as was

Tri-Faith America in the 1940s and 1950s. Indeed, so successful were the tri-faith advocates of postwar America that even their opponents struggled to win away their primary label, "Judeo-Christian." But whatever else they accomplished, perhaps their most significant victory was to limit the appeal of a return to Protestant monism, something Everett Clinchy might have been most proud of.

INTRODUCTION

1. For two recent retellings of this famous story, see Deborah Dash Moore, *GI Jews: How World War II Changed a Generation* (Cambridge, Mass.: Belknap Press, 2004), 118–21, and William R. Hutchinson, *Religious Pluralism in America: The Contentious History of a Founding Ideal* (New Haven: Yale University Press, 2003), 198–99.

2. *Time*, "Letters," April 30, 1945, 4.

3. *Congressional Record*, vol. 91, part 10, A294–A295.

4. Press release, January 14, 1960, Chapel of the Four Chaplains folder, 1960 Religious Issues files of James Wine, box 1015, John F. Kennedy Presidential Library (JFKPL), Pre-Presidential Papers (hereafter "Wine Papers"). Other Catholics invited to the event included U.S. senator Francis J. Myers of Pennsylvania and Major General William "Wild Bill" Donovan, who served as vice chairman of the chapel.

5. Letter from Daniel A. Poling to the Honorable John F. Kennedy, June 30, 1960, Wine Papers.

6. For more on the place of the Four Chaplains in mid-century American life, see Chapter 3.

7. For example, an unmarked memo in JFK's Presidential Library, dated less than two months before the election and bearing the initials of one of Kennedy's top advisors, revealed the sentiment around the Democratic camp: "Senator Kennedy *will* win in November *unless* defeated by the religious issue. This makes *neutralization* of this issue the key to the election." In all likelihood, the memorandum was from Theodore Sorenson. See "The Memo," 1, Wine Papers.

8. Daniel A. Poling, *Mine Eyes Have Seen* (New York: McGraw-Hill, 1959), 261.

9. There are several available transcripts of the famous speech and the question-and-answer period that followed it. One thorough website for John F. Kennedy research in general, which has collected all official remarks from the 1960s campaign, is www.jfklink.com. For the

Houston Ministerial Association speech, see http://www.jfklink.com/speeches/jfk/sept60/jfk120960_houston03.html (accessed March 12, 2010).

10. Ibid.

11. For a discussion of the extent to which American Catholicism served as an intellectual foil for mid-century American liberals, see John T. McGreevy, "Thinking on One's Own: Catholicism and the American Intellectual Imagination, 1928–1960," *Journal of American History* 84 (June 1997), 97–131.

12. "Pluralism—A National Menace," *Christian Century*, June 13, 1951, 701–3.

13. Michael R. Beschloss, *The Conquerors: Roosevelt, Truman and the Destruction of Hitler's Germany, 1941–1945* (New York: Simon & Schuster, 2002), 51.

14. "Editorial," *Life*, December 26, 1955, 56.

15. This story is told in Robert Wuthnow, *The Restructuring of American Religion: Society and Faith Since World War II* (Princeton, N.J.: Princeton University Press, 1990).

CHAPTER 1

1. Everett R. Clinchy, *All in the Name of God* (New York: John Day, 1934).

2. Ibid., 99; see also 124–28.

3. Ibid., 3.

4. Ibid., 168.

5. Ibid., 179.

6. Hiram Wesley Evans, *The Klan's Fight for Americanism*, a pamphlet reprinted by permission from the *North American Review* (New York: North American Review Corporation, 1926). The essay was first published in the *North American Review* 123 (March–May 1926): 33–63. The response essays were published in the June-August edition. Du Bois, of course, was the renowned intellectual then affiliated with the National Association for the Advancement of Colored People. William Starr Myers was a Princeton historian who was an active Episcopalian and a friend of Woodrow Wilson's.

7. Ibid., 1, 18.

8. Ibid., 28.

9. Ibid., 16, 12–14.

10. Ibid. 12–16, 28.

11. Ibid., 22.

12. David M. Chalmers, *Hooded Americanism: The History of the Ku Klux Klan*, 3rd ed. (Durham, N.C.: Duke University Press, 1987), 71.

13. Evans, *The Klan's Fight for Americanism*, 8, 28.

14. Ibid., 24–25.

15. Ibid., 27.

16. Chalmers, *Hooded Americanism*, 291–99.

17. At a dinner party in Sinclair Lewis's 1922 *Babbitt*, one guest dismisses the idea that Prohibition was an offense to his personal liberty by saying, "You don't want to forget prohibition is a mighty good thing for the working-classes. Keeps 'em from wasting their money and lowering their productiveness." Sinclair Lewis, *Babbitt* (Hew York: Harcourt, Brace, 1922), 114.

18. Prior to 1933, there had been perhaps five such organizations founded in all of American history. Leonard Dinnerstein, *Antisemitism in America* (New York: Oxford University Press, 1995), 112.

19. Ibid., 127.

20. George Gallup, Gallup Poll, survey 118, May 1938.

21. "Tensions," *Time*, June 13, 1938, 55.

22. "Bias Contest," *Time*, March 7, 1938, 26 and "Bias," *Time*, May 2, 1938, 49.

23. The authors studied sixteen American cities and three Canadian ones (Baltimore, Washington, D.C., Pittsburgh, Buffalo, Cleveland, Cincinnati, Chicago, Louisville, Atlanta, San Francisco, Los Angeles, Oakland, Berkeley, New York City, Philadelphia, Newark, Toronto, Montreal, and Ottawa). They spent two years writing the book, spending at least a month in each of the selected cities. Claris Edwin Silcox and Galen M. Fisher, *Catholics, Jews and Protestants: A Study of Relationships in the United States and Canada* (Westport, Conn.: Greenwood Press, 1934, reprinted 1979), vi–vii.

24. Ibid., 38.

25. Ibid., 40.

26. Ibid., 43.

27. Ibid., 41.

28. Silcox and Fisher buttressed their claims by citing the work of Heywood Broun and George Brill's book on antisemitism, *Christians Only: A Study in Prejudice* (New York: Viking Press, 1931); Bruno Lasker, ed., *Jewish Experiences in America* (New York: Inquiry, 1930); and Herman Feldman, *Racial Factors in American Industry* (New York: Harper & Brothers, 1930). See Silcox and Fisher, *Catholics, Jews and Protestants*, 42.

29. Silcox and Fisher, *Catholics, Jews and Protestants*, 42.

30. Ibid., 43.

31. Ibid., 45.

32. Ibid., 47.

33. For Catholic separateness, see, for example, Gerald Gamm, *Urban Exodus: Why the Jews Left Boston and the Catholics Stayed* (Cambridge, Mass.: Harvard University Press, 1999); Charles Morris, *American Catholic: The Saints and Sinners Who Built America's Most Powerful Church* (New York: Vintage, 1998), 141–254; and Silcox and Fisher, *Catholics, Jews and Protestants*, 69–70.

34. Silcox and Fisher, *Catholics, Jews and Protestants*, 71.

35. Ibid., 72.

36. Ibid., 73.

37. Ibid., 78.

38. Ibid., 73–74.

39. Ibid., 102–3.

40. Ibid., 174.

41. Donald Young, *American Minority Peoples: A Study in Racial and Cultural Conflicts in the United States* (New York: Harper & Brothers, 1932), quoted in Silcox and Fisher, *Catholics, Jews and Protestants*, 182.

42. "Church and State," *Time*, March 14, 1938, 55.

43. Silcox and Fisher, *Catholics, Jews and Protestants*, 357.

44. For these movements, see David Hollinger, "Ethnic Diversity, Cosmopolitanism, and the Emergence of the American Liberal Intelligentsia," *In the American Province: Studies in the History and Historiography of Ideas* (Bloomington: Indiana University Press, 1985), 56–73; John Higham, "Ethnic Pluralism in Modern American Thought," *Send These To Me: Immigrants in Urban America*, rev. ed. (Baltimore, Md.: Johns Hopkins University Press, 1984), 198–232; Diana Selig, *Americans All: The Cultural Gifts Movement* (Cambridge, Mass.: Harvard University

Press, 2008); Nicholas V. Montalto, *A History of the Intercultural Education Movement, 1924–1941* (New York: Garland, 1982); Jonathan Zimmerman, *Whose America? Culture Wars in the Public Schools* (Cambridge, Mass.: Harvard University Press, 2002); Michael Denning, *The Cultural Front: The Laboring of American Culture in the Twentieth Century* (London: Verso, 1997); and Lizbeth Cohen, *Making a New Deal: Industrial Workers in Chicago, 1919–1939* (Cambridge: Cambridge University Press, 1990).

45. For the suspicions, see Silcox and Fisher, *Catholics, Jews and Protestants*, 126–51.

46. Of thirty-six community chests examined by Silcox and Fisher, Catholics participated in twenty-seven of them, Jews in thirty. Silcox and Fisher, *Catholics, Jews and Protestants*, 125.

47. Ibid., 316.

48. The resolutions adopted at the Church Peace Union's first meeting, listing its attendees and its mission, can be found on the Carnegie Council's website, http://www.cceia.org/about/church_peace_union.html (accessed February 10, 2009).

49. Silcox and Fisher, *Catholics, Jews and Protestants*, 317.

50. John F. Piper Jr., *The American Churches in World War I* (Athens: Ohio University Press, 1985).

51. Silcox and Fisher, *Catholics, Jews and Protestants*, 329.

52. Ibid., 123–24.

53. Clinchy, *All in the Name of God*, 119–20.

54. Stanley High, "Satan, Be Warned," *Saturday Evening Post* reprint (New York: Curtis, 1940), 3; and James E. Pitt, *Adventures in Brotherhood* (New York: Farrar, Straus, 1955), 13.

55. Benny Kraut, "A Wary Collaboration: Jews, Catholics, and the Protestant Goodwill Movement," in *Between the Times: The Travail of the Protestant Establishment in American, 1900–1960*, ed. William R. Hutchison (New York and Cambridge: Cambridge University Press, 1989), 196.

56. Silcox and Fisher, *Catholics, Jews and Protestants*, 320–21.

57. The Inquiry, wrote one of the early participants, provided "one of the strongest" roots for the National Conference of Christians and Jews, and several of the NCCJ's leaders, including Father John Elliott Ross, Rabbi Lazaron, Ben Landis, Rhoda McColloch, and Silcox, began their goodwill work there. Bruno Lasker to Everett Clinchy, April 21, 1953, NCCJ history folder, box 1, NCCJ Papers.

58. Everett Clinchy to James Pitt, April 1953, NCCJ history, comments on early years folder, box 1, NCCJ Papers, Roger W. Straus, "The Story of the National Conference, Being Part of His Address at the New York Seminar," *Information Bulletin of the Nation Conference of Jews and Christians*, January 1931, 4, *Information Bulletin* folder, box 10, NCCJ Papers; and Pitt, *Adventures in Brotherhood*, 13.

59. Straus, "The Story of the National Conference," 4.

60. Notable exceptions included the *American Hebrew*, which devoted a series of issues to the problem of religious prejudice, and the Central Conference of American Rabbis, which created its own Good-Will Committee. It worked closely with the FCC's Good Will Committee, and both of which were later merged into the National Conference of Christians and Jews.

61. Straus, "The Story of the National Conference," 4.

62. Hayes to Clinchy, December 28, 1937, Carlton J. H. Hayes folder, box 9, NCCJ Papers, 2.

63. Kraut, "A Wary Collaboration," 198.

64. Pitt, *Adventures in Brotherhood*, 31–33.

65. Ibid., 14.

66. In 1905, the United Lutheran Church set up a Committee for Jewish Missions. In 1909, the Board of Home Missions of the Presbyterian Church U.S.A. consciously sought Jews. In 1914, the Christian Reformed Committee formed a Jewish Mission Committee. In 1917, the Presbyterian Church U.S. developed a department of Jewish Evangelization. In 1920, the American Baptist Home Missionary Society emerged, followed by, in 1921, the Southern Baptist Convention Work Among Jews, the Christian Missionary Alliance (also in 1921) and the Methodist Episcopal Church South (1927). Silcox and Fisher, *Catholics, Jews and Protestants*, 277.

67. Catholics also made efforts to win converts during this period. The *Catholic Directory* tabulated the number of Protestant converts to Catholicism each year (in 1918, there were 24,552; in 1919, 23,625; in 1920, 28,379). This provoked great fear in many Protestants, as demonstrated in John F. Moore's *Will America Become Catholic?* (New York: Harper and Brothers, 1931). See also Silcox and Fisher, *Catholics, Jews and Protestants*, 290.

68. For more on this, see Kraut, "A Wary Collaboration," 199, 208–10, 212–15.

69. Pitt, *Adventures in Brotherhood*, 22.

70. Ibid., 15.

71. Straus, "Story of the National Conference," 4.

72. For a more thorough list, see Pitt, *Adventures in Brotherhood*, 16.

73. By 1940, after a decade in the job, Clinchy claimed to have traveled 150,000 miles, made 5,400 speeches, and appeared with Jews and Catholics on nearly 3,000 platforms. See High, "Satan, Be Warned." Clinchy would continue in the role until 1958.

74. "Constitution, 1936," Constitution folder, box 1, NCCJ Papers.

75. Lasker to Clinchy, April 21, 1953, NCCJ history folder, box 1, NCCJ Papers.

76. Ibid.

77. Ibid.

78. There were many similar statements, such as that by Denis A. McCarthy, a Catholic, who said at one of the first tri-faith conferences: "We are not here to reduce religion to the greatest common denominator. We are met to bring to the surface the differences that keep us apart in social and civic affairs, and by explanation and understanding to create a feeling of goodwill and mutual sympathy. We do not hope to bring in the millennium, but we do hope to lessen the sharpness and the acridness of racial and religious prejudice." Bernard C. Clausen, "Significant Goodwill Conference Brings Together Protestants, Catholics and Jews," *The Baptist*, May 16, 1931, 2, NCCJ History folder, box 1, NCCJ Papers. For the quote, see Silcox and Fisher, *Catholics, Jews and Protestants*, 334–35.

79. For more on this, see Kraut, "A Wary Collaboration," 214–15.

80. Blair to Clinchy and Ashworth, June 18, 1936, Carlton J. H. Hayes folder, box 9, NCCJ Papers.

81. Kraut, "A Wary Collaboration," 215–17.

82. Ibid., 198.

83. Silcox and Fisher, *Catholics, Jews and Protestants*, 306.

84. Pitt, *Adventures in Brotherhood*, 28.

85. For instance, in 1943, NCCJ materials read: "Shortly after 1928 the United States went through the gravest economic crisis in its history. Then followed the most rapid series of social changes in American history. Throughout the 1930s the Nazi anti-Jewish and anti-Christian propaganda was reflected in the United States with the effect of considerably increasing intergroup irritation here." The NCCJ was here to help. "This One People: Annual Report 1943," Annual Reports 1940–49 folder, box 1, NCCJ Papers, 14–15.

86. "The Anti-Semitic Menace in Germany," May 29, 1931, Committee on Goodwill Between Jews and Christians folder, box 1, NCCJ Papers.

87. Clincy to Ashworth, June 3, 1931, Committee on Goodwill Between Jews and Christians folder, box 1, NCCJ Papers.

88. Ibid.

89. "1,200 Clergymen Sign Nazi Protest," *New York Times*, May 26, 1933, 13.

90. Lasker to Clinchy, April 21, 1953, NCCJ History folder, box 1, NCCJ Papers.

91. Pitt, *Adventures in Brotherhood*, 26.

92. Ibid., 24.

93. Everett Clinchy, John Elliott Ross, and Morris Lazaron, "Story of the First Trio," dictated November 11, 1933, First Trio folder, box 1, NCCJ Papers, 1–2.

94. Ibid.

95. "Tolerance Trio," *Time*, February 11, 1935.

96. Clinchy, Ross, and Lazaron, "Story of the First Trio," 1.

97. Ibid., 3.

98. Ibid., 8.

99. Ibid., and Pitt, *Adventures in Brotherhood*, 40–62.

100. Pitt, *Adventures in Brotherhood*, 29.

101. Alfred McClung Lee, "Report on the Program Effectiveness of the National Conference of Christians and Jews," NCCJ Self-Evaluation Study 1942 folder, box 7, NCCJ Papers, 5–6.

102. Ibid., 2–3.

103. Clinchy to Hayes, August 16, 1933, Carleton J. H. Hayes folder, box 9, NCCJ Papers.

104. Lee, "Report on the Program Effectiveness," 3–4.

105. High, "Satan, Be Warned," 1–2.

106. On Washington's reception during these years, see Robert J. Norrell, *Up From History: The Life of Booker T. Washington* (Cambridge, Mass.: Harvard University Press, 2009), 421-44 and Kelefa Sanneh, "The Wizard," *New Yorker*, February 2, 2009, 26–30.

107. Pitt, *Adventures in Brotherhood*, 56.

108. Ibid., 57.

109. Ibid., 58.

110. Lee, "Report on the Program Effectiveness," 3.

111. Pitt, *Adventures in Brotherhood*, 62.

112. High, "Satan, Be Warned," 2.

113. Draft of the internal "Report for the Year 1932," Annual Reports 1928–32 folder, box 1, NCCJ Papers.

114. Lee, "Report on the Program Effectiveness," 2.

115. Ibid., 5–6.

116. Ibid., 3–4.

117. Ibid., 6.

118. Clinchy, *All in the Name of God*, 157–58.

119. Lee, "Report on the Program Effectiveness," 2.

120. Silcox and Fisher, *Catholics, Jews and Protestants*, 336.

121. Carleton Hayes was the NCCJ's unofficial monitor on Catholic opinion toward the NCCJ, and on any casual anti-Catholicism that might slip into NCCJ affairs, especially within the pages of the Religious News Service. He was especially active in giving reports on anti-Catholicism during the Spanish Civil War from 1936 to 1938. For his reports and pleadings,

see Hayes to Clinchy, December 28, 1937, Carlton J. H. Hayes folder, box 9, NCCJ Papers; Hayes to Ashworth, November 24, 1936, Carleton Hayes 1936–37 folder, box 9, NCCJ Papers; Hayes to Ashworth, December 22, 1937, Carleton Hayes 1936–37 folder, box 9, NCCJ Papers; and Hayes to Clinchy, April 6, 1932, Carlton J. H. Hayes folder, box 9, NCCJ Papers. For the bishops' prohibitions, see Pitt, *Adventures in Brotherhood*, 47.

CHAPTER 2

1. A. W. Gottschall, "An Adventure in Goodwill: The National Conference of Christians and Jews Program with Armed Forces," October 26, 1945, Gottschall Reports folder, box 32, NCCJ Papers, 6.

2. Ibid., 1.

3. Andrew W. Gottschall, "National Conference of Christians and Jews Camp Program," WWII Gottschall Reports folder, box 32, NCCJ Papers, 1.

4. Gottschall collected numerous comments from base commanders and enlisted men as a way to demonstrate the Camp Program's effectiveness and, more important, raise funds. The quotation comes from ibid., 3. Many similar testimonies conclude the Gottschall essay.

5. Franklin D. Roosevelt, "Excerpts from the Press Conference," April 8, 1941, John T. Woolley and Gerhard Peters, *The American Presidency Project* [online], http://www.presidency.ucsb.edu/ws/?pid=16096 (accessed February 25, 2009).

6. The National Catholic Community Services (NCCS) and the National Travelers Aid Association (NTAA) joined the USO shortly after the USO's incorporation. The NCCS was an umbrella organization that included the Knights of Columbus and several other large Catholic organizations. The Jewish Welfare Board was also an umbrella organization of Jewish service groups. The NTAA operated under the YWCA until the interwar years, when individual Travelers Aid Societies became independent, a process not completed until after World War II. For more on the USO, see Gretchen Knapp, "Experimental Social Policymaking During World War II: The United Service Organization (USO) and American War-Community Services (AWCS)," *Journal of Policy History* 12, 3 (2000): 321–38.

7. Roosevelt, "Excerpts from the Press Conference," April 8, 1941.

8. Everett R. Clinchy to Co-Chairman, Board and Area Directors, "The National Conference in a Nation at War," December 11, 1941, Annual Reports 1940–49 folder, box 1, NCCJ Papers, 3.

9. Charles O. Purdy to John T. Kendall, December 17, 1942, Gottschall Reports folder, box 32, NCCJ Papers.

10. D. V. Gaffney to John J. Caragher, December 14, 1944, ibid.

11. A. W. Gottschall, "Manual for Army Camp and Naval Station Program," January 1, 1943, Gottschall Reports folder, box 32, NCCJ Papers.

12. "Trialogue Outline," Gottschall Reports folder, box 32, NCCJ Papers, 1.

13. Gottschall, "Adventure in Goodwill," 19.

14. Gottschall, "Camp Program," 15.

15. Alice Moldenhawer, "Clerics Tell Soldiers Why We're Fighting," *New York World-Telegram*, October 9, 1943, World War II publications folder, box 11, NCCJ Papers.

16. Gottschall, "Camp Program," 4.

17. Chilton Bennett to Andrew Gottschall, reprinted in "Manual for Army Camp and Naval Station Program," January 1, 1943, Gottschall Reports folder, box 32, NCCJ Papers, 8.

18. A list of these materials, consisting of thirty-five titles, is in Gottschall, "Camp Program," 16.

19. "Heir to Millions," Why We Fight Series, Pamphlet No. 3, World War II Publications folder, box 11, NCCJ Papers.

20. "Consolidating Victory!" World War II Publications folder, box 11, NCCJ Papers.

21. "The Answer Is Yes!" World War II publications folder, box 11, NCCJ Papers, 5.

22. Gottschall, "Adventures in Goodwill," 20–21. For the NCCJ's decision early on to create this kind of literature for chaplains, see "Minutes," May 12, 1941, executive committee 1935–41 folder, box 2, NCCJ Papers, 2.

23. "Toward Brotherhood: The 1942 Annual Report," 1942 Annual Report folder, box 1, NCCJ Papers, 17.

24. Gottschall, "Adventures in Goodwill," 21.

25. "Board of Trustees Meeting," June 22, 1944, Board of Trustees 1941–45 folder, box 2, NCCJ Papers, 3–4.

26. Gottschall, "Camp Program," 3.

27. Moldenhawer, "Clerics Tell Soldiers Why We're Fighting."

28. Richard W. Steele, "The War on Intolerance: The Reformulation of American Nationalism, 1939–1941," *Journal of American Ethnic History* 9 (1989), 27.

29. The charter is reprinted in Louis Adamic, *From Many Lands* (New York: Harper & Brothers, 1940), 347.

30. Steele, "The War on Intolerance," 11–33.

31. *Carolene Products vs. United States*, 304 U.S. 152 n.4 (1938). Footnote 4 appeared in improbable fashion—as a footnote in a decision upholding federal laws that prohibited the interstate transfer of a product called filled milk. For an account of its authorship, suggesting that Stone regularly tested radical ideas in footnotes, see Alpheus T. Mason, *Harlan Fiske Stone, Pillar of the Law* (New York: Viking Press, 1956), 512–15. For an account of its judicial importance, see Robert M. Cover, "The Origins of Judicial Activism in the Protection of Minorities," *Yale Law Journal* 91, 7 (June 1982): 1287–316. See also William E. Nelson, *The Legalist Reformation: Law, Politics, and Ideology in New York, 1920–1980* (Chapel Hill: University of North Carolina Press, 2001), 123–24.

32. Geoffrey P. Millar, "The True Story of Carolene Products," *Supreme Court Review* (1987), 397.

33. New York State Constitution of 1938, Article 11.

34. *Revised Record of the Constitutional Convention of the State of New York, 1938* (Albany: L. B. Lyon, 1938), 1066–69.

35. Quotation in Carey McWilliams, "What We Did About Racial Minorities," in *While You Were Gone: A Report on Wartime Life in the United States*, ed. Jack Goodman (New York: Simon & Schuster, 1946), 95.

36. Statement of Thurgood Marshall, December 6, 1944, Group II, A-261, NY State, General, 1944–54 folder, Papers of the NAACP, Reel 18.

37. Meeting of the Executive Committee, December 22, 1941, Board of Trustees 1941–45 folder, box 2, NCCJ Papers, 1.

38. Ibid., 4.

39. Report submitted by Everett R. Clinchy at special meeting of Board of Trustees, December 31, 1941, Board of Trustees 1941–45 folder, box 2, NCCJ Papers, 1.

40. Ibid.

41. Ibid., 2–3.

42. Ibid., 4.

43. By the end of the war, the NCCJ publicized a list titled "American Leaders Who Are Actively Interested in the Program of the National Conference of Christians and Jews for the U.S. Armed Forces." The list included Charles Francis Adams, Winthrop Aldrich, John Foster Dulles, Marshall Field, Will Hays, Thomas W. Lamont, Herbert Lehman, Alfred Lundberg, Henry Luce, Louis B. Mayer, Donald M. Nelson, John D. Rockefeller Jr., David O. Selznick, Harold E. Stassen, and Wendell Willkie. "Space forbids the listing of the many hundreds of names," it added. See "The Answer Is Yes!" World War II publications folder, box 11, NCCJ Papers, 6.

44. "Excerpts from Address of Dr. Everett R. Clinchy to National Congress of Parents and Teachers," May 21, 1941, Clinchy Writings January–December 1941 folder, box 8, NCCJ Papers, 3.

45. Advance Memorandum to Board of Trustees on Program of National Conference in Relation to National Effort, March 7, 1942, Board of Trustees 1941–45 folder, box 2, NCCJ Papers, 1–12.

46. Board of Trustees meeting, March 7, 1942, Board of Trustees 1941–45 folder, box 2, NCCJ Papers, 1–3.

47. Ibid.

48. Ibid., 4.

49. For this part of Sinatra's career see the rather thin accounts in Donald Clarke, *All or Nothing at All: A Life of Frank Sinatra* (New York: Fromm International, 1997), 91; Jon Weiner, "His Way," *Nation*, June 8, 1998, 38; and Daniel Okrent, "At the Heart of American Music," in a booklet included with *Frank Sinatra: The Columbia Years, 1943–1952—The Complete Recordings*, a 12-CD set issued by Sony Music/Legacy Record (1993). Okrent's article was reprinted in *Frank Sinatra and Popular Culture: Essays on an American Icon*, ed. Leonard Mustazza (Westport, Conn.: Praeger Press, 1998), 111–15. For Sinatra's own take on "tolerance" in this period see, Frank Sinatra, "What's This About Races?" *Scholastic*, September 17, 1945, and reprinted in *Frank Sinatra and Popular Culture*, 23–25. For the quotations, see *Time*, October 1, 1945, 61–62.

50. *The House I Live In* (1945), dir. Mervyn LeRoy, written by Albert Maltz. For the creation of *The House I Live In*, see Clarke, *All or Nothing at All*, 91.

51. For the review in *Cue*, see Gene Ringgold and Clifford McCarty, *The Films of Frank Sinatra* (New York: Citadel Press, 1971), 46–47.

52. This transition is brilliantly recreated in Wendy Wall, *Inventing the "American Way": The Politics of Consensus from the New Deal to the Civil Rights Movement* (New York: Oxford University Press, 2008), 155–59.

53. For these attacks, see Board of Trustees Meeting, June 22, 1944, Board of Trustees, 1941–45 folder, box 2, NCCJ Papers, 2.

54. Ruth Benedict and Gene Weltfish, *The Races of Mankind*, Public Affairs Pamphlet No. 85 (New York: Public Affairs, 1943).

55. "Race Question," *Time*, January 31, 1944, 56.

56. "Impersonal?" *Time*, March 13, 1944; Julia L. Mickenberg, *Learning from the Left: Children's Literature, the Cold War, and Radical Politics in the United States* (New York: Oxford University Press, 2006), 94–95.

57. Robert J. Norrell, *The House I Live In: Race in the American Century* (New York: Oxford University Press, 2005), 131–33.

58. Board of Trustees meeting, June 25, 1943, Board of Trustees 1940–45 folder, box 2, NCCJ Papers, 5.

59. Pitt, *Adventures in Brotherhood*, 157.

60. "The Answer Is Yes!" World War II publications folder, box 11, NCCJ Papers, 4.

61. Mark Silk, "Notes on the Judeo-Christian Tradition in America," *American Quarterly* 36, 1 (Spring 1984): 67.

62. "Unity without uniformity" was Clinchy's standard description, which he used throughout the 1930s. For the World War II context of the phrase, see "Trends: >From a Report of Everett R. Clinchy," December 1940, Annual Report: 1940, Annual Reports 1940–49, box 1, NCCJ Papers.

63. "Report of the Director," November 28, 1938, Annual Report folder, box 1, NCCJ Papers, 1.

64. Everett Clinchy, "Broadcast to U.S.A. from London," September 28, 1941, Clinchy Writings January–December 1941 folder, box 8, NCCJ Papers, 1–2.

65. "Heir to Millions," Why We Fight Series, Pamphlet No. 3, World War II Publications folder, box 11, NCCJ Papers.

66. Two separate observers heard the comment, and, regardless of its veracity, American Catholics cited the statement throughout the war. See, for instance, Judge Robert McWilliams, "The Catholic and Intercreedal Cooperation," *The Monitor*, July 20, 1946 and July 27, 1946 and reprinted by the NCCJ in 1946, Catholics and NCCJ folder, box 11, NCCJ Papers, 1.

67. Frank L. Weil, "Greetings," in *A Book of Jewish Thoughts*, by Joseph H. Hertz (New York: National Jewish Welfare Board, 1943) vii–viii, and excellently described in Deborah Dash Moore, "Jewish GIs and the Creation of the Judeo-Christian Tradition," *Religion and American Culture* 8, 1 (Winter 1998), 36.

68. Before the war, the NCCJ seemed content to push for a more civic version of goodwill. For the argument that tri-faith peace was a single part of a broader definition of good Americanism, see Ellis Jensen, ed., *Speak Up for Good Will* (New York: National Conference of Christians and Jews, 1941).

69. Louis Finkelstein, J. Elliot Ross, William Adams Brown, *The Religions of Democracy: Judaism, Catholicism, Protestantism in Creed and Life* (New York: Devin-Adair, 1946), iii.

70. "Toward Brotherhood: The 1942 Annual Report," 3–5.

71. "Declaration of Fundamental Religious Beliefs Held in Common by Catholics, Protestants, and Jews," in "Toward Brotherhood," 19.

72. "Heir to Millions," Why We Fight Series, Pamphlet No. 3, World War II Publications folder, box 11, NCCJ Papers.

73. "Excerpts from Address of Dr. Everett R. Clinchy to National Congress of Parents and Teachers, May 21, 1941," Clinchy Writings January–December 1941 folder, box 8, NCCJ Papers, 1–3.

74. F. Earnest Johnson to Robert A. Ashworth, March 10, 1943, John Elliot Ross folder, box 1, NCCJ Papers, 1.

75. Johnson to Ashworth, March 10, 1943, 2. The authors sought to expand on a work by Henry P. Van Dusen of the Union Seminary, which put divinely originated natural rights at the center of the intellectual life of the early Republic. For Van Dusen's essay, see Henry P. Van Dusen, "Our Dual Heritage of Freedom," *Christianity and Crisis*, October 19, 1942, 1–2.

76. Quoted in Robert A. Ashworth to L. T. Hites, March 10, 1943, John Elliot Ross folder, box 1, NCCJ Papers.

77. Johnson to Ashworth, March 10, 1943, 2.

78. Everett R. Clinchy to George F. Zook, September 20, 1943, John Elliot Ross folder, box 1, NCCJ Papers.

79. The "standard operating procedure" concept and several of these examples derive from Moore, *G.I. Jews*, esp. 120–32, 148, 154–55. See also her essay "Jewish GIs and the Creation of the Judeo-Christian Tradition."

80. Maj. Gen. Frederick E. Uhl, "The Army Way," Conference 1944–50 folder, box 10, NCCJ Papers, 9.

81. Thomas C. Reeves, *America's Bishop: The Life and Times of Fulton J. Sheen* (San Francisco: Encounter Books, 2001), 138.

82. Ibid., 146–47.

83. Ibid., 147. Sheen also devoted several pages of his *Whence Comes War* to what he said was the vital relationship between religion and democracy: "A religion can live without democracy; it can live under tyranny, persecution and dictatorship—not comfortably, it is true, but heroically and divinely. But democracy will degenerate into demagogy by selling itself to the highest bidder." Ibid., 156.

84. Board of Trustees minutes, October 7, 1942, Board of Trustees 1941–45 folder, box 2, NCCJ Papers.

85. Ibid. See also "Statement on Cooperation by the Bishops of Texas and Oklahoma," June 1944, Catholics and NCCJ folder, box 11, NCCJ Papers; and Judge Robert McWilliams, "The Catholic and Intercreedal Cooperation," reprinted from the *Monitor*, July 20 and 27, 1946, Catholics and NCCJ folder, box 11, NCCJ Papers.

86. Board of Trustees meeting, June 25, 1943, Board of Trustees 1940–45 folder, box 2, NCCJ Papers, 2.

87. Ibid.

88. McWilliams, *Brothers Under the Skin*, 17.

89. For more on this history, see "America Will Observe 'Brotherhood Day' April 29," *Information Bulletin*, April 1934, Brotherhood Week folder, box 5, NCCJ Papers, 1–4; and Pitt, *Adventures in Brotherhood*, 88–96.

90. Pitt, *Adventures in Brotherhood*, 94.

91. "Toward Brotherhood: 1942 Annual Report," Toward Brotherhood folder, box 1, NCCJ Papers, 18.

92. Franklin D. Roosevelt to Dr. Clinchy, September 14, 1943, U.S. Presidents folder, box 1, NCCJ Papers.

93. Board of Trustees meeting, June 22, 1944, Board of Trustees 1941–45 folder, box 2, NCCJ Papers, 3.

94. "Three Gold Stars in Yesterday's Sky," 1945, WWII Pamphlets folder, box 32, NCCJ Papers.

95. "Three Pals," 194-, World War II Publications folder, box 11, NCCJ Papers.

CHAPTER 3

1. Wall, *Inventing the "American Way,"* 176–77.

2. "Request of the National Conference of Christians and Jews," June 5, 1946, Christians and Jews, National Association of 1949 folder, 13/2/305, box 1, Advertising Council Archives, University of Illinois, Urbana (hereafter Ad Council Papers), 1–3.

3. Meeting minutes, March 8, 1946, 12/2/201, box 3, Ad Council Papers, 2; and Rapplier to Clinchy, June 7, 1946, Christians and Jews, National Association of, 1949 folder, 13/2/305, box 1, Ad Council Papers.

4. For example, the Ad Council sent a representative to UNCF's meetings rather than publicly support its cause. Formal support would have to wait until the civil rights movement and the Ad Council's "A Mind Is a Terrible Thing to Waste" campaign of 1972.

5. Brown to Repplier, June 14, 1946, Christians and Jews, National Association of 1949 folder, 13/2/305, box 1, Ad Council Papers.

6. This was a form letter sent to seventeen agencies. For one, see Meldrum to Whittier, July 18, 1946, Christians and Jews, National Association of 1949 folder, 13/2/305, box 1, Ad Council Papers.

7. Meldrum to Whittier, July 18, 1946, Christians and Jews, National Association of 1949 folder, 13/2/305, box 1, Ad Council Papers.

8. "Thomas Brophy, Ad Executive, Dies Trying to Save 2 Children," *New York Times*, July 30, 1967, 65.

9. Wall, *Inventing the "American Way,"* 181–82.

10. Meldrum to Clark, July 25, 1946, Christians and Jews, National Association of, 1949 folder, 13/2/305, box 1, Ad Council Papers.

11. One of the first appeared on a radio show sponsored by Ionized Yeast. The Ad Council requested the NCCJ and several other organizations to send complimentary notes to the sponsor "not mentioning the [Ad] Council but simply telling them that it is felt this is very helpful to the whole program against prejudice." See, for one request, Meldrum to Dalsimer, September 13, 1946, Christians and Jews, National Association of, 1949 folder, 13/2/305, box 1, Ad Council Papers.

12. Wall, *Inventing the "American Way,"* 184.

13. "Ugh! foreigners!" March 1949, 13/2/207, 437com, Ad Council Papers.

14. "What's his race or religion got to do with it—He can pitch!" 13/2/207, 474new, Ad Council Papers.

15. "No Catholics, Jews, Protestants," 13/2/207, 528new, Ad Council Papers.

16. See Annual Reports, 1950–51, 13/2/202, Ad Council Papers, 24.

17. Meldrum to Cavert, July 22, 1946, Christians and Jews, National Association of, 1949 folder, 13/2/305, box 1, Ad Council Papers.

18. Meldrum to Bristol, July 22, 1946, Christians and Jews, National Association of, 1949 folder, 13/2/305, box 1, Ad Council Papers.

19. Those who disagreed with this assessment included George Shuster and Monsignor Howard J. Carroll of the National Catholic Welfare Conference. Meldrum to Bristol, July 31, 1946, Christians and Jews, National Association of, 1949 folder, 13/2/305, box 1, Ad Council Papers.

20. Ashworth to Young, October 23, 1946, Christians and Jews, National Association of, 1949 folder, 13/2/305, box 1, Ad Council Papers. See also Meldrum to Bristol, November 20, 1946.

21. Meldrum to Bernheim, June 19, 1946 and Meldrum to Clark, July 25, 1946, Christians and Jews, National Association of, 1949 folder, 13/2/305, box 1, Ad Council Papers.

22. A. A. Liveright to Repplier, September 20, 1946, Christians and Jews, National Association of, 1949 folder, 13/2/305, box 1, Ad Council Papers.

23. Meldrum to Blythe, September 23, 1946, Christians and Jews, National Association of, 1949 folder, 13/2/305, box 1, Ad Council Papers.

24. Inter-Office Memorandum, December 17, 1946, Christians and Jews, National Association of, 1949 folder, 13/2/305, box 1, Ad Council Papers.

25. Wall, *Inventing the "American Way,"* 184.

26. Meldrum to Egan, September 27, 1946, Christians and Jews, National Association of, 1949 folder, 13/2/305, box 1, Ad Council Papers, and "Don't Give Me That Stuff," 1951 campaign, 13/2/207, 528new, Ad Council Papers.

27. For an excellent and funny illumination of the quotation and the context in which it was said, see Patrick Henry, "'And I Don't Care What It Is': The Tradition-History of a Civil Religion Proof-Text," *Journal of the American Academy of Religion* 49 (1981), 41.

28. And for a liberalism beyond America too. In 1950, the NCCJ founded the World Organization for Brotherhood, a global counterpart of the NCCJ, which, the plan was, would ultimately melt into the World Organization. The World Organization received pledges of support from the World Council of Churches and priests and rabbis from around Europe. "Statesmen of the Western world," said Roger Straus, "must employ all their skill" to establish international goodwill. "But only spiritual force will gain them the heights of their aspiration, because it is only the idealistic man who has the power to give life to progress." See "Brotherhood," *Time*, June 19, 1950, 59.

29. Gustave Weigel, S.J., "Americans Believe That Religion Is a Good Thing," *America*, November 5, 1955, 150.

30. These numbers come from the Princeton Religious Research Index (PRRI), a measurement of eight indicators of belief and practices. The Princeton Religious Research Center was founded by George Gallup. See George H. Gallup, *Religion in America 2002* (Princeton, N.J.: Princeton Religious Research Center, 2002), 18–34, 56–57.

31. "Readers and Religion," *Time*, August 19, 1957, 48.

32. "Dynamo in the Vineyard," *Time*, November 1, 1954, 70.

33. "Remarks Recorded for the 'Back-to-God' Program of the American Legion," February 20, 1955, John T. Woolley and Gerhard Peters, *The American Presidency Project* [online], http://www.presidency.ucsb.edu/ws/?pid=10414 (accessed April 7, 2009).

34. Dwight D. Eisenhower, "Remarks Broadcast as Part of the American Legion 'Back to God' Program," February 7, 1954, ibid., (accessed April 7, 2009).

35. This was from Truman's Brotherhood Week speech in 1950, quoted in Roger W. Straus, "Mid-Century at the Crossroads," *Conference* (1950), *Conference 1944–1950* folder, box 10, NCCJ Papers, 2.

36. Harry Truman to Eric Johnson, September 10, 1951, U.S. Presidents folder, box 1, NCCJ Papers.

37. "Text of Dulles' U.N. Appeal to Soviet for Korean Unity and Help to End World Tensions," *New York Times*, September 18, 1953, 4.

38. Joseph B. Matthews, "Reds and Our Churches," *American Mercury*, July 1953, 3–13.

39. Responses are recorded in Pitt, *Adventures in Brotherhood*, 183–84, and "Uncheckable Charge," *Time*, July 13, 1953.

40. The telegram is quoted at length in the NCCJ's in-house history. Pitt, *Adventures in Brotherhood*, 184–85.

41. Message to the National Conference of Christians and Jews, July 9, 1953, *Public Papers of the Presidents: Dwight D. Eisenhower, 1953*, 489–90.

42. "One Nation Under God: Report of the National Conference of Christians and Jews: 1954," annual reports folder, box 59, NCCJ Papers, 1.

43. The report also said that the NCCJ was, "beyond doubt, the premier agency in its field." Sterling W. Brown to All Professional Staff, February 5, 1958, Evaluation Study 1958 folder, box 7, NCCJ Papers, 1–4.

44. For a good overview, see Edward A. Purcell Jr., *The Crisis of Democratic Theory: Scientific Naturalism and the Problem of Value* (Lexington: University Press of Kentucky, 1973); John Dewey, *Liberalism and Social Action* (New York: Putnam, 1935); Robert B. Westbrook, *John*

Dewey and American Democracy (Ithaca, N.Y.: Cornell University Press, 1991); and Lionel Trilling, *The Liberal Imagination* (New York: Doubleday, 1949).

45. Martin E. Marty, *Under God, Indivisible, 1941–1960: Modern American Religion, vol. 3* (Chicago: University of Chicago Press, 1996), 299–301.

46. Budd Schulberg, *What Makes Sammy Run?* (New York: Modern Library, 1952), xiv, and first identified in Silk, "Notes of the Judeo-Christian Tradition," 65.

47. H. Stuart Hughes, "On Social Salvation," *Saturday Review of Literature*, March 3, 1951, 14, in Will Herberg, *Protestant-Catholic-Jew: An Essay in American Religious Sociology* (Garden City, N.Y.: Doubleday, 1955), 67–68.

48. This idea is similar to what James Fisher calls the "spiritual front" of the 1940s and 1950s that replaced the "popular front" of the 1930s. See James T. Fisher, *On the Irish Waterfront: The Crusader, the Movie, and the Soul of the Port of New York* (Ithaca, N.Y.: Cornell University Press, 2009), 132–33, 214.

49. "One Nation Under God: A Report on Our Moral and Spiritual Resources for Brotherhood, 1954," One Nation Under God folder, box 6, NCCJ Papers, 12–13, 6.

50. Ibid., 6. Italics mine.

51. "Religious Leaders Hail RIAL Campaign," *Religious News Service*, November 18. 1959, 3, Religion in American Life folder, box 50, NCCJ Papers.

52. "To Pray or Not to Pray," *Time*, August 8, 1960, 63.

53. Ibid.

54. Reeves, *America's Bishop*, 260.

55. Wall, *Inventing the "American Way,"* 178.

56. Ibid.

57. *Newsweek*, April 2, 1952, 118.

58. "Embarrassing Questions," *Time*, October 8, 1956, 76–77.

59. "Postage Due," *Time*, December 26, 1960, 6.

60. *Big City*, dir. Norman Taurog, MGM Films, 1948. The film never made the technological conversion to VHS, much less DVD. And even the UCLA Film and Television Archive, which houses a number of films available only in 16 mm format, does not have a copy. My information comes from several reviews, commemorative write-ups, and an interview with an actor who had a marginal role in the film.

61. Wall, *Inventing the "American Way,"* 198–99.

62. "Three Faiths in Harmony: Unique Chapels, Separate but Related, Serve Protestants, Catholics and Jews," *Life*, November 21, 1955, 113–18.

63. For more on the vibrant Christian fascination with the Old Testament during these years, see Silk, "Notes on the Judeo-Christian Tradition," 70–73.

64. For Jewish interest in, and adaptation of, Jesus, see Stephen Prothro, *American Jesus: How the Son of God Became a National Icon* (New York: Farrar, Straus & Giroux, 2003), 229–66.

65. "The Bridge," *Time*, February 27, 1956.

66. "Christianity as Culture," *Time*, May 5, 1961, 54.

67. Nelson N. Foote et al., *Housing Choices and Housing Constraints* (New York: McGraw-Hill, 1960), 407.

68. Quotation in Marty, *Under God, Indivisible*, 300.

69. For these, see Chapters 4–8.

70. Amy Vanderbilt, *Amy Vanderbilt's Complete Book of Etiquette: A Guide to Gracious Living* (Garden City, N.Y.: Doubleday, 1952), 243–49.

71. Emily Post, *Etiquette: The Blue Book of Social Usage* (New York: Funk and Wagnalls, 1945), 248–49.

72. Vanderbilt, *Amy Vanderbilt's Complete Book of Etiquette*, 244.

73. Ibid., 243–49.

74. *Emily Post's Etiquette: The Blue Book of Social Usage*, rev. Elizabeth L. Post (New York: Funk and Wagnalls, 1965), 388, 155–57. Quotation on 39.

75. Herberg, *Protestant-Catholic-Jew*, 276.

76. Will Herberg, "The Sectarian Conflict over Church and State: A Divisive Threat to Our Democracy?" *Commentary*, November 1952, 450–62.

77. Ibid., 54. Herberg was not alone in this cynicism. Several sociologists, most prominently Seymour Martin Lipset and Robin Williams Jr., questioned the depth of commitment: one study compared a survey of 1925 with one of 1950 and found a steep decline in religious activity among leading business executives, although, added Lipset, "there is no question that formal church membership has increased since the 1930's." Williams claimed, "Religious observances have been losing their supernatural or other-worldly character." Lipset, "Religion in America: What Religious Revival?" *Columbia University Forum*, Winter 1959, 19; Williams quoted in Lipset, 20.

78. For Herberg's appreciation of Riesman, see Herberg, *Protestant-Catholic-Jew*, 70–73. In addition, Herberg's copy of *The Lonely Crowd*, now in the archives of Drew University, is filled with notes and other marginalia.

79. Herberg, *Protestant-Catholic-Jew*, 69–70, 274.

80. Ibid., 51, 44.

81. Ibid., 49.

82. Ibid., 53. Emphasis in original.

83. Ibid., 55.

84. Ibid., 139.

85. Ibid., 137, 148 n. 60.

86. Ibid., 168–69.

87. Ibid., 171.

88. Ibid., 174–75.

89. Ibid., 204–5.

90. Ibid., 207.

91. Ibid., 209–10.

92. Reinhold Niebuhr, "America's Three Melting Pots," *New York Times*, September 25, 1955, BR6.

93. August B. Hollingshead, "Trends in Social Stratification," *American Sociological Review*, December 1952, 685.

94. Ruby Jo Kennedy, "Single or Triple Melting Pot?" *American Journal of Sociology*, January 1944, 331–39.

95. See, for example, Elin Anderson, *We Americans* (Cambridge, Mass.: Harvard University Press, 1938) and C. Wendell King, "Branford Center: A Community Study in Social Cleavage," Ph.D. dissertation, Yale University, 1943.

96. Berger, *Working-Class Suburb*, 40.

97. Marty, "The New Shape of American Religion," *Christian Century*, 1958, esp. 1176–79.

98. John Courtney Murray, S.J., *We Hold These Truths: Catholic Reflections on the American Proposition* (New York: Sheed and Ward, 1960), esp. 18–24.

99. Will Herberg, "Discussion of Herberg's 'Protestantism in a Post-Protestant America,'" *Christianity and Crisis*, February 5, 1962, 11.

100. Charles H. Anderson, *White Protestant Americans: From National Origins to Religious Group* (Englewood Cliffs, N.J.: Prentice-Hall, 1970), 1.

101. Reeves, *America's Bishop*, 206–11.

102. Ibid., 240.

103. For a similar take, see John McGreevy, *Catholicism and American Freedom* (New York: W. W. Norton, 2003), 211–15.

104. For a careful study of Catholic support for McCarthy, see Donald F. Crosby, S.J., *God, Church, and Flag: Senator Joseph R. McCarthy and the Catholic Church, 1950–1957* (Chapel Hill: University of North Carolina Press, 1978), esp. 228–51.

105. Peter Kihss, "City Police Cheer Talk by M'Carthy," *New York Times*, April 5, 1954, 12.

106. *American Ecclesiastical Review* 134 (January–June 1956): 414–15, and reported in "Offer in Error," *Time*, July 9, 1956, 38.

107. Silk, "Notes on the Judeo-Christian Tradition," 77 and Murray, *We Hold These Truths*, 138.

108. These numbers come from the *Official Catholic Directory, 1959* and were reported in "Catholic Growth," *Time*, May 25, 1959, 58.

109. John L. Thomas, *The American Catholic Family* (Englewood Cliffs, N.J.: Prentice-Hall, 1956).

110. See especially Andrew M. Greeley, *The American Catholic: A Social Portrait* (New York: Basic Books, 1977); Andrew M. Greeley, William C. McCready, and Kathleen McCourt, *Catholic Schools in a Declining Church* (Kansas City: Sheed & Ward, 1976), esp. chaps. 1 and 2; Andrew M. Greeley, *American Catholics Since the Council: An Unauthorized Report* (Chicago: Thomas More Press, 1985), 28–48; and Andrew M. Greeley and Peter H. Rossi, *The Education of Catholic Americans* (Chicago: Aldine 1966), 118–46.

111. *Three Brave Men*, dir. Philip Dunne, Twentieth Century-Fox Film Corporation, 1956. Goldsmith is played by the evidently pan-religious Ernest Borgnine, who played a Catholic in the previous year's *Marty*, which won Best Picture at the 1956 Academy Awards.

112. The case is described in Stuart Svonkin, *Jews Against Prejudice: American Jews and the Fight for Civil Liberties* (New York: Columbia University Press, 1997), 151–60; quotation on 152.

113. Ibid., 161–77.

114. Edward S. Shapiro, *A Time for Healing: American Jewry Since World War II* (Baltimore, Md.: Johns Hopkins University Press, 1992), 36.

115. Sholem Asch, *One Destiny: An Epistle to the Christians*, trans. Milton Hindus (New York: G. P. Putnam, 1945), 70, 83; Moore, "Jewish GIs and the Creation of the Judeo-Christian Tradition," 38.

116. Morris Freedman, "New Jewish Community in Formation: A Conservative Center Catering to Present-Day Needs," *Commentary*, January 1955, 36–47.

117. For this, see Jonathan D. Sarna, *American Judaism: A History* (New Haven, Conn.: Yale University Press, 2004), 279–82, and Stephen J. Whitfield, *The Culture of the Cold War* (Baltimore: Johns Hopkins University Press, 1996), 77–100.

118. Joshua L. Leibman, *Peace of Mind: Insights on Human Nature that can Change your Life* (New York: Citadel Press, 1994 [1946]), 145–47, 152.

119. Moore, *G.I. Jews*, 200–48.

120. Hasia R. Diner, *We Remember with Reverence and Love: American Jews and the Myth of Silence After the Holocaust, 1945–1962* (New York: New York University Press, 2009).

121. "Work Done," *Time*, March 30, 1953, 15, and Wayne A. Ratzlaff, "Saving Grace: Carl McIntire and the Anti-Communist Crusade Against Bishop G. Bromley Oxnam," unpublished paper, University of Illinois at Chicago, 2006.

122. Drew Pearson, "One Church for Protestant GIs?" *Washington Post and Times Herald,* July 14, 1957, E5; Chaplain Charles I. Carpenter to Stanley Lichtenstein, July 26, 1957, Military Chaplaincy and State folder, box 34, NCCJ Papers.

123. Will Herberg, "The Sectarian Conflict Over Church and State" (1952), in *From Marxism to Judaism: Collected Essays of Will Herberg,* ed. David D. Dalin (New York: Markus Weiner Publishing, 1989), 196.

124. "Era of Good Feeling?" *Time,* June 2, 1958, 66–67.

125. Robert McAfee Brown and Gustave Weigel, S.J., *An American Dialogue: A Protestant Looks at Catholicism and a Catholic Looks at Protestantism* (Garden City, N.Y.: Anchor Books, 1961), 14.

CHAPTER 4

1. Herbert Gans, *The Urban Villagers: Group and Class in the Life of Italian-Americans* (New York: Free Press of Glencoe, 1962); e-mail correspondence with author, October 2, 2008; Herbert Gans, *The Levittowners: Ways of Life and Politics in a New Suburban Community* (New York: Vintage, 1969), xvii–xviii, 3–4.

2. E-mail correspondence with author, October 2, 2008.

3. The phrase "myth of suburbia" comes from Berger, *Working Class Suburb,* chapter 1, which also contains a good analysis of it. The most famous portrait of this myth is John Keats, *The Crack in the Picture Window* (Boston: Houghton Mifflin, 1956).

4. E-mail correspondence with author, October 6, 2008.

5. Gans, *The Levittowners,* xvii.

6. E-mail correspondence with author, October 6, 2008.

7. Gans, *The Levittowners,* 22.

8. Ibid., 413–14.

9. E-mail correspondence with author, October 6, 2008.

10. Gans, *The Levittowners,* vi, xviii–xix.

11. Ibid., 68–80.

12. Ibid., 49, 53, 63, 76.

13. Ibid., 50, 64, 90, 96, 97, 113–14.

14. Ibid., 121.

15. Ibid., 44, 61.

16. E-mail correspondence with author, October 1, 2008.

17. E-mail correspondence with author, October 6, 2008.

18. Gans, *The Levittowners,* 84.

19. Ibid., 84.

20. See Nathan Glazer and Daniel Patrick Moynihan, *Beyond the Melting Pot: The Negroes, Puerto Ricans, Jews, Italians and Irish of New York City* (Cambridge, Mass.: MIT Press, 1963).

21. Gans, *Urban Villagers.*

22. "The Cardinal on Housing," *Providence Visitor,* February 19, 1959, 3.

23. "Catholic Leader Hits Living Restrictions as 'Legal Ghettos,'" American Council on Race Relations Report, June 1946, 1.

24. "Statement on Churches' Concern for Housing," November 18, 1953, Non-AJC folder, box 104, Papers of the American Jewish Committee, YIVO Institute for Jewish History, New York, New York.

25. See, for example, "Building Brotherhood, February 19–26, 1950," Cartoons folder, box 97, RG 347.17.10, Papers of the American Jewish Committee.

26. *American Jewish Year Book, 1951* (New York: American Jewish Committee, 1951), 54.

27. Ibid., 54–55.

28. *Shelley v. Kraemer* 334 U.S. 1 (1948).

29. Sidney Fine, *Frank Murphy: The Washington Years* (Ann Arbor: University of Michigan Press, 1984).

30. *Shelley v. Kraemer* (1948). See also William C. Berman, *The Politics of Civil Rights in the Truman Administration* (Columbus: Ohio State University Press, 1970).

31. *Barrows v. Jackson*, 346 U.S. 249 (1953).

32. The story appeared throughout the popular press. A recent recapitulation can be found in Stephen Richard Highley, *Privilege, Power, and Place: The Geography of the American Upper Class* (Lanham, Md.: Rowman & Littlefield, 1995), 41–42.

33. U.S. Commission on Civil Rights, *Report of the United States Commission on Civil Rights, 1959*, Housing [19]42–62 folder, box 103, RG 347.17.10, Papers of the American Jewish Committee.

34. *ADL Bulletin*, January 1959, 1.

35. "AJC Speaks Up for Fair Housing," housing 1946–61 folder, box 103, Papers of the American Jewish Committee.

36. Dr. Dan W. Dodson, "The Role of Church and Synagogue in the Racially Changing Community," in *Race: Challenge to Religion: Original Essays and* An Appeal of the Conscience *from the National Conference on Religion and Race*, ed. Mathew Ahmann (Chicago: Henry Regnery, 1963), 80.

37. U.S. Commission on Civil Rights, *Report of the United States Commission on Civil Rights, 1959*.

38. "Dixie Likes Levittown," *Pittsburgh Courier*, August 31, 1957, 2.

39. "Suburbia: High Cost of Democracy," *Time*, December 7, 1959, 22. Several articles, meanwhile, challenged the assertion that African Americans brought down property values; see Charles Abrams, "Gresham's Law of Neighborhoods," *Journal of Real Estate Appraisers*, March 1952, and Luigi Laurenti, "Effects of Nonwhite Purchases on Market Prices of Residencies," *Journal of Real Estate Appraisers*, July 1952.

40. Morris Zelditch, "Suburbia," an address delivered at the (Jewish) National Community Relations Advisory Council, June 16, 1955, Integration-Identity folder, box 210, Papers of the American Jewish Committee.

41. Andrew M. Greeley, *Why Can't They Be Like Us? America's White Ethnic Groups* (New York: Dutton, 1971), 104.

42. Ibid., 108, 110–11.

43. Ibid., 110–11.

44. Ibid., 106–7, 112, 117.

45. E-mail correspondence with Marian Ronan, January 27, 2003.

46. "Memories of a Catholic Boyhood" is the first chapter of Garry Wills, *Bare Ruined Choirs: Doubt, Prophecy, and Radical Religion* (New York: Dell, 1971), 15–16, 37.

47. August Hollingshead, "Cultural Factors in the Selection of Marriage Mates," *American Sociological Review*, October 1950, 624, 627.

48. Gerhard Lenski, *The Religious Factor: A Sociological Study of the Impacts of Religion on Politics, Economics, and Family Life* (New York: Doubleday, 1961), 48–49.

49. John L. Thomas, "The Factor of Religion in the Selection of Marriage Mates," *American Sociological Review* 16, 4 (August 1951): 487–91.

50. Ibid.

51. Wills, *Bare Ruined Choirs*, 19.

52. Marshall Sklare and Joseph Greenblum, *Jewish Identity on the Suburban Frontier* (New York: Basic Books, 1967), 271, 277. See also the companion volume, studying the same community, Benjamin B. Ringer, *The Edge of Friendliness* (New York: Basic Books, 1967) and parts of each volume that were combined and excerpted in Marshall Sklare, ed., *The Jewish Community in America* (New York: Behrman House, 1974).

53. Sklare, ed., *The Jewish Community in America*, 342.

54. Ibid., 350.

55. Ibid., 351.

56. Sklare and Greenblum, *Jewish Identity on the Suburban Frontier*, 280.

57. Marshall Sklare, Joseph Greenblum, and Benjamin B. Ringer, *Note Quite at Home: How an American Jewish Community Lives with Itself and Its Neighbors* (New York: Institute of Human Relations Press, 1969), 35.

58. Jay P. Dolan, *The American Catholic Experience: A History from Colonial Times to the Present* (Garden City, N.Y.: Image Books, 1985), 382.

59. Albert I. Gordon, *Jews in Suburbia* (Boston: Beacon Press, 1959), 232.

60. Ibid., 170.

61. Ibid., 232.

62. Edward S. Shapiro develops the same point in his *A Time for Healing*, 129. For the quotations, see Harry Golden, "Jews of the South," in *Mid-Century: An Anthology of Jewish Life and Culture in Our Times* (New York: Beechhurst Press, 1955), 216, 220, 218, 221.

63. Nathan Glazer, "Judaism in Suburbia," *ADL Bulletin*, February 1958, 5.

64. American Jewish Committee, "Background Memorandum for Executive Board Meeting," January 21–22, 1961, Community Relations 1961–62 folder, box 62, RG 347.17.10, Papers of the American Jewish Committee, 2.

65. Zelditch, "Suburbia," 8.

66. Sklare and Greenblum, *Jewish Identity on the Suburban Frontier*, 294, 307–11, 314–16.

67. Sklare, ed., *The Jewish Community in America* (New York: Behrman House, 1974), 348–49.

68. Ibid., 358–59.

69. John T. McGreevy, *Parish Boundaries: The Catholic Encounter with Race in the Twentieth Century Urban North* (Chicago, Ill.: University of Chicago Press, 1998), 83–84. It is also the central theme of Gamm, *Urban Exodus*.

70. Foote et al., *Housing Choices and Housing Constraints*, 407–8.

71. Lenski, *The Religious Factor*, 141, 92, 196, 198, 60, 63–64, 33–34.

72. Ibid., 110, 197, 198, 206, 209, 240, 251.

73. Ibid., 60, 20, 124.

74. Ibid., 29, 54–55.

75. Ibid., 291, 288, 17–18, 289.

76. Ibid., 296, 326, 328, 329, 31.

77. Howe quotation in Deborah Dash Moore, *To the Golden Cities: Pursuing the American Jewish Dream in Miami and L.A.* (Cambridge, Mass.: Harvard University Press, 1994), 6.

78. Greeley, *Why Can't They Be Like Us?*, 115.

CHAPTER 5

1. Spencer Rich, "Religion in Public Schools: A Case History," *Congress Weekly*, found in CLSA Materials: July–December 1957, a collection compiled by the American Jewish Congress, New York, N.Y. Thanks to Marc Stern for granting me access to these files. "Suburb Districts End School Votes," *New York Times*, May 3, 1956.

2. Rich, "Religion in Public Schools."

3. Ibid.

4. The first disestablishment occurred at the time of the nation's founding, through four foundational documents: James Madison's 1785 "Memorial and Remonstrance Against Religious Assessments," Thomas Jefferson's 1786 "Virginia Statute of Religious Freedom," Article VI of the U.S. Constitution (1787), and the First Amendment (1789). Together, these four documents ensure that the nation cannot mandate religious tests for those vying for political office, cannot establish a national religion (or impose taxes in support of one), and cannot infringe upon someone performing religious activities (within certain limits). In general, in Madison's words, they ensure that "the Religion of every man must be left to the conviction and conscience of every man."

5. This story is recounted in Naomi W. Cohen, *Jews in Christian America: The Pursuit of Religious Equality* (New York: Oxford University Press, 1992), 146.

6. Will Herberg, "The Sectarian Conflict over Church and State," *Commentary* 14 (November 1952): 450–64.

7. *America*, September 1, 1962, 665–66.

8. James W. Fraser, *Between Church and State: Religion and Public Education in a Multicultural America* (New York: St. Martin's Press, 1999), 131–44; R. Laurence Moore, "Bible Reading and Nonsectarian Schooling: The Failure of Religious Instruction in Nineteenth-Century Public Education," *Journal of American History* 86 (March 2000): 1581–99; and David Tyack and Elisabeth Hansot, *Managers of Virtue: Public School Leadership in America, 1820–1980* (New York: Basic Books, 1982).

9. Will Herberg, "Summary Statement on 'the American Tradition on Church and State,'" Articles Unpublished File, RG 14.2, Will Herberg Papers, Will Herberg Collection, Drew University, Madison, N.J.; George Gallup et al., *The Gallup Poll: Public Opinion, 1935-1971* (Wilmington, Del.: Scholarly Resources, 1972), 3:1779. The most famous crèche, legally speaking, was that in Ossining, New York, which first appeared in 1956. On Ten Commandments plaques, see Leo Pfeffer, "Memo of Law in Opposition," May 15, 1957, CLSA Materials: July–December 1957, a collection compiled by the American Jewish Congress, New York, N.Y.

10. The NEA data are reprinted in the *American Jewish Year Book, 1951* (New York: American Jewish Committee, 1951), 48–49.

11. Douglas's famous quotation comes from his opinion in *Zorach v. Clauson*. For the National Council of Churches of Christ quotation, see the *American Jewish Year Book, 1954* (New York: American Jewish Committee, 1954), 50.

12. *New York Times*, March 1, 1947, 16. For the argument of the New York Board of Rabbis, see Harold H. Gordon, "Letter to the Editor," *New York Times*, March 5, 1947, 24.

13. The story is recounted in the *American Jewish Year Book, 1954*, 52–53, and *America*, January 31, 1953, 471.

14. "New Concepts," *Time*, November 27, 1947.

15. Henry P. Van Dusen, *God in Education* (New York: Scribner, 1951).

16. Luce is quoted in the *American Jewish Year Book, 1947–1948* (New York: American Jewish Committee, 1948), 25; the 1953 bills on Bible reading are discussed in the *American Jewish Year Book, 1954*, 52.

17. Herberg, "Sectarian Conflict," 191.

18. Howard M. Squadron, testifying on behalf of the American Jewish Congress at House subcommittee hearings held in New York, July 10, 1995, cited in Fraser, *Between Church and State*, 144–45.

19. For the Catholic bishops quotation, see the *American Jewish Year Book, 1954*, 49; Benjamin Fine, "Catholic Schools Raise Enrollment to 4,000,000 Peak," *New York Times*, May 30, 1952, 1; and for the development of elite Catholic schools, see Milton M. Gordon, *Assimilation in American Life: The Role of Race, Religion, and National Origins* (New York: Oxford University Press, 1964), 210–12.

20. The Cleveland case and the Dundee Elementary School are discussed in the *American Jewish Year Book, 1951*, 50–51. Regarding the "Protestantization of American Judaism," Shapiro also emphasizes the changing nature of Jewish worship and the timing of sermons. Edward S. Shapiro, *A Time for Healing: American Jewry Since World War II* (Baltimore: Johns Hopkins University Press, 1992), 166–68.

21. Leo Pfeffer and Phil Blum, "Public School Sectarianism and the Jewish Child," May 1957, 2, in CLSA Materials January–June 1957.

22. Quoted from Pfeffer and Blum, "Public School Sectarianism," 11.

23. The letter is Exhibit P-1 in the "Appendix to Appellant's Brief," *Ralph Lecoque and Bernard Tudor v. Board of Education of the Borough of Rutherford and the Gideons International*, 14 N.J. 31, 100 A.2d 857 (1953), State of New Jersey, *Supreme Court of New Jersey*, vol. 305 (Newark, N.J.: Adams Press, 1954), 99a–100a.

24. "Brief for Plaintiff-Appellant," ibid., 4.

25. "Appendix to Appellant's Brief," ibid., 9a, 100a, 71a–73a, 101a.

26. Ibid., 24a.

27. Ibid., 3a.

28. Ibid., 24a–25a.

29. On Catholics and Jews joining forces, *New York Times*, October 4, 1953, 65; Will Maslow and Shad Polier, two prominent attorneys from Jewish organizations, joined Pfeffer when the *Tudor* case was appealed to the U.S. Supreme Court.

30. "Appendix to Appellant's Brief," *Tudor v. Board*, 28a–29a.

31. Several of the Advertising Council posters for its "United America" campaign of 1949–50, for example, showed schoolchildren being discriminated against because of race or religion. Civil rights liberals, business interests, and the federal government all supported the Ad Council. The posters can be found in file 474, New United America, Advertising Council Archives.

32. On "democratic education," see *Tudor v. Board*, 58a–59a; on the "unconstitutional preference," see "Brief for Plaintiff-Appellant," *Tudor v. Board*, 6.

33. Ibid., 11–13.

34. For Chein's quotation, see "Appendix to Appellant's Brief," *Tudor v. Board*, 42a–43a; for the second expert, ibid., 56a.

35. *Doremus et al. v. Board of Education of the Borough of Hawthorne et al.* 342 U.S. 429 (1952); for its use in the *Tudor* case, see "Appendix to Appellant's Brief," *Tudor v. Board*, 65a–66a.

36. "Appendix to Appellant's Brief," *Tudor v. Board*, 75a–76a.

37. Ibid., 81a–91a.

38. Ibid., 96a.

39. *New York Times*, October 4, 1953, 65.

40. Ibid.

41. *Bernard Tudor v. Board of Education of the Borough of Rutherford and the Gideons International* 14 N.J. 31 (1953).

42. Ibid.

43. *Life*, December 26, 1955, 56; and Herberg, "The Sectarian Conflict," 450–64.

44. That anti-Catholicism sits at the root of most of the separation discussion since the 1840s is the main argument in Philip Hamburger, *Separation of Church and State* (Cambridge, Mass.: Harvard University Press, 2002). See also Gregg Ivers, *To Build a Wall: American Jews and the Separation of Church and State* (Charlottesville: University of Virginia Press, 1995).

45. Cohen, *Jews in Christian America*, 167.

46. Stephen D. Solomon, *Ellery's Protest: How One Young Man Defied Tradition and Sparked the Battle over School Prayer* (Ann Arbor: University of Michigan Press, 2007), 61–62.

47. American Jewish Congress, "In Defense of Religious Liberty," Church + State Misc. folder, box 37, RG I-77, Papers of the American Jewish Congress.

48. *Church v. Bullock*, 109 S.W. 115, 118 (Tex. 1908).

49. Leo Pfeffer, "The Gideons March on the Schools," *Congress Weekly*, October 10, 1953, 7–9, and December 21, 1953, 3–4, in Cohen, *Jews in Christian America*, 192.

50. Solomon, *Ellery's Protest*, 263, 319–20.

51. *Proposed Amendments to the Constitution Relating to Prayers and Bible Reading in the Public Schools*, 1964, 825–29 (statement of Bishop Fulton J. Sheen), in Solomon, *Ellery's Protest*, 320.

CHAPTER 6

1. Alfred McClung Lee, *Fraternities Without Brotherhood: A Study of Prejudice on the American Campus* (Boston: Beacon Press, 1955), 15–16.

2. Ibid., 26–27.

3. Lawrence Bloomgarden to Maurice W. Jacobs, June 28, 1960, Teich-Jacobs Correspondence, box 88, RG 347.10, Papers of the American Jewish Committee.

4. Lawrence Bloomgarden to Vigdor W. Kavaler, February 26, 1959, Alpha Epsilon Pi folder, box 89, Papers of the American Jewish Committee.

5. A similar debate, and outcome, occurred in collegiate sororities as much as a decade later, though fraternities set the precedent. See Shira Kohn, "'The World Is Not Ready for This': Jewish Sororities and the Desegregation Question," Association for Jewish Studies 39th Annual Conference, Toronto, Canada, December 16–18, 2007.

6. Nelson Antrim Crawford, "Goddesses of Learning," *American Mercury*, November 24, 1931, 290–98, in Clyde S. Johnson, *Fraternities in Our Colleges* (New York: National Interfraternity Foundation, 1972), 217.

7. For a description of what he calls "Aryanism," see Lee, *Fraternities Without Brotherhood*, ix–xi. See also James Rorty, "Greek Letter Discrimination," *Commentary*, February 1956, 121; and *Time*, June 25, 1965, 53.

8. Numbers quoted from Dean A. Ray Warnock, "Letter," *New York Times*, December 5, 1948.

9. Rorty, "Greek Letter Discrimination," 120.

10. "National Fraternities Prepare for a Record Year," *New York Times*, June 9, 1946, 70; for the case at Brown University, Vince Heath Whitney, "Fraternities at Brown University," *Social Problems* January 2, 1955, 154.

11. Buell G. Gallagher, "Prometheus Rampant," *Vital Speeches of the Day*, 1946, History of Problem folder, box 1, Clyde S. Johnson Papers, University of Illinois Archives (hereafter CSJP).

12. "National Fraternities Prepare for a Record Year," *New York Times*, June 9, 1946, 70.

13. By 1943, many people had been talking about the possibility of the federal government subsidizing the economic burden of veterans returning to college with the potential for increased enrollments (as it did with the GI Bill of Rights), and at least one observer envisioned "a Greek letter fraternity renaissance" after the war. L. G. Balfour, quoted in Lionel Crocker, "Fraternities and Democracy: The Brotherhood of Man," *Vital Speeches of the Day*, October 1, 1943, 768.

14. For these numbers, see *Time*, February 9, 1948, 75–76; and *Life*, September 24, 1956, 141; see also "College Fraternities Are Again Enjoying an Era of Expansion," *New York Times*, November 30, 1947, E11.

15. One estimate at the University of Texas put the figure as high as 85 percent. See "College Fraternities Are Again Enjoying an Era of Expansion," *New York Times*, November 30, 1947, E11; and "Education in Review," *New York Times*, December 4, 1949, E13.

16. Phil R. Hussey to Clyde S. Johnson, October 26, 1965, Maine U-Frty Study folder, box 7, CSJP.

17. Wade Thompson, "My Crusade Against Fraternities," *Nation*, September 26, 1959, 171.

18. *Time*, February 9, 1948, 75.

19. In Anthony W. James, "The College Social Fraternity Anti-Discrimination Debate, 1945–1949," *Historian* 62, 2 (2000): 309.

20. Lee, *Fraternities Without Brotherhood*, 48–49.

21. Alfred S. Romer, "The Color Line in Fraternities," *Atlantic Monthly*, June 1949, 28. See also Morris Kaplan, "Rumblings in the Fraternities," *New York Times Sunday Magazine*, January 23, 1949, 17.

22. That it was a regional movement is one of the central arguments of James, "The College Social Fraternity Anti-Discrimination Debate, 1945–1949," *Reporter* [periodical of the National Association of Intergroup Relations Officials], June 1951, 303, in "College Fraternities Are Lowering Race Bars," *Christian Century*, July 11, 1951, 812.

23. "Brief History—The Fraternity Autonomy Problem," in Surveys—Herb Brown folder, box 1, CSJP.

24. Ibid., 7.

25. Quotation in "Pledging of Negro Brings Suspension," *New York Times*, November 13, 1948, 17.

26. Stephen Steinberg, *The Academic Melting Pot: Catholics and Jews in American Higher Education* (New Brunswick, N.J.: Transaction Books, 1977), 9, 20.

27. Edwin J. Lukas and Lawrence Bloomgarden, "White Men of Full Aryan Blood," April 21, 1953, Fraternities and Sororities folder, box 88, Papers of the American Jewish Committee.

28. Lee, *Fraternities Without Brotherhood*, 127.

29. The American Jewish Committee admits as much in Mrs. Horace S. Manges, "Report on Jewish Fraternities," November 13, 1956, Fraternities and Sororities folder, box 88, Papers of the American Jewish Committee, 3–4.

30. Among this group were professors Melville J. Herskovits, Max Lerner, and Alfred McClung Lee; clergymen John Paul Jones and L. Maynard Catchings; and civic leaders Edwin H. Wilson, the humanist leader, and Robert C. Weaver, who would become under President Johnson the nation's first black cabinet member.

31. Lee, *Fraternities Without Brotherhood*, 34, 47, 42, 47.

32. Ibid., 130, 34, 199.

33. Interfraternity Conference Minutes, Sessions 39–40 (1947–1948), 39th Annual Session, November 28–29, 1947, 122–26.

34. Ibid., 125.

35. This central tension within liberalism is identified in William Galston, "Two Concepts of Liberalism," *Ethics* 105, 3 (1995); John Rawls, *Political Liberalism* (New York: Columbia University Press, 1993); and Will Kymlicka, *The Rights of Minority Cultures* (New York: Oxford University Press, 1995), 15.

36. *Interfraternity Research and Advisory Council (IRAC) Bulletin*, March 13, 1957, 2.

37. General Letter to the Executive Board #20-b from Warren W. Etcheson, January 23, 1952, Autonomy, Delta Chi folder, box 2, CSJP, UIA.

38. Ibid.

39. Letter to the Honorable Frank H. Myers from Fred H. Turner, April 15, 1954, IRAC May–June 1954 folder, box 2, Papers of the IRAC Bulletin Editor, University of Illinois Archives (UIA); and "Memo," April 23, 1954, IRAC May–June 1954 folder, box 2, Papers of the IRAC Bulletin Editor, UIA.

40. Letter to the Honorable Frank H. Myers from Fred H. Turner, April 15, 1954, in IRAC May–June 1954 folder, box 2, Papers of the IRAC Bulletin Editor, UIA; and "Memo," April 23, 1954, IRAC May–June 1954 folder, box 2, Papers of the IRAC Bulletin Editor, UIA.

41. "Report of IRAC Investigation," "Letter from Marilyn Stevens," March 22, 1954, and Margaret O'Leary to Fred H. Turner, May 5, 1954, IRAC May–June 1954 folder, box 2, Papers of the IRAC Bulletin Editor, UIA.

42. "Operation Brotherhood," SDA folder, box 1, CSJP, UIA.

43. L. G. Balfour to Clyde S. Johnson, April 22, 1957, Autonomy, AB758 Misc 1950s folder, box 1, CSJP, UIA.

44. After listing the number of schools where fraternities had been expelled from campuses for their restrictive clauses, one NIC member wrote: "We cannot fool with this any longer. We are going to have a show-down and I think New York offers the opportunity." Letter to Joseph A. McCusker from unnamed, October 31, 1952, Williams 1952–3 folder, box 1, CSJP.

45. *Webb v. State University of New York*, Civ. A. No. 5063, 125 F. Supp. 910, June 7, 1954 and upheld, 348 U.S. 867, November 8, 1954.

46. See, for instance, Rorty, "Greek Letter Discrimination," 119.

47. Survey in the ADL's *Rights: Reports on Social, Employment, Educational and Housing Discrimination*, 5, 5 (October 1964): 108. For specific examples, see "Columbia to End Fraternity Bias," *New York Times*, May 11, 1953, 1; and "Colorado U. Ends Fraternity Bias," *Christian Century*, April 18, 1956, 494.

48. Numbers come from Simon Marcson, "Introduction: A Symposium on Segregation and Integration in College Fraternities," *Social Problems*, January 2, 1955, 130; and Herbert Brown, *The Problem of Social Rights for Fraternities* [NIC pamphlet], NIC Policies folder, box 1, CSJP, UIA.

49. Balfour to C. S. Johnson, December 28, 1951, IRAC Correspondences folder, box 6, CSJP, UIA.

50. Balfour to C. S. Johnson, September 2, 1959, Survey of Disaffiliated Locals folder, box 1, CSJP, UIA.

51. Herb Brown to C. S. Johnson, September 18, 1959, Survey of Disaffiliated Locals folder, box 1, CSJP, UIA.

52. Herbert L. Brown, "The Problem of Social Rights for Fraternities," NIC Policies folder, box 1, CSJP, UIA.

53. See, for instance, "Here's to AEΠ," *Fraternity Month*, May 1949, 34–35.

54. Interfraternity Conference Minutes, Sessions 39–40, 85. The resolution was also printed in the *New York Times*, "Fraternity Group Defers Bias Vote," November 28, 1948, 72.

55. Interfraternity Conference Minutes, Sessions 39–40, 87–88.

56. "Fraternities Keep Negro Exclusion," *New York Times*, November 27, 1948, 15.

57. Ibid.

58. "Fraternity Group Defers Bias Vote," *New York Times*, November 28, 1948, 72.

59. For other examples of "gentleman's agreements" excluding Jews, see Evelyn Lauter, "Fraternity Integration: Ideal or Foolhardy?" *National Jewish Monthly*, November 1961, 11. On the SAEs, letter to Grand Officers of ATO, August 12, 1954, membership committee 1954 to 1956 folder, box 1, ATO Board of Directors/High Council, Membership Clause Files, 1941–1974, UIA.

60. Lukas and Bloomgarden, "White Men of Full Aryan Blood," 7.

61. 42nd Congress Proceedings, box 34, ATO Congresses, Conferences and Workshops, UIA, 281.

62. Ibid., 283.

63. Ibid.

64. Report on the Committee on Study of Selectivity Clauses to the 44th Congress of the ATO Fraternity, Houston, Texas, August 27–30, 1958, Committee on Study of Selectivity Clauses 1957–1960 folder, ATO-BOD, UIA.

65. Draft report of the committee on the Study of Selectivity Clauses, 1960, Committee on Study of Selectivity Clauses 1957–1960 folder, ATO-BOD, UIA.

66. Bloomgarden to Irma Cohen, October 18, 1958, NIC folder, box 89, RG 347.17.10, Papers of the American Jewish Committee.

67. Comments on questions posted by Dr. Karlem Reiss to Clyde S. Johnson, November 12, 1965, Tulane Fraternity Study folder, box 12, CSJP, UIA.

68. Report on Jewish Fraternities, November 13, 1956, Fraternities and Sororities folder, box 88, RG 347.17.10, Papers of the American Jewish Committee, 2.

69. Simon Marcson, "Introduction: A Symposium on Segregation and Integration in College Fraternities," *Social Problems*, January 2, 1955, 130.

70. See Lee, *Fraternities Without Brotherhood*, ix; and "Bias at Williams Is Reported Cut," *New York Times*, May 19, 1957, 70.

71. "Dartmouth Tells 4 Fraternities to End Discrimination by Fall," *New York Times*, April 17, 1960, 31.

72. Noel P. Gist, "Fraternal Membership Policies and Minority Groups," *Social Problems* January 2, 1955, 168.

73. Vincent Heath Whitney, "Fraternities at Brown University," *Social Problems* January 2, 1955, 157.

74. "Bias at Williams Is Reported Cut," *New York Times*, May 19, 1957, 70.

75. John Slawson to Lawrence Bloomgarden, April 18, 1962, Discrimination in Education folder, box 74, RG 347.17.10, Papers of the American Jewish Committee.

76. Report on Jewish Fraternities, November 13, 1956, Fraternities and Sororities folder, box 88, RG 347.17.10, Papers of the American Jewish Committee, 2.

77. Lawrence Bloomgarden to Manheim Shapiro, November 13, 1958, Minnesota folder, box 89, Papers of the American Jewish Committee.

78. Report on Jewish Fraternities, November 13, 1956, Fraternities and Sororities folder, box 88, RG 347.17.10, Papers of the American Jewish Committee, 4.

79. Maurice Jacobs, "The Case for Jewish Fraternities," *National Jewish Monthly*, November 1961, 40.

80. Ibid.

81. Letter from Fred Turner to L. G. Balfour, January 3, 1958, L. G. Balfour 1954–1958 folder, box 2, Papers of the Editor of the IRAC Bulletin, UIA.

82. Letter from L. G. Balfour to Fred Turner, January 9, 1958, L. G. Balfour 1954–1958 folder, box 2, Papers of the Editor of the IRAC Bulletin, UIA.

83. Lawrence Bloomgarden to Maurice Jacobs, June 28, 1960, Teich-Jacobs correspondence folder, box 88, RG 347.17.10, Papers of the American Jewish Committee.

84. Quotation in Lukas and Bloomgarden, "White Men of Full Aryan Blood," 4.

85. Report on Jewish Fraternities, November 13, 1956, fraternities and sororities folder, box 88, RG 347.17.10, Papers of the American Jewish Committee. Emphasis in original.

86. *National Jewish Post and Opinion*, June 28, 1957, 15.

87. Maurice Jacobs to Irving Engel, July 7, 1955, Teich-Jacobs correspondence folder, box 88, RG 347.17.10, Papers of the American Jewish Committee.

88. Arthur Teich to American Jewish Committee, January 27, 1955, Teich-Jacobs correspondence folder, box 88, RG 347.17.10, Papers of the American Jewish Committee.

89. Alvin Sapinsley, to Pearson E. Neaman, October 11, 1956, fraternities and sororities folder, box 88, RG 347.17.10, Papers of the American Jewish Committee.

90. James Seder to Lawrence Bloomgarden, April 20, 1960, University of Michigan folder, box 88, RG 347.17.10, Papers of the American Jewish Committee.

91. Lawrence Bloomgarden to James Seder, April 25, 1960, ibid.

92. Found in Thomas B. Morgan, "The Vanishing American Jew," *Look*, May 5, 1964, 46.

93. "Jewish Fraternities," October 1, 1958, Jewish fraternities folder, box 89, RG 347.10, Papers of the American Jewish Committee, 1.

94. Maurice Jacobs, "The Case for Jewish Fraternities," *National Jewish Monthly*, November 1961, 40.

95. "History," found at http://www.k-state.edu/phikap/history.htm (accessed June 15, 2010).

96. Evelyn Lauter, "Fraternity Integration: Ideal of Foolhardy?" *National Jewish Monthly*, November 1961, 38.

97. "Social, but Not Civil," *Commonweal*, December 13, 1957, 277.

98. For these examples, see Harold Braverman, "The Right of Privacy," *ADL Bulletin*, April 1957, 1–7.

99. Irving Spiegel, "Bias Drop Noted in Fraternities," *New York Times*, May 28, 1957, 26.

100. Wallace Turner, "Colleges Face U.S. Aid Cutoff if They Permit Fraternity Bias," *New York Times*, June 18, 1965, 1.

101. Will Kymlicka argues that in order for minority groups to be as free as the dominant majorities, they need some system of increased group rights, some kind of affirmative action, to counteract the pervasive influence of the dominant culture. He was one of the first to make the case on behalf of minority cultures. Will Kymlicka, *Multicultural Citizenship* (New York: Oxford University Press, 1995), esp. chap. 9.

102. For a description of the play and an interview with Karp, see "When the Frat Recruited a Jew," *New York Times*, May 17, 2005, A22.

CHAPTER 7

1. "Appraisal of census programs," February 1954, folder 8, box 5, A. Ross Eckler Files, Records of the Bureau of the Census, RG 29, National Archives, Washington, D.C.

2. Ibid.

3. Gallup, for instance, broke down both the 1952 and 1956 presidential election data into numerous segments, including Protestant, Catholic, and Jew. Gallup, *The Gallup Poll*, 2:110, 1453. Religion, while important to Gallup's segmentation, was often relegated to a secondary role, in favor of education, occupation, and age as Gallup's key divisions.

4. See for instance, Gallup, *The Gallup Poll*, 2:1031–32.

5. Ibid., 2:1317–18.

6. For some of these stories, see "99 to 1," *Time*, October 20, 1954, 64, and "I Believe in God," *Newsweek*, October 20, 1952. For a distillation of these numbers, see James Hudnut-Beumler, *Looking for God in the Suburbs: The Religion of the American Dream and Its Critics* (New Brunswick, N.J.: Rutgers University Press, 1994), 29–40.

7. Questions about the number of churches and synagogues, their seating capacity, and their monetary value had been asked in 1850, 1860, and 1870, but never had the Census Bureau asked about an individual's faith. For the institutional resistance to asking a question on religion, see "Question on Religion in the CPS (Notes of a Meeting of the Census Advisory Committee on Population Statistics)," April 2, 1976, Religion Files, Records of the Bureau of the Census, Bureau of the Census, Suitland, Md.

8. On the Rhode Island farmer, see William Petersen, *The Politics of Population* (Garden City, N.Y.: Doubleday, 1964), 264; Philip Hauser, "Memo," n.d., Religion folder, Philip Hauser Files, Records of the Bureau of the Census, National Archives, Washington, D.C.; and Foster, *Question on Religion*, 6.

9. For the quotation, see Robert W. Burgess to Irving M. Engel, October 16, 1957, Decennial 1960 File, box 45, RG 347.17.10, Papers of the American Jewish Committee.

10. Conrad Taeuber interview by Robert Voight, April 12, 1989, in U.S. Census Bureau, *Conrad Taeuber—Oral History*, http://www.census.gov/prod/2003pubs/oh-Taeuber.pdf; *New York Times*, September 24, 1999, B11. On the meeting with Rupert Vance, see Foster, *Question on Religion*, 6. Conrad Taeuber and Irene B. Taeuber, *The Changing Population of the United States* (New York: John Wiley, 1958).

11. The quotations come from Robert W. Burgess's obituary, *New York Times*, May 28, 1969, 47.

12. U.S. Bureau of the Census, "First List of Questions Concerning the 1960 Censuses of Population and Housing," November 30, 1956, box 21, Religion Files, Records of the Bureau of the Census, Bureau of the Census, Suitland, Md.

13. "Getting Religious Statistics," *America*, September 1, 1956, 406; "Taking the Census," *America*, October 13, 1956, 22.

14. "Getting Religious Statistics," 406. Census information is not "anonymous" but "confidential." In anonymous surveys, the respondent's name is never known by the surveyor. In confidential surveys, the name is known but not disclosed. Thanks to Judith Tanur for pointing this out.

15. Robert W. Burgess, "Taking the Census," *America*, October 13, 1956, 22.

16. U.S. Census Bureau, "General Statement Regarding Testing of a Possible Question on Religion or Religious Affiliation," n.d., Robert Burgess File, Records of the Department of

Commerce, RG 40, National Archives. On the timing of the press release, see Foster, *Question on Religion*, 8–9.

17. Ibid.

18. U.S. Bureau of the Census, *Current Population Reports: Population Characteristics*, series P-20, no. 79, February 2, 1958, 1; Petersen, *Politics of Population*, 257.

19. Actually, three households refused, making it slightly more than one-half of 1 percent. U.S. Census Bureau, "General Statement Regarding Testing of a Possible Question on Religion," 1.

20. CPA Board of Directors Memo, October 8, 1956, file 3, box 21, collection 10, Papers of the National Catholic Welfare Conference, Catholic University of America, Washington, D.C.

21. Foster, *Question on Religion*, 9.

22. For Thomas B. Kenedy's position, see *New York Times*, July 19, 1957, 18, and an article in the Washington, D.C., archdiocesan newspaper, *Washington Catholic Standard*, January 18, 1957, clipping, Decennial 1960 File, box 45, Papers of the American Jewish Committee. On those for and against the question on religion, see U.S. Bureau of the Census, "A Partial List of Reactions of Organized Groups and Newspapers to a Question on Religion in the 1960 Census," November 19, 1957, in Memo from T. Kenedy, November 26, 1957, file 3, box 21, collection 10, Papers of the National Catholic Welfare Conference; and Donald J. Bogue, *The Population of the United States* (Glencoe, Ill.: Free Press, 1959), 688 n. 2.

23. On midcentury suspicions of Catholics, see McGreevy, "Thinking on One's Own," 97–131. For the Catholic organizations and publications supporting the census question, see Bureau of the Census, "Partial List of Reactions of Organized Groups and Newspapers to a Question on Religion in the 1960 Census."

24. Jewish groups had accused H. S. Linfield of raising the specter of a question on religion for at least a decade. See Fine to Philip Waterman, March 8, 1948, 1950 Census File, box 45, Papers of the American Jewish Committee.

25. See Marshall Sklare to John Slawson, December 12, 1956, Decennial 1960 File, box 45, Papers of the American Jewish Committee. For the development of strategies and the clear recognition of the principal opponent, see Theodore Leskes to Sol Rabkin, July 19, 1957, ADL-AJC Joint Statements file, box 45, RG I-77, Papers of the American Jewish Congress, American Jewish Historical Society, New York; Jules Cohen to NCRAC Membership, August 6, 1957, U.S. Census to YMCA, 1957 File, box 26, RG I-337, Papers of the National Jewish Welfare Board, American Jewish Historical Society, New York; "Minutes," June 17, 1957, file 103, box 6, Papers of the American Jewish Congress; Rabkin to Herman Edelsberg, April 26, 1957, Decennial 1960 File, box 45, Papers of the American Jewish Committee.

26. For the American Jewish Congress's strategy of having rabbis and community members write the U.S. Census Bureau, see Shad Polier to Division and Chapter Presidents, October 22, 1957, CLSA Memoranda file, box 24, Papers of the American Jewish Congress. For the American Civil Liberties Union's new position, see *New York Times*, August 2, 1957, 17; Israel Goldstein to Editor, *New York Times*, August 2, 1957, 21.

27. Burgess to Engel, October 16, 1957, Decennial 1960 File, box 45, Papers of the American Jewish Committee. For the American Jewish Congress's official stand, see, for example, American Jewish Congress, "Religion Question in the Census: Resolution Adopted by the Executive Committee of the American Jewish Congress," June 17, 1957, file 103, box 6, Papers of the American Jewish Congress.

28. For Rabbi S. H. Markowitz's bulletin, see *National Jewish Post and Opinion*, January 17, 1958, 1. Markowitz was an active committee member of the Jewish Statistical Bureau. Sklare

to Slawson, December 12, 1956, Decennial 1960 File, box 45, Papers of the American Jewish Committee; American Jewish Committee memorandum, attached to Fine to Franck, February 25, 1957, ibid.

29. For Roosevelt's claim, see Beschloss, *Conquerors*, 41; Good, "Questions on Religion in the Census," 9. On the "emotional reaction" to the question, see Earl Morse to the American Jewish Committee, September 17, 1957, Decennial 1960 File, box 45, Papers of the American Jewish Committee.

30. See Götz Aly and Karl Heinz Roth, *The Nazi Census: Identification and Control in the Third Reich*, trans. Edwin Black (Philadelphia: Temple University Press, 2004), 8–55, esp. 10–14, 18–22; and William Seltzer and Margo Anderson, "The Dark Side of Numbers: The Role of Population Data Systems in Human Rights Abuses," *Social Research* 68, 2 (Summer 2001), 481–513.

31. Most Jewish organizations, including the American Jewish Congress, were concerned about group maintenance in a suburbanizing America. Its director of membership complained about the lack of data on the location of America's Jews, especially considering "the tremendous exodus to the suburbs which has characterized population trends, including Jewish," since World War II. Notes from the Officers Committee Meeting, May 13, 1957, file 72, box 4, Papers of the American Jewish Congress; Sanford Solender to Samuel D. Gershovitz, June 28, 1957, United States Census to YMCA, 1957 File, box 26, Papers of the National Jewish Welfare Board.

32. See Solender to Gershovitz, June 28, 1957, United States Census to YMCA, 1957 File, box 26, Papers of the National Jewish Welfare Board; Gershovitz's response penciled at the bottom of Solender's initial correspondence, ibid.; Solender to Gershovitz, August 6, 1957, ibid.; and Cohen to Solender (forwarded to Gershovitz), August 26, 1957, ibid. For the Jewish Community Relations Council's decision not to publicize its desire for a question on religion, see Harry Winton to Philip Jacobson, September 18, 1957, Decennial 1960 File, box 45, Papers of the American Jewish Committee. For the only public break, made after the matter had been settled, see New York Association of Rabbis press release, December 30, 1957, Decennial Census: Organization Responses File, ibid.

33. "God and the Census," *Christian Century*, August 21, 1957, 979.

34. "God and the Census," 979; Burgess to Engel, October 16, 1957, Decennial 1960 File, box 45, Papers of the American Jewish Committee, 3; Bureau of the Census, "Partial List of Reactions of Organized Groups and Newspapers to a Question on Religion in the 1960 Census"; *New York Times*, August 6, 1957, 25.

35. For example, an authoritative Christian Science manual reads, "Christian Scientists shall not report for publication the number of members of The Mother Church, nor that of the branch churches. According to the Scriptures they shall turn away from personality and numbering the people." Mary Baker Eddy, *Manual of the Mother Church: The First Church of Christ Scientist* (Boston, 1910), 48. Bureau of the Census, "Partial List of Reactions of Organized Groups and Newspapers to a Question on Religion in the 1960 Census."

36. Leo Pfeffer, "Is It the Government's Business?" *Christian Century*, October 30, 1957, 1283; "God and the Census," 979.

37. "Religion in the Census?" *Commonweal*, August 2, 1957, 438; Joseph B. Schuyler to Editor, "Religion in the Census," ibid., September 13, 1957, 591–92.

38. For the number of clippings, see Foster, *Question on Religion*, 11; *Minneapolis Tribune*, July 1, 1957.

39. For the decision to forge a strong public reaction, see Polier to Division and Chapter Presidents, October 22, 1957, CLSA Materials July–December 1957, American Jewish Congress, New York. The author is indebted to Mark Silk and Marc Stern for helping him access these

files. For the bombardment of letters, see A. L. Feinberg, memo, October 23, 1957, Decennial 1960 File, box 45, Papers of the American Jewish Committee.

40. Foster, *Question on Religion*, 19.

41. Thomas Kenedy to Archbishop John Francis O'Hara, November 26, 1957, file 3, box 21, collection 10, Papers of the National Catholic Welfare Conference. For the press release, see Foster, *Question on Religion*, 19–20.

42. Francis Cardinal Spellman to Sinclair Weeks, April 12, 1958, file 3, box 21, collection 10, Papers of the National Catholic Welfare Conference.

43. For the quotation from *Business Week*, see Burgess to Engel, January 15, 1958, Ch-St/U.S. Census File, box 45, Papers of the American Jewish Committee; Bogue, *The Population of the United States* 688–89; American Jewish Committee, *American Jewish Year Book, 1958* (New York: American Jewish Committee, 1958), 4.

44. Foster, *Question on Religion*, 12; *New York Times*, December 13, 1957, 30; "Minutes, Executive Committee," December 17, 1957, file 103, box 6, Papers of the American Jewish Congress.

45. This explanation is inferred from the language used in Bureau of the Census, *Current Population Reports*, 1.

46. Ibid.

47. Ibid., 2.

48. Ibid., table 2.

49. For the first complaint, see Rabkin to David A. Brody, March 13, 1958, Ch-St/U.S. Census File, box 45, Papers of the American Jewish Committee. For the second, see H. S. Linfield, "The New Statistics of Religious Groups," March 1958, Ch-St/U.S. Census File, box 45, Papers of the American Jewish Committee.

50. Nathaniel H. Goodrich to Edwin J. Lukas, May 20, 1958, Ch-St/US Census File, box 45, Papers of the American Jewish Committee. Cf. Foster, *Question on Religion*, 14.

51. For Jewish leaders' awareness of Robert W. Burgess's attitude to their argument, see Engel to Burgess, January 10, 1958, and Burgess to Engel, January 15, 1958, Ch-St/U.S. Census File, box 45, Papers of the American Jewish Committee. On the meeting of "like-minded others," see Goodrich to Jacobson, April 21, 1958, Ch-St/U.S. Census File, box 45, Papers of the American Jewish Committee. For politicians' attention, see Brody to Rabkin, May 12, 1958, and Rabkin to H. S. Linfield, July 1, 1958, Ch-St/U.S. Census File, box 45, Papers of the American Jewish Committee.

52. Burgess to Linfield, May 15, 1958, Ch-St/U.S. Census File, box 45, Papers of the American Jewish Committee.

53. For Frederick H. Mueller's communication to Burgess, see Foster, *Question on Religion*, 19.

54. Ibid., 14.

55. Good, "Questions on Religion in the Census," 11–12; Petersen, "Religious Statistics in the United States," 178, 173.

56. Sidney Goldstein has graciously shared copies of the data with me. See Sidney Goldstein, "Socioeconomic Differentials among Religious Groups in the United States," *American Journal of Sociology* 74 (May 1969): 612–31.

57. U.S. Bureau of the Census, "Tabulations of Data on the Social and Economic Characteristics of Major Religious Groups, March 1957," unpublished report (in Kevin M. Schultz's possession). For Catholic transitions, see Andrew M. Greeley, *The American Catholic: A Social Portrait* (New York: Basic Books, 1977); Andrew M. Greeley, William C. McCready, and Kathleen McCourt, *Catholic Schools in a Declining Church* (Kansas City: Sheed & Ward, 1976);

and Andrew M. Greeley and Peter H. Rossi, *The Education of Catholic Americans* (Chicago: Aldine, 1966), 118–46. For Jewish transitions, see Marshal Sklare, *The Jews: Social Patterns of an American Group* (Glencoe, Ill.: Free Press, 1958); Marshall Sklare, "Intermarriage and the Jewish Future," *Commentary* 37 (April 1964): 46–52; Marshall Sklare, Joseph Greenblum, and Benjamin B. Ringer, *Not Quite at Home: How an American Jewish Community Lives with Itself and Its Neighbors* (New York: Institute of Human Relations Press, American Jewish Committee, 1969); and Thomas B. Morgan, "The Vanishing American Jew," *Look*, May 5, 1964, 42–46.

58. As Glen Jeansonne and Naomi W. Cohen have shown, postwar American Jewish institutions used numerous tactics to control the discourse, hushing their most bigoted critics (such as Gerald L. K. Smith) or successfully removing prayers and Bible reading from public schools (as in *Engel* and *Schempp*). Glen Jeansonne, "Combating Anti-Semitism: The Case of Gerald L. K. Smith," in *Anti-Semitism in American History*, ed. David A. Gerber (Urbana: University of Illinois Press, 1987), 152–66; Cohen, *Jews in Christian America*, 123–239; *Engel v. Vitale*, 370 U.S. 421 (1962); *Abington School District v. Schempp*, 374 U.S. 203 (1963).

59. Schuyler, "Religion in the Census," 592.

60. Will Herberg did not comment publicly or, according to his private papers, privately on the census debate, perhaps because he was not a part of the Jewish communal groups and perhaps because demography was less interesting to him than moral and theological issues. Herberg, *Protestant-Catholic-Jew*, 52–55, and Will Herberg Papers, Will Herberg Collection, Drew University, Madison, N.J.

61. "Pluralism—A National Menace," *Christian Century*, June 13, 1951, 701–3.

62. Burgess to Engel, October 16, 1957, Decennial 1960 File, box 45, Papers of the American Jewish Committee, 2.

CHAPTER 8

1. "Summit Conference on Race, Religion," *Ebony*, April 1963, 47.

2. "Religion-Racial Conference Gets Kennedy Pledge," *Chicago Sun-Times*, January 15, 1963, 3.

3. For the convening of the conference, see the introduction to *Race: Challenge to Religion: Original Essays and* An Appeal of the Conscience *from the National Conference on Religion and Race*, ed. Mathew Ahmann (Chicago: Henry Regnery, 1963), iv–xi; for King's speech, see 161. For King's quotation on the event, see Stanley Pieza, "Rev. King Urges Boycott by Churches in Fight Bias," *Chicago American*, January 16, 1963.

4. Sister Margaret Ellen Traxler, "American Catholics and Negroes," *Phylon* 30, 4 (1969): 366. The lack of citations for this and other stories suggests that Traxler may have been at the conference.

5. For Ahmann's role, see Rabbi Balfour Brickner, "Notes on the National Conference on Religion and Race," Civil Rights Movement–Interreligious Action folder, box 17, NCCJ Papers, 1–2, 12.

6. Ahmann, *Race: Challenge to Religion*, 171 for "our most serious domestic evil," and viii for "guilt."

7. Brickner, "Notes on the National Conference on Religion and Race," 2.

8. Ahmann, *Race: Challenge to Religion*, 5, 55.

9. Ibid., 91, 99.

10. On Albert Cardinal Meyer's trip to Vatican II in Rome, see "Cardinal Sums Up Racial Meet Aims," *New World*, January 11, 1963; for the other quotations, see Brickner, "Notes on the National Conference on Religion and Race," 12.

11. Ahmann, *Race: Challenge to Religion*, 42–43. This was also the theme of Franklin H. Littell's book *From State Church to Pluralism: A Protestant Interpretation of Religion in American History* (New York: Anchor Books, 1962).

12. Brickner, "Notes on the National Conference on Religion and Race," 10 and Ahmann, *Race: Challenge to Religion*, 41, 43.

13. Ahmann, *Race: Challenge to Religion*, 166–69.

14. Ibid., 171–73.

15. Dave Meade, "10-City Attack on Race Bias Urged in Conference Report," *Chicago Daily News*, January 17, 1963. For similar statements, see "Call History-Making Racial Parley Here," *Chicago Tribune*, June 21, 1962, "Church Leaders to Meet," *Chicago Daily News*, June 21, 1962, and Dolores McCahill, "Slate Historic Meeting on Race Bias," *Chicago Sun-Times*, December 29, 1962.

16. "Special Tonight," *Chicago Tribune*, January 19, 1963 and Paul Malloy, "Here, There, on the Air," *Chicago Sun-Times*, January 19, 1963, 26.

17. Louis Cassels, "Historic Race-Religion Parley to Open," *Chicago Defender*, January 12–18, 1963.

18. The cities were Atlanta, Chicago, Detroit, New Orleans, Oakland, Pittsburgh, San Francisco, San Antonio, St. Louis, and Seattle.

19. Each community engaged in different activities. For the initial round of social action, see National Conference on Religion and Race, *Newsletter* 1, 3 (May 1963): 1–10, in folder 2, box 1, Chicago Conference on Religion and Race (CCRR) Collection, Special Collection of the University of Illinois at Chicago (UIC) Library (hereafter CCRR Collection).

20. This list is mostly catalogued in Background Information on the Chicago Conference on Religion and Race, folder 4, box 1, CCRR Collection, 1–7. For the Tri-Faith Employment Project, see "Background Information: The Tri-Faith Employment Project," April 28, 1967, folder 5, box 1, CCRR Collection, and National Conference on Religion and Race, *Newsletter*, January–February 1967, folder 5, box 1, CCRR Collection.

21. Gordon W. Lovejoy, "Follow-Up to National Conference on Religion and Race," February 1, 1963, civil rights movement-interreligious folder, box 17, NCCJ Papers.

22. After 1963, the NCCJ expanded its advocacy into issues related to race, gender, class, sexuality, and disability, leading the organization, in 1998, to change its name to the National Conference for Community and Justice—still the NCCJ, but absent any religious identity.

23. Ahmann, *Race: Challenge to Religion*, 6.

24. The religious language of the civil rights movement has an extensive historiography. For an overview, see Davis W. Houck and David E. Dixon, eds., *Rhetoric, Religion, and the Civil Rights Movement* (Waco, Tex.: Baylor University Press, 2006), and Mark A. Noll, *God and Race in American Politics: A Short History* (Princeton, N.J.: Princeton University Press, 2008), chap. 4.

25. Martin Luther King Jr., "Letter from Birmingham Jail," *Why We Can't Wait* (New York: Signet Classics, 2000), 83.

26. Martin Luther King Jr., "Paul's Letter to American Christians," November 4, 1956, *Papers of Martin Luther King, Jr: Birth of a New Age, December 1955–December 1956*, eds. Clayborne Carson, Ralph Luker, Stewart Burns, and Penny A. Russell (Berkeley: University of California Press, 1997), 414–20.

27. Quotation in Chappell, *Stone of Hope*, 68.

28. Ibid., 76.

29. "Attack on the Conscience," *Time*, February 18, 1957, 17.

30. Jane Dailey, "Sex, Segregation, and the Sacred After *Brown*," *Journal of American History* 91 (June 2004), 126–27.

31. William Martin, *With God on Our Side: The Rise of the Religious Right in America* (New York: Broadway Books, 2005 [1996]), 63.

32. Dailey, "Sex, Segregation, and the Sacred," 120.

33. Ibid., 132.

34. Ibid., 138.

35. Milton M. Gordon, *Assimilation in American Life: The Role of Race, Religion, and National Origins* (New York: Oxford University Press, 1964), 14.

36. Ibid., 14.

37. Ibid., 109 10.

38. Ibid., 130–31.

39. Horace M. Kallen, *Cultural Pluralism and the American Idea: An Essay in Social Philosophy* (Philadelphia: University of Pennsylvania Press, 1956), 97. For a critique of Kallen and a commentary on his vague use of the term "pluralism," see Stephen J. Whitfield's Introduction to Horace M. Kallen, *Culture and Democracy in the United States* (New Brunswick, N.J.: Transaction, 1998), xxxiii, 113.

40. Nathan Glazer, "Ethnic Groups in America: From National Culture to Ideology," in Monroe Berger, Theodore Abel, and Charles H. Page, eds., *Freedom and Control in Modern Society* (New York: D. Van Nostrand, 1954).

41. Stewart G. Cole and Mildred Wiese Cole, *Minorities and the American Promise* (New York: Harper and Brothers, 1954); George E. Simpson and J. Milton Yinger, *Racial and Cultural Minorities*, rev. ed. (New York: Harper and Brothers, 1958), and George R. Stewart, *American Ways of Life* (Garden City, N.Y.: Doubleday, 1954).

42. Pitt, *Adventures in Brotherhood*, 6.

43. Ibid., 201.

44. Ibid., 205.

45. Ibid., 200.

46. Ibid., 153.

47. Ibid., 206.

48. "The Purpose, Nature, and Function of the NCCJ," February 5, 1958, Evaluation Study 1958 folder, box 7, NCCJ Papers, 2.

49. McGreevy, *Parish Boundaries*, 90.

50. Svonkin, *Jews Against Prejudice*, 11–40 and Clive Webb, *Fight Against Fear: Southern Jews and Black Civil Rights* (Athens: University Press of Georgia, 2001).

51. "Civil Rights Passage Predicted by Johnson," *Oklahoma Courier*, May 8, 1964, 20, in Civil Rights Movement—Inter-Religious Actions folder, box 17, NCCJ Papers.

52. Everett Tilson, *Segregation and the Bible: A Searching Analysis of the Scriptural Evidence* (New York: Abington Press, 1958), 95.

53. Chappell, *Stone of Hope*, 97, 140–44.

54. Found in T. B. Maston, *Segregation and Desegregation: A Christian Approach* (New York: Macmillan, 1959).

55. Ibid., 164–66.

56. "Prelate Critical of Priests, Nuns Demonstrating in Selma Drive," *Religious News Service*, March 19, 1965, 1–2.

57. The editorial added, "This is not a call for retreat from involvement on the part of the clergy. It is a call for a witness which will become still more effective as it sharpens the united moral witness or religious leaders." See: "*Ave Maria* Urges Conference on Appropriate Clergy Protest," Religious News Service, March 16, 1965, 12.

58. This is the argument in Wuthnow, *The Restructuring of American Religion*.

59. Modjeska Simkins, column for May 17, 1947, *Norfolk Journal and Guide*, in Chappell, *Stone of Hope*, 63.

60. Ahmann, *Race: Challenge to Religion*, 3–4.

61. Michael B. Freidland, *Lift Up Your Voice Like a Trumpet: White Clergy and the Civil Rights and Antiwar Movements, 1954–1973* (Chapel Hill: University of North Carolina Press, 1998), 74.

62. "Suburbia: High Cost of Democracy," *Time*, December 7, 1959, 22.

63. "One Nation Under God: Report of the National Conference of Christians and Jews 1954," annual reports folder, box 59, NCCJ Papers, 2.

64. "Churches: The Hidden Revival," *Time*, February 1, 1963, and "A Letter from the Publisher," *Time*, January 3, 1964, 11.

65. "Wailing for Them All," *Time*, April 24, 1964, 52.

CONCLUSION

1. Martin, *With God on Our Side*, 77–79. The book, based on a public television series of the same name, includes numerous long quotations from many of the leaders of the religious right. Martin himself conducted most of the interviews, many of which appeared in the television series.

2. Ibid.

3. Ibid., 70–71.

4. E. V. Toy Jr., "The National Lay Committee and the National Council of Churches: A Case Study of Protestants in Conflict," *American Quarterly*, Summer 1969, 190–209.

5. Martin, *With God on Our Side*, 157.

6. Ibid., 212.

7. For an illumination of the expansion of these Christian schools, and of the way they are re-interpreting American history, see Jeff Sharlet, "Through a Glass Darkly: How the Christian Right Is Reimagining U.S. history," *Harper's*, December 2006, 33–43.

8. This is Paul Weyrich's argument (Weyrich was a key conservative activist at the time): "What galvanized the Christian community was not abortion, school prayer, or the ERA. I am living witness to that because I was trying to get those people interested in those issues and I utterly failed. What changed their mind was Jimmy Carter's intervention against the Christian schools, trying to deny them tax-exempt status on the basis of so-called de facto segregation." Martin, *With God on Our Side*, 173.

9. Martin, *With God on Our Side*, 122.

10. Ibid., 193.

11. Ibid., 217.

12. Ibid., 215.

13. Jay Reeves, "Campus Christians Going Greek," *Chicago Tribune*, November 16, 2008, 15.

14. See, for instance, Barry A. Kosmin and Ariela Keysar, *American Religious Identification Survey: Summary Report 2008* (New Haven, Conn.: Trinity University, 2008), 5.

15. Greeley's most conscientious attempt to break myths about postwar Catholics can be found in Andrew M. Greeley, *The American Catholic: A Social Portrait* (New York: Basic Books, 1977). See also Andrew M. Greeley, William C. McCready, and Kathleen McCourt, *Catholic Schools in a Declining Church* (Kansas City: Sheed & Ward, 1976), esp. chaps. 1 and 2; Andrew M. Greeley, *American Catholics Since the Council: An Unauthorized Report* (Chicago: Thomas More Press, 1985), 28–48; and Andrew M. Greeley and Peter H. Rossi, *The Education of Catholic Americans* (Chicago: Aldine, 1966), 118–46.

16. Greeley and Rossi, *Education of Catholic Americans*, 118–23.

17. Peter Novick, *That Noble Dream: The "Objectivity Question" and the American Historical Profession* (New York: Cambridge University Press, 1988), 364–66.

18. While Catholics had risen to top positions at General Motors and Ford Motor Company, they were otherwise underrepresented in big business as well. For Jewish acculturation, see Shapiro, *A Time for Healing*, 39–44. For the persistence of antisemitism in big business see, Steven L. Slavin and Mary A. Pradt, *The Einstein Syndrome: Corporate Anti-Semitism in America Today* (Washington, D.C.: University Press of America, 1982), 39–44, 47–61.

19. Shapiro, *A Time for Healing*, 39–44.

20. Morgan, "The Vanishing American Jew," 45.

21. "Jewishness and the Younger Intellectuals," *Commentary*, April 1961, 350.

22. Ibid., 353–54.

23. Since his college years, Hacker's markers of assimilation had changed. In 1961, the elite college he taught at now accepted "dumb Jews," not just a handful of smart ones. He found it "a sign of progress" that "dumb Jews" now had "equality of treatment with dumb Gentiles." Ibid., 326–27.

24. Ibid., 327.

25. Daniel Bell, "Reflections on Jewish Identity," *Commentary*, June 1961, 471.

26. Ibid., 473–75.

27. Ibid., 478.

28. He quoted A. B. Hollingshead and Frederick C. Redlich's study *Social Class and Mental Illness*, which found that 83 percent of New Haven analysts "came from Jewish homes" and that 64 percent of these were intermarried. Marshall Sklare, "Intermarriage and the Jewish Future," *Commentary*, April 1964, 50.

29. Ibid.

30. Peter Novick, *The Holocaust in American Life* (New York: Mariner Books, 2000), 133–42.

31. For one American Jew's guilt at not being in Israel in 1967 or 1973, see Alan M. Dershowitz, *Chutzpah* (New York: Simon and Schuster, 1992), 16.

32. For the centrality of the Holocaust to American Jewish life, see Novick, *Holocaust in American Life*, 170–205 and its corrective Diner, *We Remember With Reverence and Love*.

33. Daniel Callahan, "The New Pluralism: From Nostalgia to Reality," *Commonweal*, September 6, 1963, 528–31.

34. Francis Canavan, "New Pluralism or Old Monism," *America*, November 9, 1963, 556–60.

35. Philip Gleason, "Pluralism and the New Pluralism: Before We Can Talk Sense About 'Pluralism,' We Have to Know What It Means," *America*, March 7, 1964, 308–12.

36. Donald J. Thorman, "Today's Layman: An Uncertain Catholic," *America*, January 14, 1967, 39–41.

37. Philip Gleason, "The Crisis of Americanization," in *Contemporary Catholicism in the United States*, ed. Philip Gleason (Notre Dame, Ind.: University of Notre Dame Press, 1969), 3–31.

INDEX

Page numbers in italics denote illustrations.